CORRECTIONS

Page 109: For 'Tab-eel,' read 'Tob-al.'

Pages 220-222: For 'Assyria' and 'Assyrians,' read 'Babylonia' and 'Babylonians.'

MEN OF PROPHETIC FIRE

Men of Prophetic Fire

by

ROLLAND EMERSON WOLFE

with illustrations by

PHILLIPS E. OSGOOD

THE BEACON PRESS · BOSTON

Foreword

THIS STUDY IN THE PROPHETS of the Old Testament is intended specially for young people. No attempt is made to cover all the material which has come down to us from those religious leaders. This presentation deals with the high lights in the colorful careers of the prophets. These scenes are developed with the hope that each reader may gain something of that profound religious insight which the prophets of Israel have given to the world.

Inasmuch as this is a book for young people, the manuscript has been submitted for criticism to those who are specialists in working with youth. Highest appreciation goes to Mrs. Sophia L. Fahs, of New York City, who has gone over the manuscript several times with meticulous care. Readers from Massachusetts, to whom the author is indebted for more or less extensive comments, are Rev. Ernest W. Kuebler of Boston, Rev. Raymond B. Johnson of Hingham, and Rev. Clifton G. Hoffman of Fairhaven. Thanks go to several residents of Cleveland for reading the material and offering help, particularly to Rev. Robert H. MacPherson, Mrs. Elizabeth G. Sprague, and Mrs. Marguerite L. Ashbrook. Mention should be made of my sons Frank and Homer, twenty-one and eighteen at the moment, who have played a large part in giving me what little insight I may have into the spirit of youth. It is needless to remark that I stand indebted to numberless Biblical scholars, teachers, and authors for making it possible to accumulate the facts on which this book is based; however, these persons are too numerous for individual mention.

A special word may be addressed to any Biblical scholar, minister, teacher, or more inquiring adult who may read this book. Study of the prophetic writings is complicated because so many secondary materials have been added to them in the course of early centuries. Consequently it is often difficult to get a clear picture as to the original prophets. The passages used in this study are only those which are regarded as genuine. A key to the secondary additions, and a treatment of them, is found in the author's Harvard doctoral dissertation entitled, "The Editing of the Book of the Twelve." A forty-page summary of the same, with identical title, was published in the *Zeitschrift für die alttestamentliche Wissenschaft,* Berlin, 1935, Vol. XII, pp. 90-129.

Thanks are due Harper and Brothers for permission to use parts of the author's translations from the book "Meet Amos and Hosea" which was published by them in 1945. Outside of a few minor alterations, one major change has been made. The term Yahweh, which was the name for the god of the Hebrew people and was used by the pre-exilic prophets, is replaced here by the designations God or Lord. Inasmuch as these translations are presented for appreciation rather than specialized study, the change in divine name brings them more into harmony with present-day religious thought.

It is hoped this study may open the field of the prophets to those for whom this has been an unknown or only slightly known literature, and that this may be the beginning of an increasingly rewarding acquaintanceship with those notable religious leaders.

ROLLAND EMERSON WOLFE

Harkness Professor of Biblical Literature
Western Reserve University
Cleveland, Ohio

Contents

JEREMIAH

SECOND ISAIAH

JONAH

PROPHETS OF LATER CENTURIES

Illustrations

MEN OF PROPHETIC FIRE

I

The Prophets—WhoWereThey?

IN THE PROPHETS OF ISRAEL we make acquaintance with one
of the most remarkable groups of religious leaders in all
history. The great men of that movement were sixteen in
number, and lived in Palestine long before the days of Jesus.
The succession which they formed covered a period of approximately five hundred years. As preserved in our Bibles,
their writings fill almost one-third of the Old Testament.
Those leaders pioneered in the field of religion, developing
the crude primitive faith of the Hebrew people into something
ethically mature and worthy. It was due primarily to their
amazing religious contributions that Palestine came to be
called "The Holy Land."

Misunderstandings

Nevertheless, few groups throughout the centuries have
been so misunderstood. [In their own days the prophets were
regarded as unpatriotic and subversive, and were often treated
as traitors.] To later generations, however, it has gradually
become evident that these prophets were the true patriots.
[Their only crime was that they saw clearly the pathway of right
for their nation and insisted that their corrupt rulers and fellow citizens follow it]

By many, the prophets were regarded as atheists and irreligious because they attacked the shallow rites of their times. Yet, as we look back upon these men today, they appear as spiritual geniuses who had conceived a higher type of religion than the people in those ages had yet begun to envision.

By the forces of evil they were regarded as meddlers, and were urged to go and mind their own affairs. Their maligners frequently succeeded in turning the masses of people against the prophets, even though they were the friends of mankind in working for a just society and in resisting the exploitation of the many at the hands of the few.

Because of these, and other misunderstandings, the prophets were usually regarded in their days as dangerous characters, and people stood in fear before them.

A Youth Movement

One of the most general present-day misconceptions regarding these religious leaders concerns their age. Most people think the prophets were old men. Particularly in sculpture and art they have frequently been portrayed as aged individuals with long beards and bald heads.

The truth is the exact reverse. For the most part the prophets were young men. Almost all the early ones seem to have begun their ministries in their twenties or early thirties. It appears that Jeremiah felt called to this task even as early as his teens. Persecution and martyrdom prevented most of them from enjoying a prolonged hearing.

For some reason, information concerning the deaths of these individuals was either not placed in the narratives or was later censored from them. Specific accounts are found only outside the prophetic records, for the Old Testament supplies nothing but general statements. These, however, carry the suggestion that many of the prophets met violent deaths. For instance, Jeremiah 2:30 tells how the sword had devoured the prophets "like a destroying lion." As recorded in Matthew 23:37-39 and Luke 13:34-35, Jesus wept over Jerusalem because it was a city which was accustomed to kill its prophets. By this method, opponents of the prophets were frequently able to dispose of these religious leaders before they had a chance to say much. This prevented many of them from attaining an advanced age. Most of their work was therefore done in the days of young manhood.

A few such as Isaiah and Jeremiah, who were allowed to continue their activity for forty and forty-two or more years respectively, grew old in the course of their labors. Nevertheless, it must not be forgotten that even these were called to their tasks as young men. They had been set on fire with a new spirit in the days of their youth. Their contributions began as the product of youth's nobility, and the precedents they established were set by them as young men. With those few who were fortunate enough to escape martyrdom and grow old in the course of their labors, this spirit of youth's idealism was kept bright. This was why they were able to continue as prophets in spite of advancing years.

Recognizing the essential youthfulness of the prophets, whether in years or in spirit, is an important consideration in appreciating their contributions. When properly understood, the work achieved by these great leaders of Israel may rank as one of the most significant religious youth movements of all time.

Predictors of the Future?

Perhaps the greatest misunderstanding of the Hebrew prophets abroad today is the common belief that they were primarily predictors of a far-distant future. Some religious groups and speakers go so far as to say that everything which is happening in the world of our day, and will happen in the future, has been predicted by the prophets. This persisting belief, that foretelling the future was the prophet's primary role, is one of the greatest religious absurdities of our time.

How does it happen that many good people continue to believe that these writings contain valid predictions for our era and the years that lie ahead? This is largely because most individuals have no knowledge of the issues that were uppermost in the days of the prophets, and are not aware of the historical happenings which were then taking place. Therefore, these people are unable to relate the prophetic teachings to the problems of those times. To such persons the predictions contained in those writings seem aimed at our age.

This mistaking of the prophetic objectives has been made possible largely because the moral and spiritual life of mankind has moved forward so little through the centuries. The fundamental issues of existence which the prophets were talking about — the problems of war, poverty, justice, hatred, etc. — were much the same as those with which we are concerned today.

Abandoning the idea of finding in the prophetic writings predictions as to what will happen in the immediate and distant future, we find in them collections of wise advice, as valid and valuable today as these words of counsel were at the time the prophets spoke. This is quite different from saying they gave predictions of our day. There is something eternal about their teachings. They minister to our age almost as pointedly as to the times in which they were first uttered. In fact they speak more forcibly than most voices of the present, which have grown so timid. In order to gain some of their courage and insight, we take time to study the prophets today.

Predictors of Jesus?

A further misconception is the common belief that the primary role of these religious pioneers was to predict in advance the coming of Jesus and to describe the manner of his expected ministry. Those who hold this misunderstanding tend to forget everything else about these men of God. For such misinterpreters, the prophets become simply God's announcers, to the people in Old Testament times, of his intention to send Jesus at a certain designated date some seven centuries later.

Best research shows that this belief also is baseless, for there are no predictions of Jesus in the prophets. Most of these supposed "Messianic" passages were not even in the original collections, but became added in the years after the exile when Palestine had lost her king, for which Messiah was but another name. These passages anticipated a day when political independence would be restored, and a righteous king would again sit on the throne of Israel. In a mood of extreme idealism, they described the nature of the new ruler and outlined the policies which they expected him to follow. In their bondage and persecution, people after the exile envisioned the king, who they hoped would rule over them some day, as well-nigh perfect. They anticipated the joy when he would be born, and told of the righteous acts he would perform.

Although in most Christian circles today it is still taken for granted that these passages refer to Jesus, when they are examined closely it is found they do not fit. If space were available to look at each expectation carefully, it could be seen that they refer to leaders hoped for in the immediate future and not centuries later in the person of Jesus.

Jesus said he came "to fulfill" the law and the prophets, but not in the mechanical sense most Christians usually take it. By reversing the two parts of the verb we get his meaning better. He conceived that it was his mission to "fill full" the law and the prophets. The Sermon on the Mount describes how he did this, and how he wishes his followers to do it. To be sure, Jesus was influenced much by the prophets. Their ideals of righteous leadership constituted one of his chief sources of inspiration. This, however, is quite different from saying they predicted Jesus.

Mighty Men of God

The chief trouble with these misunderstandings is that they have blinded people to the real significance of this remarkable succession of individuals. If they were not old men, if they did not possess a blueprint of the distant future, and if they were not predictors of Jesus, what then was their work?

The answer is simple. They were the great teachers and preachers of those times. They differed from the good religious leaders of today only in degree, and not in essence. They had no more supernatural knowledge or predictive ability than the wide-awake teacher or preacher of the present who is well-informed and a person of vision.

Today such high quality leaders are amazingly few in number. The situation in the times of the prophets was similar. The same is true in almost any age. As Isaiah said, the eyes of most people are closed, their ears are shut, and they are unable to think (Isa. 6:10).

Today the prophets would be called social reformers. Few eras in history have had sufficient idealism to receive such uncompromising people with good grace. The forces of wickedness in every age hate the social reformer and leave no stone unturned in setting the populace against him. Usually they succeed. Forsaking the wise counsels of the prophets, the generations seem to prefer the way of destruction. Man seems much like swine, always returning to wallow in the mire.

The prophets were the liberals of their day. They gave their lives to free the people from the cramping orthodoxies which had enslaved their mental and spiritual outlooks. They were the radicals of their times. They were people of fire and determination.

They devoted no time to the past and seldom gave even any backward look. In this the prophets differed sharply from the average individual who worships the past and longs to return to it. These were men of the progressive spirit, living for the things that yet should be, rather than for the past or a greedy enjoyment of the present. The attention of the prophets was directed chiefly toward the future. They were always several steps ahead of the people among whom they lived.

They were pained by seeing the citizens of those generations thoughtlessly and ignorantly jeopardizing the welfare of their country and endangering its security by undermining the moral foundations upon which alone a nation can continue to exist. Faced with such a situation, the prophets gave their lives to insure the continuance of their country for a glorious future by encouraging wise restraints and by urging upon the citizenry a redevotion to the cause of duty and regard for the rights of others.

Those in the prophetic succession were *forthtellers* rather than *foretellers*. They had courage to speak out boldly regarding all forms of corruption wherever it was found, in high places as well as low, without fear or favor. They refused to compromise in their battles for what they considered to be right. Although overwhelmed by persecution and silenced by imprisonment again and again, they continued on. So long as they had breath, they would accept no such thing as defeat.

In final essence, the prophets were spiritual pioneers who spent their lives helping mankind push back the moral frontiers. They were the voices of righteousness in times of political and moral degeneracy. In the regions of Palestine, they were the conscience of their age.

Literary Considerations

Most of the prophets were poets. This has been discovered in recent years, and editions of the Bible more and more are arranging these writings in verse form. Poetry may be described as memorable speech. By forging their utterances into poetic form, these individuals made more certain their messages would be remembered by future generations. Like Jesus, most of them were only speaking prophets, and never wrote anything. They inscribed their messages neither on paper nor on stone but on the human heart.

Memories were much more highly developed in those days than at present. People took pride in treasuring the words of their teachers accurately, and in passing them on to others without change. There seldom was any effort to remember whole addresses, but only the most striking portions of them. What we have in the books which bear the prophets' names might therefore be fittingly described as high points in the teachings of these men.

Their Importance

The importance of the prophetic writings can hardly be overstressed. They are the heart of the Old Testament, as the gospels are the heart of the New. There would have been no New Testament if it had not been for Jesus, for the whole of it is but the shadow cast by his personality. In the same way, there would probably have been no Old Testament if it had not been for the prophets, for most of it is but a projection of their teachings.

All the great religions of the Western world find their unity in the prophets. These writings are sacred to Jews, Mohammedans, and Christians. In spite of the barriers that have developed between these various groups, there is hope that in common study of the prophets we shall grow into a greater unity that in time may surmount these tragic divisions.

An Imaginative Approach

It must be remembered that the Bible is merely a collection of dry words. The rich vibrant life which was taking place in those days has, as it were, been dehydrated of all its spirit and reduced to lifeless words on pages of paper. Hours, days, weeks, or even years of activity are frequently concentrated into a small paragraph of scratches.

In order to appreciate the Bible, and the prophets in particular, it is necessary to reverse this process. The dry words, paragraphs, and pages must be made to live again by turning them back into life. This can be done by approaching these writings imaginatively.

It is not necessary to be fanciful. One needs only to use the clues found in the text, and then reconstruct the scenes and action in harmony with those indications. A few liberties may be taken in piecing out the picture, as a scientist reconstructs a skeleton, though some of the parts may be missing. Even such restorations, however, can have a high degree of accuracy.

Every prophetic utterance had its own distinctive background against which alone it can be truly understood. Practically nothing with regard to these historical settings has been preserved in the Bible. In order to appreciate the addresses at all adequately today, it is necessary to reconstruct the approximate scenes of the oral delivery. This can be done fairly successfully from a careful study of what evidence is available in the addresses themselves, combined with the facts of history from those times. By sizing up the audience, as it were, looking at the prophet-speaker, listening to what he has to say, and noting the reactions of his hearers, we can make these writings grow more meaningful; thus it becomes possible to enter into greater comprehension of the prophets. The only reverent approach to the Bible is the imaginative approach in which the reader tries to relive the experiences there recorded.

No attempt will be made to study all sixteen of the great prophets. It seems best to concentrate on certain of the more significant ones, and gain a rather intimate acquaintance with them. Consequently, only seven will be treated here. Even among these, only a small portion of their appearances and addresses will usually be considered. The purpose is rather to get the flavor of the prophets and gaze unhurriedly on certain of the more representative scenes in the course of their activities. In this way it is hoped that we may catch something of their spirit.

Becoming acquainted with this remarkable group of religious geniuses, whose real significance still remains largely unknown for most people, can be a literary and religious adventure. The prophets of Israel are able to lead us into the paths of right as they showed the way to the people of their generations. If we approach them with anticipation and imagination, the result can be a most rewarding acquaintance with these religious pioneers who set the world on fire with a new spirit.

Amos

2

The Shepherd of Tekoa

PROPHECY DID NOT BREAK FORTH suddenly in mature form.
There was a long buildup that covered a period of five
centuries. Among the score of forerunners were such discerning religious pioneers as Moses, Samuel, and Nathan. In the
work of Elijah, Elisha, and Micaiah ben Imlah the prophetic
movement had begun to gain considerable momentum; however, it remained for Amos to bring it into full swing. As
the first of the great prophets, he was to render a decisive service toward the religious development of his own people and
all mankind.

Home at Tekoa

It might be assumed that an individual of such influence
enjoyed remarkable opportunities in his youth. Yet, in this
instance, the truth of matters is quite the reverse. The place
in which Amos happened to be born was one of the most
unpromising regions in Palestine from which to expect any
greatness. This matter of the location reduced to a minimum
the prospects of anything good coming from him.

The territory in which Amos spent his early years and grew
to maturity was located in the wilds of a frontier area. It
was in the Jeshimon Mountains, which lay between the

populated highland region of Judah on the west and the desolation of the Dead Sea on the east. That was the no man's land of Palestine. It was a region of rocky hills and lonely gullies. There was little good soil remaining, for most of it had eroded away. Pastures were sparse, and for much of the year water was extremely scarce. Usually it was with great difficulty that sufficient grass could be found to keep the flocks alive.

Tekoa was the name of the particular spot where Amos lived, but that place was hardly worthy of being called a village. It was little more than a camping place in the isolated mountain regions where perhaps a dozen shepherd families were accustomed to pitch their tents and persist in trying to eke out a bare existence. It would seem that anyone born into such an outpost country would have been automatically destined for oblivion.

The times in which Amos lived were also inauspicious for anyone in younger years. The boy grew up in an age when children did not count, and were given practically no opportunities by their parents. Young folks were virtually slaves of the family. Their only role was to do work, and more work. Even for the most privileged child of that day, opportunities for cultural development were almost wholly lacking.

In a world which at best gave practically no consideration to children, Tekoa offered to a growing youth the extreme minimum in advantages. In that isolated location there was no place of religious gathering where he could attend services of worship and instruction. Weekday education also was something unknown. Consequently Amos never went to school a day in his life. He never had the opportunity of going to a museum. He never attended a lecture. He never scanned a newspaper. He never read a book. In fact, during all the years he lived in Tekoa, this young man probably never even as much as saw a book. Undoubtedly he could neither read nor write.

Strange as it may seem, what slight education Amos may be said to have possessed consisted largely of his knowledge concerning the outside world. Much of what he learned in this regard consisted of rumors left by an occasional traveler who by chance visited this village. Also, the men of Tekoa went annually, after the time of sheep shearing, to sell their wool and do some buying. When they returned, all the families of Tekoa would gather at the close of day and for many evenings would listen to tales concerning the things which the men had seen while absent from home. They heard stories about the luxury, softness, immorality, and low manner of life as observed in the cities. Such tales seemed unbelievable to these residents of the hills where the struggle for existence was so grim that they could be thankful when they had the barest necessities of life. At other times of the year there were tales of Israel's past. Those evenings about the campfires of Tekoa were the nearest Amos ever came, during childhood and youth, to anything that might be called schooling.

Except when he led his flocks across the Jordan to the pasture lands of Bashan in time of drought, it is doubtful if Amos himself had ever been out of the isolated regions about Tekoa. Travel into the populous parts of the outside world was reserved for the male adults. Women, children, and young men were denied such contacts. These underprivileged groups remained at home and worked while their elders were away on these occasional marketing trips. During those periods, the most arduous tasks fell to young men like Amos.

This lad of Tekoa undoubtedly yearned to see the villages, cities, and farmlands of Palestine with his own eyes. Perhaps some day this opportunity would come. For the time being, however, he was left, behind the curtain of the hills, to dream of the great outside world with its wonder, its luxuries, and its sins.

The Shepherd's Life

Tekoa was a village of one occupation, the raising and herding of sheep. This had been the traditional vocation of the Hebrew people. With the passing of time, the early pastoral manner of life had gradually given way, over much of Palestine, to agricultural pursuits. Orchards, vineyards, and grain fields had come increasingly to replace the sheepfold. Accompanying this development was the ever-encroaching dominance of town and city.

By contrast, in Tekoa life remained primitive, much as in the days of Abraham, Isaac, and Jacob, who tented on the highlands of Judah, only a short distance to the westward. Amos probably often recalled the patriarchal stories about those ancestors who first gained a foothold for his people in this "promised land."

To be a shepherd in the regions of Tekoa was a hazardous experience. The Jeshimon Mountains were infested with wild beasts, especially bears and mountain lions. While out alone with his flock in the most dangerous areas, Amos may have thought of the time the "young lion roared against" Samson, and how that strong man had mastered and slain it bare-handed (Judges 14:5-6). There were also reminiscences of David who, as a shepherd boy several centuries earlier and only a few miles from Tekoa, had encountered bears and lions and slew them with pebbles from his sling, much as he later did the giant Goliath. This fearless boy David had once even grabbed a lion by its beard as it proceeded to attack him, and had succeeded in dispatching it lonehanded in the Samson manner (I Sam. 17:34-37). There was also the recollection from the time of the prophet Elisha when two enraged she-bears came out of the woods and ate or mangled a group of forty-two children playing nearby (II Kings 2:23-25).

This deserted region, in which Amos conducted his shepherd activities, was full of limestone caves. These constantly reminded him of the time when David, as a young man, had fled in desperation into these havens of safety to escape from maddened King Saul, who was using every means possible to catch and kill him. It is likely that, on many a night, Amos reviewed the exploits of David, the boy-king, in these same caves, reliving those narrow escapes from death at the hands of Saul's armies (I Samuel 23:14-25:13; 26:1-25).

The constant fear of wild beasts that haunted the Tekoan shepherd was more acute by reason of the fact he was practically harnessed to his flock. He was frequently forced to stay out on the hills with his sheep, by night as well as day. In seasons of drought, these shepherds were gone from their homes with the flocks for weeks, and even months, without returning. At times they went to distant regions in search of better pastures. At night the shepherd would try to secure his flock from harm in some cave or protection among the rocks. Often it was impossible to find shelter. Those nights had to be spent in danger, out on some hillside slope.

In other ways the shepherd had an easy life. Most of the time there was no real labor. All he needed to do was lead his flock from place to place where there were pastures, remain with them, and protect them. It was a life of relative leisure. David had employed his time as a shepherd by observing nature, mastering the harp, and learning accuracy with the sling. By contrast, Amos was inspired to deep

thought during those days when he had so much time for
reflection.

As Moses had the most significant experience of his life
while watching his flocks at "the back of the wilderness" (Ex.
3:1), so Amos may have had his moments of greatest illumination when he went occasionally to those far eastern ranges that
overlook the Jordan Valley and the Dead Sea. He thought
of the day when Lot, making his disastrous choice, stood with
his uncle Abraham on one of those same hilltops from which
they could see "all the plain of the Jordan, which was well
watered . . . like the garden of the Lord" (Gen. 13:10-13).

From those easterly slopes Amos may often have looked
down over the Dead Sea area where he could see the remains
of Sodom and Gomorrah, those two prosperous but wicked
cities that had been burned in the days of Abraham (Gen. 19).
As the ever-rising waters of this salt sea had not yet come
to the point of covering those ruins, they offered their silent
witness to the catastrophe which had engulfed the "civilization" of those carefree cities of the plain. Looking at their
fallen walls and crumbled houses, several miles below him at
the foot of the ranges, Amos probably was made to think
of the immoralities developed in those places. He recalled
how their perversions had brought the deserved fate of extinction to those prosperous city-states that were once located in
the rich valley of the Jordan.

Now the whole country had come to follow the ways of
wickedness in which these twin cities had pioneered. As
Amos looked at the site of their ruins, he could hardly help
but reflect upon his country's past, present, and probable
future. So, in the wilds of Judah, the young shepherd Amos
had time to think of good and evil, and about the great issues
of life.

Called to Become a Prophet

Most of the prophets had what is usually described as a *call*. This refers to the particular experience which inspired each one to take up the prophetic task. Frequently, some physical occurrence, personal contact, or notable experience was of strategic importance in producing these effects. In such situations, the particular happening usually had a deep meaning for the individual specially concerned, out of all proportion to what its nature would suggest. It is the same today, for many young people are directed into their life's vocation by some chance circumstance such as the meeting of a particular person, some sickness, an accident, a death in the family, experiences in war, or any number of other occurrences.

The speed with which a person was transformed into a prophet varied considerably. Occasionally some sudden catastrophe, or other event, caused an ordinary individual to decide, in almost a moment of time, to become a prophet. In other instances, the inner urgings that led a young man to take up this work exerted a gradual pull, over a considerable period, before he became resigned to the task.

The call of Amos was of the sudden type. It happened when he was probably far from home, on one of those nights when he could not find shelter for the flock, and they were huddled together on some hilltop. The joy of this evening under the Palestinian stars was suddenly turned to terror as a lion darted out of the darkness, pounced upon the flock, seized one of the lambs, and departed with it.

The best way to appreciate the call of Amos is to go to a zoo fifteen minutes before the lions are fed, and listen to the beasts roar. As they belch forth their rising crescendos, that

make the whole building vibrate, you begin to be concerned
about whether the bars will be able to hold the beasts in case
they should decide to have their dinners a little early, and
choose some of the choice morsels before them. However,
you take your chance with the other people, and endure the
terrifying sounds which accompany the lions' performances.
To appreciate the experience of Amos on that night, we
must be mindful that there were no bars protecting him and
his flock. Also, the shriek of a lion pouncing on some prey
and tearing it to death is infinitely more terrifying than the
simple roar of a hungry beast that wants some food.

We can understand something concerning the sense of
relief that came over Amos as the lion departed. Nevertheless,
we can imagine his continuing fright and thumping heart.
There was danger the lion might return and seize another of
the flock, or even the shepherd himself. We can be sure there
was not much sleep that night.

The Unfolding Mission

Why should this experience have happened to Amos? In
those days, all such natural occurrences were regarded as
direct acts of God for some special purpose. There could be
no doubt but that God must have sent the lion, and for a
particular reason. The puzzling question was, What was God's
purpose in this event? That was difficult to answer. We
could have seen Amos buried in thought as he tried to solve it.

After considerable time, his face lit up as he felt he had
reached the answer. The terrified shepherd came to see in
this occurrence a parable that God had enacted. The lamb,
which had been torn into shreds, represented the country of
Israel. The lion was a symbol of God himself. The whole
episode showed how the deity had become so enraged over

A Lamb from Amos's Flock

the sinfulness of his people that he was about to pounce
on them, and tear his nation into shreds. What occurred that
evening to one lamb, on an isolated hilltop, was what soon
would happen to Israel as a nation.

This was God's warning to Israel. Yet no one but Amos
had heard it. How then could the Israelite people know of
it? Apparently they would remain unaware of the danger
unless he should inform them. Inasmuch as he was the only
one who knew of this impending development, it seemed
necessary for him to go and tell them. This would require
that he leave his home at Tekoa, and his flocks.

These considerations forced Amos to conclude that he must
go out into the thick of Palestinian life and journey from
village to village, and from city to city, announcing the
message of warning which he had received on that fateful
night. In other words, he felt *called* to become a prophet.
Up to that evening, Amos was only an ordinary upright young
man. The tense moments of that night, however, had begun
to transform him into a prophet of the Most High.

When a sheep was seized and carried away by wild animals,
it was regarded as the obligation of the good Palestinian
shepherd to rescue the animal alive if possible. If this could
not be done, it was his duty to recover what was left of it. He
was expected to follow the wild beast and rescue the remains,
even if forced to go to its very den. The passage in Amos
3:12 may well be the prophet's description of how he went
searching, on the following morning, for what was left of
that lost lamb. He found nothing but "two shinbones" and
the "scrap of an ear." These constituted the only remaining
evidence concerning the tragedy of the nighttime.

When Amos later described that decisive night of his life,
he told how he previously had been "only a shepherd and a

dresser of mulberry trees" but that God took him from following the flock, and God said unto him, "Go, prophesy unto my people Israel" (Amos 7:15). That he should have obeyed was as inevitable as that he had become terrified on that night. To be a prophet was not his choice. He felt himself seized by a divine compulsion. There was no escape.

Days of Preparation

In the days that followed, Amos was overshadowed with a sense of new responsibility. He did not appreciate how presumptuous it would seem for a hill-bred illiterate young man, who had never been to school and probably had never even seen a city, to think of going out and trying to alter the whole course of national trends. Apparently it never occurred to him that there could be any doubt but that the people would be attentive and responsive to his messages.

What was he going to say? That was the chief problem. Since there were no theological schools to which he could go for training, whatever preparation was to be made for these coming tasks had to be done by himself, out under the sun and stars.

In the course of his thinking as to what he would say before the various cities and villages, the utterances of this young prophet took shape. As there was nothing prosaic about the mind of Amos, his proposed speeches came forth in the form of excellent poetry. Apparently he began practicing them at once, using the sheep as his audience. After rehearsal many times before the flock, these addresses assumed a literary polish that has seldom been equaled. It matters not that Amos was unable to read or write. In his skillful use of the spoken word he became one of the greatest literary masters of Bible times.

The next step was to free himself from his shepherd duties. After weeks of intensive preparation in the wilds, he decided his hour for action had come. So he turned homeward with his flock. Now the big question was, What would his parents say about these ambitious plans? Was he naive enough to think they would be proud of him and bid him Godspeed on his important project? Did he think the people of Tekoa would be pleased to have one of their number go forth as a prophet?

It is probable Amos found a response far more hostile than he could have anticipated even in his most pessimistic moments. As a youth in his twenties, he was told that he was too young to be a prophet. His place was taking care of the flocks. His relatives were resolved to purge these crazy ideas from his mind. He would bring disgrace upon the family, and they could not tolerate this.

Nevertheless, the young man Amos was not deterred by these oppositions. He met them with an irresistible resolve. It was perhaps to meet the attempted persuasions of his family, and the assembled neighbors of Tekoa, that he spoke to justify his decision. As the days of psychological terms had not yet dawned, he found himself handicapped in trying to express his inner feelings. In those times there were not even words for "cause" or "effect." So he felt compelled to make use of figurative language. By a series of examples illustrating cause and effect, he tried to impress on the people of Tekoa that when a given cause has occurred, the corresponding effect is inevitable. The experience of that memorable night was the cause, and his going forth as a prophet was the unavoidable effect.

> Do two people travel together,
>   Unless they have met?
> Does a lion roar in the forest,
>   Unless he has found prey?

Does a young lion utter his growl,
  Unless he has seized something?
Does a bird fall to the earth,
  Unless a net is set for it?
Does a trap spring from the ground,
  Unless something has tripped it?
Can a trumpet be blown in the city,
  And the people not become terrified?

The lion has roared,
  Who will not fear?
The Lord has spoken,
  Who can but prophesy?

Amos 3:3-6a, 8

Did the family of Amos and the townspeople relent in their attitudes, and withdraw their prohibition of his going? Or did they become all the more bitter against this young upstart, and his proposed plans, as he proceeded with preparations to leave Tekoa? These are questions that probably never can be answered with certainty.

Civic pride was an important factor in this matter. The reputation of Tekoa was at stake. We can guess that the villagers were especially disgusted over the plans of this misguided youth, as they regarded him. The residents of Tekoa did not propose to allow one of their number to go out and bring the good name of their fair village into disgrace.

Little did those people realize that Amos was about to do the very opposite. If it had not been for this prophet, the name of Tekoa would have passed into oblivion centuries ago. Instead of bringing a blighting disrepute upon its reputation, the memory of Amos has made that little camping place among the hills immortal.

3

An Unexpected Speaker

WHATEVER THE CIRCUMSTANCES of his leaving, the important fact is that Amos finally departed from Tekoa, and went forth as a prophet to the people of his day. As he left home, he probably had with him only a small bundle of the most essential items. He was not dressed in his best Sunday suit, for he had none. In respect to clothing, he possessed only one outfit. The garb that served him for years in the pastures of the wilderness would be obliged also to take care of his needs as a prophet in the cities of Israel.

The Trip North

We can still see the eager step with which Amos walked down those winding trails in the direction of Bethlehem. There he struck the main road of the Judean highlands leading toward the north. If we mistake not, Amos was never to set eyes upon Tekoa again.

Jerusalem, the capital of the Southern Kingdom, may well have been his first stop. Perhaps he spent a few days there, observing what city life was like. He went into Solomon's Temple and probably was disappointed with the manners of worship and conduct there. To one who had lived the bare existence that was possible in Tekoa, the show of luxury throughout much of the city was beyond anything he had ever conceived. He had suddenly moved into a wholly different world. What troubled him most were the evidences of immorality and corruption which he detected on almost every side. It was to combat these tendencies that he had come forth as a prophet.

Although there was ample need here, it seemed to Amos that Jerusalem was not the best place to begin his work. He had heard that the cities of the Northern Kingdom of Israel were even more corrupt. So he decided to go there and spend his efforts where wickedness was at its worst. There was nothing cowardly about Amos. As on the pastures about Tekoa, he was determined to beard the beast of corruption in its very den.

Resuming his journey northward, he probably made his first stop at Gibeah, the ancestral home of King Saul. Several miles farther on he came to Ramah, made memorable because the prophet Samuel's home was there in his later years. Next was Bethel, hallowed by so many memories that were associated with the patriarchs during the first days of the Hebrew sojourn in Palestine. Then he passed through other villages that carried special memory associations with Jacob and his son Joseph.

While going from city to city, there developed within Amos the increasing resolve that he would not stop until he had reached Samaria. His attention became centered on this place because he had heard along the way that, of all the cities of Israel, this capital of the Northern Kingdom was the worst.

Eventually he arrived at his destination. As he approached, the city towered above him with its elaborate fortifications. Samaria did not go in deeply for things religious. It did not have a shrine that could compare with Solomon's Temple, but in other ways the show of luxury in this northern capital was such as the residents of Jerusalem could not begin to equal.

If you wish to find the real America, it is not advisable to go to some such place as a library, a church, or a college. The best way to get a cross section of America is by walking up Broadway or Fifth Avenue in New York City in the Times Square area, with open ears, listening to what people are saying on your right, your left, in front, and behind. Usually it is possible to "tune in" on a conversation in one of these quarters. The same can be done on Tremont Street in Boston, Euclid Avenue in Cleveland, State and Randolph Streets in Chicago, and in crowded key areas of other cities. It may be guessed that Amos used something of this technique in amassing his knowledge concerning the interests of the people in Samaria. He probably also entered into many conversations with them.

The worst fears of Amos were substantiated with regard to what he found in Samaria. The manner of life he observed there was even more degenerate than reports he had heard in cities along the way had indicated. It was not long before he had seen so much that he was at the point of overflowing with things he felt ought to be said.

Where would he do his first speaking? The response might depend considerably on his choice of occasion. So he waited, continuing his observations and walks about the city, until the time should be opportune.

Judgment upon the Nations

Not many days later, the appropriate occasion arrived for which the young prophet had been waiting. It seems that a national gathering, of special political significance, was about to take place in Samaria. The city was rapidly filling with people who had come from all parts of Palestine and beyond. The large square before the palace was becoming crowded with visitors, expectantly awaiting the scheduled ceremonies and addresses. The platform for the dignitaries was in readiness. It was only a matter of minutes until the festivities and program would begin.

Apparently Amos suddenly concluded this would be his opportunity. While the crowd was awaiting the men of the day, he ascended the speaker's stand. Not one person in the audience knew who he was or from where he had come. The appearance at such a place of a man in this crude shepherd's garb must have served notice on the people that something unusual was about to happen. Before anyone had a chance to rush up and take him away, he began to speak.

The first stanza of his poetic address on that occasion was devoted to Syria, whose capital was at Damascus. That neighbor country on the northeast had been a thorn in the side of Israel ever since the Hebrew people had settled in Palestine. Amos reminded his audience of atrocities recently committed in a raid against the Israelite dwellers east of the Jordan River, in the land of Gilead. The Syrians apparently had herded their captives together and had driven over them with iron-toothed threshing sledges drawn by oxen, trampling and cutting their victims to death. Amos began this address by announcing to his hearers that this irresponsible border incident was due for punishment.

Thus the Lord has spoken:
"Because of three transgressions by Damascus,
    And now four, I cannot withhold punishment;
Because they drove over the Gileadites,

On threshing harrows with teeth of iron.
Therefore I will set fire to the house of Hazael,
    And it shall consume the palaces of Ben-Hadad. . . ."
The Lord has spoken.

Amos 1:3-5

This was good news for an Israelite audience. Even the
most important occasion could be postponed until the crowd
had heard more of it. The applause was amazing. The Israelites always had hated these people, and it was good to hear
someone come forth with the assurance that the Syrians were
about to get what was coming to them. The applause died
down only because that gathering wished to hear more.

As words began to pour again from the lips of the prophet
from Tekoa, he attacked another of Israel's traditional enemies,
the Ammonites. They also lived to the east, across the Jordan,
somewhat farther south than the Syrians. This concerned a
border clash, also with the Israelite territory of Gilead. In
the course of enlarging their national boundaries, the Ammonites had committed unspeakable deeds of barbarity against
civilian populations. Amos described these as an outrage,
and called for punishment.

Thus the Lord has spoken:
"Because of three transgressions by the Ammonites,
    And now four, I cannot withhold punishment;
Because women with child they ripped up in Gilead,
    For the sake of enlarging their boundaries.
Therefore I will set fire to the walls of Rabbah,
    And it shall consume the palaces thereof. . . ."
The Lord has spoken.

Amos 1:13-15

The applause this time probably was louder and more prolonged than before. Two of Israel's worst enemies to be

punished! This was almost too good to be true. The Ammonites were scum of the earth, and it would be a pleasure to be rid of them.

In the third stanza, the edict of divine wrath settled upon Moab, another country east of the Jordan, but farther south than the other two. Moab also had been a source of irritation to the Israelites ever since the latter had entered the "promised land." Amos called to his hearers' attention an indignity committed by Moab against the Edomites, the people who lived on their southwestern border. The Moabites had captured the king of Edom and had cremated his body, which was regarded as an intolerable practice in those times. The text may indicate they used the lime derived from his burned bones to plaster their houses. This made the crime all the more revolting. Accordingly, Amos announced that the judgment of God was about to fall upon the Moabites.

> Thus the Lord has spoken:
> "Because of three transgressions by Moab,
>   And now four, I cannot withhold punishment;
> Because the bones of the king of Edom,
>   They have burned even into lime.
> Therefore I will send into Moab a fire
>   That shall consume the palaces of Kerioth. . . ."
> The Lord has spoken.

Amos 2:1-3

After this third stanza of the address, one can imagine that the rejoicing and applause of Amos's audience was almost uncontrollable. All of Israel's three most formidable enemies to be punished! No better news could have been brought to an Israelite gathering. Some of the prominent listeners may already have been consulting together, planning how they would place this speaker at the head of the Palestinian armies, so he could help God in executing these judgments upon their hated neighbors.

The applause was probably so prolonged that Amos may have felt compelled to raise his hand, for the purpose of quieting the people, so he could resume speaking. His hearers dared to hope he would continue by heaping ever-greater judgments upon their enemies. Perhaps, before getting through, he would announce that all foes and rivals of Israel would be annihilated. As it became apparent that Amos was beginning to speak, there was a sudden hush of silence. No one wanted to miss his words.

Judgment upon Israel

The people were astounded as they heard the name "Israel." Could it be possible that this crudely dressed shepherd was pronouncing judgment upon his own people? There must have been some mistake. Apparently he had gotten his words mixed.

No! There was no mistake. With full intent, Amos waded into the sins of Israel, sins of such magnitude that the crimes of the three nations just mentioned fell into insignificance. Before his astonished audience, he lay bare the record of Israel's acts.

Thus the Lord has spoken:
"Because of the three transgressions by Israel,
  And now four, I cannot withhold punishment;
Because they have sold the righteous for silver,
  And the needy for a pair of shoes.
They trample on the heads of the poor,
  The meek are denied access to the courts."

"A father and his son go to the same woman,
  And so my holy name is profaned;

Sprawled out, they lie beside every altar,
   Even upon garments taken in pledge;
Gulping down, in the house of their God,
   The wine left as payment for penance."

Hear this word which the Lord has spoken
   Against you, O people of Israel:
"You only have I known
   Of all the families of the earth,
Therefore I will punish you
   For *every one* of your iniquities."

Amos 2:6-8; 3:1-2

Conditions in Israel

The words of Amos reveal clearly the conditions which were prevailing in Palestine. He had grown deeply conscious of the crimes against the poor in that land which had come to be ruled by the rich. By their oppressions, they were minting the lives of the masses into cold cash. This was done by foreclosing on them. Properties were seized by those to whom their owners were indebted. Often debtors were sold into slavery when they were unable to pay at the moment of demand. The nation had degenerated to the point where poor people received no consideration in court. Judges would decide in favor of a rich creditor for even such a small bribe as a pair of shoes.

The overlords of Palestine were as truly trampling "on the heads of the poor" as were the Syrians when they ran over the Gileadites with their threshing harrows. Only, the offending Israelites were so merciless as to do this to their own citizenry. To Amos, the champion of the poor and oppressed, this exploitation and enslavement of one's fellow men was the most revolting of all crimes.

Personal immorality was another chief curse of the day.

Prostitution was practiced openly in Palestine, yes, even *sacred prostitution*. Today gambling schemes such as bingo, raffles, etc. are included in the activities of some churches for purposes of raising money. In those times, prostitution was similarly carried on with the blessing of the religious authorities, provided they received their racketeering rake-off. It was like some cities today which still license prostitutes, and use the accrued money for the support of libraries, or some other worthy end. In the days of Amos, practically every holy place had its "sacred precincts" where women worshipers would go into seclusion with the "holy men," the priests. Similarly, male pilgrims would seek out the "holy women" or priestesses.

At times of national gathering, when the booths could not accommodate the people, couples lay "sprawled out . . . beside every altar" on improvised beds made of garments which the priests had kept as security when loans were made, and had never been returned. Upon these "stolen" pieces of clothing, the celebrants carried on their licentious and drunken carousals, gulping down the wine which had been exacted from offenders by the priests "as payment for penance."

Amos reminded his audience of an especially revolting scene, perhaps observed only shortly before, when a father and son went together and patronized the same prostitute. Although all these acts were done in the holy name of their God, Amos called them a profanation of religion.

Before those days of regression, the Israelites had been forward looking in religion. They had prided themselves on being God's "chosen people." Amos expressed this when he represented the deity as saying, "You only have I known of all the families of the earth."

Because the people of Israel had better opportunities in

the way of religion than other countries, however, Amos insisted that their responsibilities were also correspondingly greater. To whom much is given, much is also to be expected, among nations as well as individuals.

In the case of Damascus, Ammon, and Moab, these nations were to be punished for an exceptional sin in which each had gone too far in overstepping the bounds of propriety. By reason of her greater advantages, Amos declared that Israel, by contrast, was about to be punished for "every one" of her iniquities. Because her opportunities were greater, her punishment would be correspondingly severe.

Although Israel had gotten started on the higher religious pathway ahead of surrounding peoples, she had now fallen behind. It had come to the point where she had been weighed in the balances, and had been found wanting. So the divine favor was giving way to wrath. The time of punishment had finally come.

The Stunned Audience

The closing portion of this first address by Amos fell as a bombshell in the audience at Samaria that day. To have a patriotic rally spoiled, by making such accusations in public, seemed to the people unforgivable. Faces were pale. By contrast with the roaring applause that followed the previous portions of his presentation, these last words were greeted with a deathlike silence, especially the final pronouncements in which he had heaped bitter judgment upon his own people.

At the close of his remarks, Amos probably stepped from the speaker's stand, walked out through the throngs, and took his departure. The people seemed glued to the spot, however, and were unable to move.

This was one of the great addresses in history. Seldom

has a speaker been such a master of his audience. At first he played upon their prejudices and international hates until he had won their confidence and had completely disarmed them. Then, suddenly, and without warning, he drove home his message with such vigor that it never could be forgotten. Although the science of psychology was yet unknown, Amos was in reality a master psychologist.

The text of this utterance has been spoiled considerably in our Bibles through interpolation within it, by later writers, of sections pronouncing judgment on other "bad" nations. Even so, its surpassing excellence can still be appreciated. For powerfulness in declaring to the people their sins, nothing comparable to these words had ever been heard in Israel before, and the people hardly knew what to make of them. We can imagine parents telling their children about those tense moments when they heard the prophet Amos speak. Around the evening campfires, from generation to generation, the record of that day must have continued as one of the most exciting stories.

Although this was the first speech by Amos as a prophet, the care with which he chose his occasion and the strategy of surprise, made possible by the fact no one knew him or what he was likely to say, rendered this one of the most notable addresses in all the annals of the prophets. In skillfulness of execution, and command of the audience, this was a masterpiece. Through the centuries it has remained a model and inspiration for all aspiring prophets. If he had delivered no more, this one address would have been sufficient to have made the memory of the prophet from Tekoa immortal for all time.

4

Prophet of Justice

BECAUSE OF ITS ELEMENT OF SURPRISE, that first address by Amos had afforded the golden opportunity of his ministry. On later occasions, people knew approximately what to expect when they saw him coming. Nor did he ever have the privilege of addressing such a large crowd again. From this time on, he faced the necessity of speaking before smaller groups. For some days he apparently continued around the capital at Samaria, giving messages wherever occasion afforded. One is left to imagine where he spent his nights. The major portion of each day was undoubtedly occupied in making observations about the city. Attention is devoted here to only three of his remaining addresses delivered at this capital of the Northern Kingdom. Nevertheless, among this trio of scenes from his life are found some of Amos's most significant appearances.

Before the Women's Club

One of the unusual experiences of this prophet was before the women of Samaria, possibly at some subsequent hour on the same day that he gave his address to the large political gathering. Or, the time may have been a day or two later. At any rate, it probably occurred while that prolonged national celebration was still in progress. Amos had not planned

to seek out the women and speak to them. This came about
in a curious manner, and so suddenly that it must have been
a shock even to him.

The best guess is that Amos was walking down the street on
which the palace was located at the time the "upper four
hundred" of Israel were gathering at the queen's invitation for
afternoon tea. Possibly the prophet paused before the palace
for a time to watch this gay procession enter.

The person today who has greatest possibility of compre-
hending the feelings of Amos, during those moments before
the palace, is an unemployed person, in time of depression,
on the opening night of grand opera. There he stands, outside
the Metropolitan Opera House in New York City, or the
Opera House in Boston, with tattered clothing and gnawing
hunger. As the ladies enter they pass him in a carefree mood,
with their ermine coats, their bejeweled fingers, their multiple-
stringed necklaces of pearls, and with a dizzying whirl of per-
fumery that follows them. This show of wealth, and social
caste, becomes offensive to the unemployed man. He finds
it difficult to see how anyone should be allowed such luxury
at a time when great human needs all about are calling for
attention.

Amos, the "vagrant," standing across the street in Samaria,
was amazed by the show of luxuries he saw as these women
approached the royal mansion. The make-up and conscious
heightening of sex appeal was something he had never seen
before. Although not privileged to come in expensive limou-
sines with liveried chauffeurs, some of these guests arrived
in the ancient equivalent, the sedan chair or palanquin, which
was borne by four servants. This was one way these women
had of displaying their fashionableness and exhibiting their
snobbishness. Amos was most amazed at their haughtiness

LADIES OF FASHION

and pride, as each presented herself at the palace door. The prophet from Tekoa continued to stand there, stunned by this demonstration of arrogance and wealth.

Suddenly Amos became agitated. This was an urgent matter. Something must be done about it, and at once. Go into that gathering? Yes! Yes, he must go in immediately, and give them a message. There could be no better time than now, when they were all together. So he crossed the street and went through that same door which, a few minutes before, had received that conceited procession.

As Amos made his way into that place of meeting, we can imagine what a turmoil he created. The contrast was picturesque. Before him were the highly perfumed women of Israel, in all their gorgeous array. Before them stood Amos in the crude, smelly garb of a shepherd.

As the prophet found a place of vantage, and faced his audience, he was speechless for a moment. The fatness of the women almost unnerved him. How concepts even in feminine beauty change! The Hollywood and Paris standards in those days dictated that a woman must weigh two hundred, three hundred, or four hundred pounds in order to rate at any beauty contest.

As Amos looked at these potential aspirants for the role of "Mrs. Israel of 750 B.C.," he was reminded of other days. He recalled a time of drought when, to seek food for his flock, he had led the sheep far beyond his usual territory, across the Jordan River, and into the rich grazing lands of Bashan. There he had seen a herd of fat heifers that had gorged themselves to the full, and were lying down on one of those hillside pastures, chewing their cuds. Inasmuch as these chunks of flesh which he faced reminded him of those fat cattle, Amos began his remarks by addressing them as "cows of Bashan."

Afflicted with the malady of "keeping up with the Joneses," these women had developed insatiable desires and appetites. In order that their mania for properties, possessions, and material luxuries might in a measure be satisfied, their husbands were forced to go out and exploit those with whom they had dealings. When these men came home from their day's activities in the evening, their wives had them serve up the drinks, so they might dine in state and make merry.

The first part of Amos's message to those women that afternoon was extremely short, but he spared no vigor in chiding them for their part in oppressing the poor and crushing the needy.

> Listen to these words —
> You cows of Bashan,
>   Who are in Mount Samaria;
> Who oppress the poor,
>   Who crush the needy,
> Who say to your husbands,
> "Serve, and let us drink."
>
> *Amos 4:1*

The tragedy in all this was that these people of influence were weakening the structure of their country, making it vulnerable to attack from foreign quarters. Such a civilization, whose benefits went to the few rather than to the many, would not hold up in time of conflict. A dispossessed and discontented citizenry cannot be counted upon to make an effective defense of a country. Amos knew that the Assyrians in Mesopotamia were eyeing Palestine for conquest at that very moment. He therefore ended by telling these vampires, who were sucking the life out of their nation, what would inevitably happen to them when the threatened military invasion should take place.

When Amos had previously walked about the high citadel
of Samaria, he had noticed the dump in the valley. On that
side there were small holes in the city wall. Through these
the refuse was pushed that it might roll down to the dump in
the valley below. There was no garbage or waste collection
in those days. Even if a donkey died, his owner dragged him
to one of these holes, and chucked him through the wall.
Down in the dumps below, flames and worms did their part in
trying to clear the valley.

Amos reminded these women that, with the arrival of
military siege, they would be worth no more than one of those
dead donkeys. Later on, the words of Amos were thought
too terrible for reading in the synagogue, and so were pur-
posely corrupted at this point into something relatively mean-
ingless. This censored version is what is read in our Bibles.
Today it is becoming possible to go back to old manuscripts
and reconstruct, from clues in ancient versions, what presumably were the real climaxing words of Amos as he spoke
on that occasion.

> The Lord has sworn by his holiness, that,
> "Behold, days shall come upon you
> When you shall be dragged by the nose with hooks,
> And by your buttocks, with fish spears;
> Even as dung you shall be hauled out, one by one,
> To be cast forth on the dump heap naked."

Amos 4:2-3

To some people today this may seem the utterance of a
wild man. Just the reverse, they were the words of a person
with deep sincerity, who spoke what he foresaw. Amos had
no use for prudish restraints, or the mincing of words. He
told these women exactly what would come upon them as a

result of their deeds. They would be raped by the military invaders until dead. Then someone would grab a hook in a meat shop, or a harpoon or spear in a fish market, jab it into the buttocks of their naked bodies and drag them through the streets, as a dead donkey, to the dump. They would have nothing more in the way of a burial service than was enjoyed by the least of animal carcasses.

After Amos had concluded his few minutes with these representatives of royalty, and elite women of Israel, they knew that something had happened. Whether some of the more enraged ones forced him from their midst can probably never be determined. The only certainty in the situation is that a perfectly wonderful afternoon tea had been *completely spoiled* for these women.

Nevertheless, the biting condemnation of their corroding luxury, and its accompanying exploitation, must have produced some effect upon Amos's listeners. Especially impressed were those who had not been in the audience but heard the rumors of this "prophetic tea" as they spread over the country. The prophet Elijah never dared to face the wicked Queen Jezebel. Amos, by contrast, had the courage to confront a host of Jezebels.

A Day in Court

Next we follow Amos as he went into one of the places where court was in progress. In those days there were no formal judicial bodies, housed in expensive buildings, as we have them. Their courts were informal, and usually held at the city gate. The elders of the community were self-appointed judges. Formerly they had taken pride in meting out justice; however, a change in this area also had come over Israel. Now the lure for graft on the part of the judges had replaced their passion for right. In his first address, Amos had given a severe indictment concerning the judicial processes of his day but apparently it had produced little effect, at least in this particular court.

As Amos observed the proceedings, he was more amazed than ever at the miscarriage of justice. It had come to the point where the courts seemed wholly allied with the forces of corruption. What was handed out in the name of justice served as a boon to the undeserving and unscrupulous. To the innocent, who were being defrauded, this thing *called* justice was a bitter pill.

When witnesses tried to testify truthfully, the typical judge proceeded to confuse, silence, and get rid of them by denying the admissibility of their evidence. The size of the bribe, rather than standards of legal procedure, was what counted. Since the poor could not afford bribes, they stood no chance in court. When anyone stood up during a session to challenge this corruption, he found himself hated and practically run out of the community by the forces in control. The judicial system had degenerated to the point where it even supported racketeering by which these conniving forces seized a portion of every farmer's grain crop each year as their price for *protecting* him.

After watching for a while, the prophet Amos was so outraged by what he saw that he arose in court, interrupted the crooked proceedings, and made that open space before the city gate ring with his vigorous call to justice.

> Thus the Lord has spoken
> To the house of Israel;
> "Who turn justice into bitterness,
> And cast righteousness to the earth;
> They hate him who reproves in the gate,
> And abhor those who speak truthfully;

Harassers of the righteous, takers of bribes,
They even turn aside the needy in the gate."

"Therefore, because you trample upon the poor,
And take from them exactions of grain;
Though you have built houses of hewn stone,
You shall not dwell in them;
Though you have planted delightful vineyards,
You shall not drink their wine;
For I know how many are your transgressions,
And how great are your sins."

Amos 5:4, 7, 10-12

These court officials may have regarded Amos as a *meddler*, but he at least knew that "Righteousness exalts a nation, while sin is a reproach to any people" (Prov. 14:34). He could see that these judges, and their patrons, were really guilty of treason. They would have resented this charge, asserting they were *one hundred percent* Israelites. They may not have been in negotiation with foreign countries, but far worse, they were giving their lives to make the heart of their native land judicially rotten. Amos knew that honorable procedure is an essential for governments as for individuals, and that adherence to right principles is the only sure foundation upon which any nation can endure. When this ceases to be present, the stability of a people is weakened, and they soon become easy victims for conquest from without.

As he spoke, Amos may well have pointed at the massive mansions of hewn stone that were in process of construction on every side about Samaria. This elaborate building program seemed to indicate tremendous prosperity. In reality, it was a witness to the opposite, for a considerable part of the money being channeled into those rising structures was tainted wealth amassed by extortioners. Amos told the owners they would never get to live in those houses. The enemy would take care of that.

Among other projects by these same magnates were the extensive vineyards which were being planted and equipped in the regions of Samaria. Amos may have pointed at them too, on the surrounding hillsides. He told the landlords who were setting out those vast vineyards that they would never taste wine from those young vines. The enemy would take care of that also.

If there had been newspapers at that time and an unscrupulous reporter who loved the spectacular had been present, he would have rushed out of that court with the startling news which soon would have found its way into big headlines. These would have stated that Amos was working to destroy the judicial machinery of Israel and was conspiring with foreign nations for the overthrow of his own country by violence. The offended parties in this situation served as the ancient equivalent, spreading such scandal by word of mouth, over all the land of Palestine. Even then, patriotism was used as the last refuge of scoundrels while the prophetic voice of conscience was suspect. Amos did not go into that court to chide and complain. He went there to save his country.

High credit, both at that time and today, should go to those judges who are impartial and scrupulous in dispensing justice. Also, those attorneys merit praise who have a passionate desire to see the poor get their rights and are willing to give their best services in such defense, even though the client may not be able to render a fee.

Nevertheless, we need not assume, in our self-righteousness, that we have achieved complete exemption from the judicial maladies which were plaguing civic life in the days of Amos. He could find plenty of room for protest in some of our courts. Winks between opposing lawyers often speak volumes concerning connivances to prolong trials and mutually increase fees. It is still not unknown for judges to receive bribes and for juries to be "fixed."

In modern times the chief obstruction to justice is not so much corruption in court, but rather the fact that money is so often able to buy the verdict. The side with the most financial reserve can command the best legal services, and usually win its case. In most instances, the cost of appeal automatically eliminates the poor man from a fair opportunity for a final decision, almost as effectively as in Palestine where he was pushed physically from the court area as his case was refused a hearing. If the significance and implications of Amos's day in court could be more adequately appreciated today, it might do considerable to create new interest in the cause of justice among men.

In the Market Place

Inasmuch as Amos was one who believed that the basic principles of religion have a pertinent bearing on business practices, it is not surprising that he was found wandering through the market place on a Saturday afternoon. The shopkeepers were accustomed to break the Sabbath by getting at their work before the holy day was over. On this occasion, Amos went to see them in operation in their market stalls while the silence of the holy day still prevailed, and there was only an occasional customer.

As he walked about, with ears open, he overheard shop-

keepers tell each other about their various means of defrauding the people. He must have seen their balances that were
adjusted to give scant weight. Perhaps he took up one of
their measures, only to be amazed at finding it had a false
movable bottom. Defrauding through misrepresentation, and
poor quality of goods, was another story. On that afternoon
he saw the merchants, with their wares displayed and their
schemes for fleecing the people perfected, awaiting impatiently
the moment when the Sabbath would end so unjust gain might
again flow into their coffers.

In harmony with Amos's ability to seize an opportunity at
an instant's notice, and make the most of it, the thought
suddenly occurred to him that this would be a good time to
address the merchants in relative privacy and quiet. It would
need to be done at once for, following the close of the Sabbath, such places of trade soon would become a bedlam with
their din of barter. At that strategic moment, Amos spoke
out in exasperation and made that market place resound as
he denounced the merchants' dishonest business practices.

> Listen to this!
> You who trample upon the needy,
>   And would destroy the poor of the land;
> You who say,
> "When will the new moon be past,
>   That we may again sell wheat?
> And the day of the Sabbath,
>   That we may open the grain sacks?"
> Making the measure scant and the price high,
>   Trading dishonestly with deceitful scales;
> Buying out the poor for silver,
>   And the needy for a pair of shoes.
>
> The Lord has sworn by the pride of Jacob,
> "I never will forget any of your doings.

Do I care more for you than for the Cushites,
O people of Israel?
Behold I have my eyes on this sinful kingdom,
And will destroy it from the face of the earth."

Amos 8:4-7; 9:7-8

Even though Amos was pained to see such unscrupulous business malpractices carried on, he concluded that God, with infinitely higher ethical sensitiveness than any prophet, was undoubtedly far more distressed. How could the deity permit such dishonest proceedings to go on? Amos regarded these Israelites as so degenerated that he conceived they must have appeared worse to God than any other people of the world. They were presumably more despicable in his sight than the most hated Cushites, who lived on the upper reaches of the Nile. Those Israelites, who once had been the chosen of God, as they thought, had now slipped until they left the Cushites in second place and had become, in the sight of both God and man, the most despised of all peoples.

Amos felt assured God would not allow such a wicked nation to continue much longer. So he announced to the merchants how their deeds were making it inevitable that God would "destroy" this corrupt Israelite kingdom "from the face of the earth." These were no uncertain words, and we may imagine there was no hesitancy in the voice of Amos as he spoke them.

Business can be "a great civilizer" if carried on with a measure of moral principle. When this is gone, business can cause blight and bring destruction to a whole nation. This is what Amos perceived was happening in Israel. A business policy that is wise, and has regard for its future, will not cast its burdens on the poor. Here the message of Amos was not only to Palestine but to us as well. His words were like the warning given by Goldsmith to England:

Ill fares the land, to hastening ills a prey,
Where wealth accumulates, and men decay.

Only One Idea

After all, Amos was a young man of only one idea. He had glimpsed something concerning the importance of justice, and had developed a passion for the standards of right upon which it is dependent. Whatever he said in the various cities of Israel was but the outworking of this one master concept. The effect of Amos upon other prophets, upon posterity in general, and even upon us in our present times, is an eloquent testimony to what one person can accomplish, even if he has only one idea, provided he does something about it.

5
Religious Pioneer

WE CAN ONLY SPECULATE as to the circumstances attending
Amos's departure from the capital at Samaria. Had he been
driven from the city by force? Or did he leave voluntarily?
Had he become discouraged with his work as he proceeded
from Samaria? Or was he in a mood of satisfaction over
what had been achieved at the capital? Knowing he was
not the type of person who would yield to despair, we can
be certain Amos was still driven by hope. Whatever the reason for going, his interest now was in moving on to new fields.

By the Altar at Gilgal

The prophet of Tekoa apparently journeyed in the direction
of Gilgal because he wanted to attend an important religious
event that was about to take place there. Gilgal was an ancient
shrine, used by the Canaanites before the Hebrews ever entered Palestine. The distinctive thing about this holy place
was its circle of sacred stones, in which it was originally
thought different deities dwelt.

It must be remembered that Amos had come from a place
where there was no institutional religion. In his home town
there had been no temple, no synagogue, no church, and no
priesthood. Rituals and formalities played no part in worship
among his people. At that place religion consisted only in the

soul's outreach toward God, all wakeful hours of the day and night.

In light of this background, it was quite a jolt to Amos when he came to Gilgal. The shallowness of the religion, as practiced at that shrine, made the greatest impression upon him. Here religion seemed merely a matter of forms, rituals, and sacrifices. Proper care to these details summed up practically the whole religious duty of man. These people attended their temples and went through their rites to please God, but they had no regard for their fellow men.

The ten commandments of Moses seemed forgotten. To all intents and purposes there was no connection between religion and everyday living. It was like a man today who got up at a midweek testimonial meeting and said, "I've cursed, I've sworn, I've stole, I've committed adultery, and I've murdered, but I thank God I've never lost my religion." While we hope this is an exception today, it was pretty much the rule in the age of Amos.

The people of Israel burned their choice animals, grains, and vegetables so the appetizing smell of the roasting beef, and other foods, would rise up to God and be pleasing to him. They were sure that if they sacrificed in abundance and the deity smelled all these good things, he would overlook their evils and only do them good. They never conceived that he would ask any questions as to how they lived, or concerning the good or nasty things they did to others. They thought the attitude of God toward them depended upon how appetizing were the odors they sent up to him from their altars.

Amos was so aroused over this condition of things that he could no longer refrain from speaking. He rushed to the altar where preparations were under way for presenting the great offerings on this special occasion. This provided another picturesque scene. His crude shepherd garb and slim appearance contrasted with the fatness of the black-robed priests.

At first Amos resorted to ridicule. His initial words were spoken in a tone of bitter sarcasm.

> Come to Bethel — and transgress!
> To Gilgal — and commit more wrongs!
> And present your sacrifices each morning,
> Your tithes, on the three annual festivals,
> Burn incense of leavened bread as thank offering,
> And announce your gifts — make them known;
> For in such things you take delight,
> O people of Israel.
>
> *Amos 4:4-5*

Such religion, which consisted in offering material gifts to the deity, favored the comfortable and the rich. Their wealth could supply the most delectable items for sacrifice, and in great abundance. If this was religion, they could break every one of the ten commandments, and not lose it.

Under such a system of standards, the poor man, who had nothing to offer, was completely outclassed and had no religious status. It was like the gospel hymn, "If religion were a thing that money could buy . . . the rich would live and the poor would die." So religion was veering away from the masses, in the days of Amos, becoming the exclusive practice of the wealthy.

Although sacrifices were thought primarily to assure the offerer credit with God, there was also a more *practical* aspect. The worshiper gained among his fellows a prestige proportional to the size of his bounties. At times the priests sounded a gong in their temples when an especially big gift was about to be presented, so all the people would be sure to witness the act. You could see the givers of large sums of money and sacrifices pointing out the fact on the lists of gifts posted on temple bulletin boards. If there had been an Israelite Daily News, donors would have insisted on having such items published there also. These people loved to bask in the honor that came from their large bequests.

After his moments of sarcasm, Amos got down to seriousness with these worshipers. With stinging words he proclaimed that such practices amounted to degrading religion into greed for fame. This he regarded as despicable in the sight of both God and man.

In reference to their belief that God was leaning out over the parapet of heaven so as not to miss one slight smell from their altars, Amos presented a decidedly contrasting picture. He showed them a God who was holding his nose shut so he would not need to smell the odor of the sacrifices that came from such corrupt people. Amos described God as turning his back on them so he would not need to see the disgusting rituals and absurd antics carried on about his shrines.

There was also the sound of music that came from their instruments and festival songs. It was assumed that God would at least like to hear the soothing strains from their harps. But no! proclaimed Amos. God would not even listen to that. It might make him more indulgent toward them. So he stuck his fingers in his ears and stopped them up, that he might no longer be able to hear their songs.

Perhaps it is best that one should listen to the actual words of Amos as he uttered them.

"I hate, I despise your feasts,
And I take no delight in your assemblies;
Even though you bring me burnt sacrifices,
I will not gaze on them with favor;

Neither will I accept your meal offerings,
    Nor look upon your peace-offerings of fatlings.
Take away from me the noise of your songs,
    The melody of your harps I refuse to hear.
But let justice roll forth as a fountain of water,
    And righteousness as an ever-flowing stream."

Amos 5:21-24

Amos probably did not intend to say that all religious ritual, including the assembling together for public worship, was repulsive. He meant that it was disgusting when carried on by bad people. The citizens of Israel in that day came under this classification. So Amos conceived of God as nauseated by their whole round of rituals and worship. The trouble was that there was no stress on religious living.

A religion that is not backed up by deeds is worthless. Yes, it is worse than worthless. Often it is actually a corrupting influence. Throughout the world's history a distressingly large portion of what has passed for religion has really been the false product which destroys the lives of its worshipers. Religion has always tended to degenerate, as Charles Kingsley first said, into becoming the opium of the people, lulling them to sleep and doing them evil rather than good.

The prophet Amos, standing by the altar at Gilgal, glimpsed a vastly higher concept of religion than had yet been known in his day. It was expressed tersely in his last two lines where he summed up the whole of religion in the ideals of justice and righteousness. Whatever aids these primary ends, has place in religion. What does not, should be eliminated from it. These two final lines from Amos, on that occasion, comprise one of the mountain peaks of religious definition for all time.

These deductions were possible only because Amos had revolutionized the idea of God. In earlier times it had been assumed that the deity was a creature characterized by caprice, and therefore unpredictable. Amos was the first person in the Bible to conceive of God as a being who is always on the side of right, and therefore dependable.

From that discovery concerning the fundamental nature of God, Amos made the further deduction that the deity desires right and just living on the part of his people in their daily contacts with each other. The talk of *worshiping God* is pretty much idle twaddle. After all, the only way we serve God is by serving our fellow men. By advancing the concept of a just society, it was made plain that henceforth religion must register in daily life. Thus Amos introduced the idea of the social gospel as the heart of religion.

Other activities followed that address, the festivities came to a close, and the prophet took his departure, but ever since that day there have been reverberating over our world those final words of Amos.

> But let justice roll forth as a fountain of water,
> And righteousness as an ever-flowing stream.

Encounter with the Priest of Bethel

The most thrilling experience of this prophet's short but dramatic ministry was connected with his final public appearance. Up to this time, it seems that Amos for some reason had by-passed Bethel in his preaching. Religiously, that place was the capital of the Northern Kingdom. The shrine there had been built to compete with Solomon's Temple after the division of the kingdom. By constructing such an attractive holy place on a hallowed spot near the border of the Southern Kingdom, the northerners proposed to head off a large percent of pilgrims to Jerusalem, getting them to stay at Bethel and worship there instead.

Bethel had two sources of special appeal. The original altar on this site was the first to be built in Palestine by Israel's great ancestor Abraham after his arrival from Ur of the Chaldees (Gen. 12:8). Also, here on these bare heights was the spot where Abraham's grandson Jacob was sleeping one night when he had that remarkable dream of the ladder reaching to heaven, with angels ascending and descending (Gen. 28:10-22). In the temple at Bethel King Jeroboam had placed the golden calves which had become the pride and worship of the north country, but the complaint of the south (I Kings 12:25-33). By the time of Amos, this temple had come to be regarded as a royal sanctuary, under the special patronage of the king.

Toward this hallowed place the shepherd-prophet finally made his way. He wished to deliver his message at this religious capital of the north as he had already done at Samaria, the political, commercial, and judicial center of that country. He was in a mood of special expectation as he neared that hallowed place of pilgrimage.

In some way the news that Amos was approaching the city had gone ahead, for Amaziah, the chief priest of Bethel, was awaiting him in person. As the prophet came up toward the temple, Amaziah probably came out and met him in the open court before it. This provided another in the series of dramatic scenes that attended Amos's ministry.

Priest Amaziah was clad in rich black robes, with fringes, tassels, scepter, mitre, and the fragrance of the highly perfumed anointing oil which he administered to those in physical need. By contrast, the shepherd from Tekoa stood there in his crude bleached garments which had become no less smelly during these homeless days in the north country. At last the priest and the prophet had met.

As Amos approached, he probably was overjoyed to think the priest had come out to welcome him, and that he would have the prospect of a successful ministry at this strategic spot of Bethel.

With the first words from Priest Amaziah, these hopes were cruelly crushed. It became apparent at once that Amaziah was bitter in his opposition. He had come out to tell Amos he was not to enter the sacred precincts of that temple. Furthermore, he would not be allowed to do any prophesying in Bethel.

This was the most severe blow to Amos in all his life. He would have expected more from a priest, especially such a prominent one. Was not the priest interested in the good life, and in fostering it by every means possible?

This chief priest of the Northern Kingdom had been the victim of popular misunderstandings. Unthinkingly, Amaziah had believed the slanders against this prophet which had come from those whose toes he had tramped on during his clear speaking in defense of right. This lethargic, easygoing, well-fed, and luxury-enjoying priest of Bethel was content to see things move slowly, if at all. He felt himself forced to oppose the youthful Amos who probed deep in detecting wrong and expected the cause of right to move more rapidly.

If these two had merged their energies, there might have been a religious reformation in Israel and a remaking of the nation. As it was, they became bitter enemies and we have one of the most tragic spectacles of the ages. This is when the forces of religion fight each other rather than co-ordinate their efforts in the conquest of evil.

It turned out that, even before Amos arrived, Amaziah had sent a note to the king which read,

> Amos has conspired against you
> In the midst of the house of Israel.
> The nation cannot tolerate all his words.

Amos 7:10

After sending this note, the priest thought how futile it was in the emergency of the moment. The capital at Samaria was some twenty-five miles away. It would take time for a courier to carry his message there and return with a directive telling what should be done with this character. Also, the king might be away from the capital. In that event Amaziah would wait in vain.

It seemed apparent to the priest that he must take matters into his own hands, and at once, in order to stop this seditious radical before he should have a chance to do any damage at Bethel. From that moment, things began to happen rapidly. Inflating his pompous self to the full, Amaziah gave an ultimatum to the prophet.

> O visionary, go!
> Flee to your homeland of Judah,
> Eat your bread in that country,
> And do your prophesying there;
> But never prophesy again at Bethel,
> For this is the king's sanctuary,
> It is even a royal structure.

Amos 7:12-13

Two insinuations in this speech hurt Amos particularly. First, in an uncomplimentary manner, Amaziah had called him a "visionary," or dreamy idealist, as it would be phrased today. Whether then or now, no term is more stinging to the upright reformer who is sacrificing and enduring hardships for the cause of right. Also, Amaziah insinuated that Amos was in this work only for what he could get out of it, just a way of making a living and getting his stomach filled. This is what was implied when he told Amos to go and "eat your bread" in Judah. He had virtually called Amos a beggar.

This failure of the priest to perceive the worthiness of Amos really indicated the bankruptcy of idealism within the priest himself. When he labeled Amos an insincere person, who was in his work only for the personal advantage that would accrue to him, Amaziah was in reality projecting upon the prophet his own selfish, if not evil, designs.

Amaziah had something to learn about the individual whom he had before him on this occasion. This was the type of prophet who would not back down, even to the high priest of Bethel. Amos felt himself sent by God, and all the priests in Palestine could not stop him. His message must be spoken, and he was going to deliver it, in spite of any number of prohibitions on the part of Amaziah. So Amos said to the chief priest of Bethel:

> I am neither a prophet,
> Nor the son of a prophet;
> For I am only a shepherd,
> And a dresser of mulberry trees.
> But the Lord took me from following the flock,
> And the Lord said unto me,
> "Go, prophesy unto my people Israel."

> *Amos 7:14-15*

When Amos said that he was "neither a prophet nor the son of a prophet" he meant he was not a member of the prophetic guilds or schools. This was his manner of indicating that he was not a trained prophet but a person directly commissioned by God. Realizing that Amos was getting started in delivering one of his addresses, and was thereby disobeying the priestly order, Amaziah concluded he must stop the prophet at once. So the priest interrupted and said, presumably in the most decisive manner he was able to command,

> "Don't prophesy against Israel" and
> "Don't rave about the house of Isaac."
>
> *Amos 7:16*

In this pair of commands, Priest Amaziah had made a further insinuation that was insulting to Amos. He had virtually called Amos a madman. The specific Hebrew word he used indicates a person who foams at the mouth because he has gone mad. Perhaps Amos had a little salivary difficulty by reason of the hot weather and his extreme earnestness. To dismiss him however as a madman, or an insane person as we would say today, was going a little too far.

So Amos fired a volley back at the priest in four final biting lines. In these the prophet described what Amaziah and his family might expect in the coming conquest of Palestine which its unscrupulous leaders, including himself, were making inevitable. Those were days, of course, when the priests still married. These were strong words for utterance to the chief priest of Bethel, but he had them coming to him.

> Your wife shall become a harlot in the city,
> Your sons and daughters shall fall by the sword,
> Your land shall be divided with a measuring line,
> And you yourself shall die on ground that is unclean.
>
> *Amos 7:17*

What daring for an unlearned and unknown shepherd from Tekoa to utter such severely pointed words before the great

Amaziah! This must have confirmed the priest all the more in his judgment that the one before him had gone mad. What was to be done with Amos?

This scene at Bethel is a classic representation of the eternal conflict between two types of religion, the priestly and the prophetic. Priestly religion is always interested in magic, miracle, rituals, rites, forms, ceremonies, pageantry, ecclesiastical dress, fees, conservatism, and the past. Prophetic religion, by contrast, is concerned with ethics, morality, personal living, reform, community service, the social gospel, progress, liberalism, and the future. Although it is seldom that either one is wholly pure, without any admixture of the other, most religions can be classed rather easily in one or the other of these groups.

There should be co-operation between these two, for both purport to be striving for the same ends. Yet, from the time of Amos to the present, a lamentable opposition continues between them, for neither is able to appreciate the other. Even in our day, this cleavage remains as a great gulf, dividing the religious forces of our world into two potentially hostile camps.

The Fate of Amos

At this point the record concerning the activities of Amos suddenly became strangely silent. We are not told what happened to the prophet. On this point the reader is left to speculate. Various theories have been advanced. The one which seems most likely is that Priest Amaziah had his visitor from the south arrested and imprisoned before he could utter anything more. Perhaps, when the king finally proceeded to action in the matter, Amos may have been given the semblance of a trial, but probably was executed as a traitor. In that

The Wrath of the Professional Priestcraft

event, Amos would rank as the first of the many prophet-martyrs of the Hebrew people.

The ministry of Amos was likely much shorter than has generally been supposed. It had lasted perhaps only two or three months. Although brief, it was a period of intense work. Looking back to the time when he left Tekoa, we recall the amazing eagerness with which he had set out on this work. Now, what had happened? It had all come to an inglorious end. His cause must have seemed hopelessly lost. In his dying moments, with no relatives or friends about, this young prophet too may have poured forth his soul in something like the despairing cry of the Twenty-second Psalm, "My God! My God! Why have you forsaken me?"

Then, as in all ages, the blood of the martyrs became the seed of the faith. Even at the time of his presumed execution, Amos was still a relatively unknown person. However, the spectacular manner of his death, and its apparent injustice, drew popular attention to Amos and his cause. By this event, all Palestine was led to inquire concerning the nature of the prophet's utterances. What had he said that was worthy of death? Many were the people who could see nothing wrong with his words. To the exploited of that country they sounded increasingly like the welcome voice of a liberator.

In getting rid of Amos, Priest Amaziah and King Jeroboam thought they had killed an insane and dangerous person. Instead, they had unknowingly dramatized a notable cause. So, a great prophetic movement was to grow from the work of Amos, perhaps not in spite of his martyrdom but, as with Jesus, because of it. With the passing of this prophet, other minds in the land of Israel were to rethink his messages, and other lips were to spread his words.

Hosea

Hosea

6

The Farmer-Preacher

HOSEA WAS SECOND IN THE SUCCESSION of great prophets, and quite a different person from Amos. In many respects the variations between them were so great that they become a study in contrasts. Hosea apparently began speaking in public about seven years after Amos. When the shepherd of Tekoa delivered his prophecies in the capital city of Samaria, Hosea was probably a young man in his late teens. If Amos had done his work at approximately the year 750 B.C., the time from 743 to 735 B.C. seems most likely for the prophetic activity of Hosea.

Home and Boyhood

By contrast with Amos, the shepherd who came from the barren wastes and was interested in such things as lions, sheep, lambs, flocks, and pastures, Hosea was a farm boy. This conclusion seems warranted from the observation that he spoke almost entirely in terms of items with rural interest such as grain, new wine, fresh oil, heifers, threshing, bulls, harrows, yokes, plows, and fig trees.

From the cities mentioned in his writings, together with these agricultural items, it is possible to form a fairly clear picture of the location of the farm on which he was born. Jezreel, the ancient capital of the Northern Kingdom, seems

71

to have been the nearest city. This was located at a point where the Plain of Jezreel, coming west from the Jordan River, meets the Plain of Esdraelon, extending east from the Mediterranean. In a military way, this city-fortress stood command over northern Palestine.

These two plains, and the smaller ones which joined them, constituted the agricultural heart of Palestine. To us their total acreage would not seem a very large area, but in that country, where fertile ground was scarce, this was the greatest expanse of farming land known to the Israelites. Esdraelon and Jezreel formed the granary of Palestine. The territory had once been lake bottom, but in the course of centuries had filled in. This made the richest type of soil.

The farm on which Hosea was reared seems to have been located in this great plain area. The attention in his writings to wine and grapes, as well as grain, may point to the conclusion that this particular farm was situated on the edge of the valley, with part of its acreage lowland and part hill country.

Clues in the Book of Hosea indicate that the farm home in which he grew up was a rather prosperous one. Amos's hard life, with constant dread of wild animals and fear lest the sparse pastures vanish through drought, was almost completely absent here. In the home of Hosea's boyhood there seems to have been an air of comfort.

By contrast with the isolation of Amos, Hosea grew up quite literally at the crossroads of the nations. If there was a central spot in the world of that day, the Plain of Esdraelon was it. For millenniums it had been the battleground of the nations. Season after season, through ancient times, armies had come from far distances and met in battle on this plain. More blood had been shed on that soil than was true of perhaps any other spot on the earth's surface. Lying between the highlands of Ephraim on the south and the hills of Galilee on the north, this plain was like an immense amphitheater, surrounded by hilltop bleachers. In the surrounding hills, there were five passes through which the armies of ancient times made their entrances and exits.

As a strategic location, this plain had significance in times of peace as well as war. It was a center of communication. Five major highways of the Near East came together on the level stretches of that plain. It was like a union depot where caravan trains met, bartered, exchanged, and rerouted their wares for the long treks ahead into far countries. Here Hosea as a boy was more or less in contact with travelers from distant nations. Having seen traders from Egypt, Assyria, Arabia, and the more fabulous Orient, he may often have been entertained by tales from those lands of grandeur.

Life for Hosea, however, was by no means all entertainment. He was a farmer's son, and the farmer's life is at no time an easy lot. Work in the fields under the hot Palestinian sun was tiring. There was also the task of caring for the oxen. The training of heifers and cattle, which they impressed into their service, was a daily chore. Although not an easy life, it was pleasant and rewarding.

Courtship, Marriage, and Call

Then, as now, a young man's fancy occasionally turned to thoughts of love. On some nearby farm there was a young woman named Gomer, to whom Hosea was attracted. This apparently was not a rushing love affair, but something which extended and grew through the years. We might have seen Hosea often at his work, in absent-minded manner, dreaming, hoping, and planning.

The extent to which the parents chose the bride, and arranged all items connected with marriage, cannot be determined in this particular case. In some Palestinian homes, young people had a fairly free voice in determining their own lives. In others, all such matters were fixed by the parents, with no consideration for the wishes of the young people involved. One would like to think Hosea lived in a home of the former type. Even so, the formal marriage agreement would have been negotiated by the parents, and the details connected with the wedding, and the establishing of domestic life, would have been arranged by them.

Whatever the exact circumstances, the time finally arrived when Hosea and Gomer were to be married and live a common life. Inasmuch as no details concerning that event have survived, they are left to the fancy of each reader.

During the days immediately before that wedding, we can imagine the joy of Hosea. He was the domestic type of person who would take delight in wife, home, and family. We can see him review his expectations in this regard. He was sure he was getting a wonderful wife, and that theirs would be one of the happiest of homes.

Among high-minded young people, nothing is comparable to the time of courtship and the early days of marriage for developing idealism, clarifying purposes, and crystallizing goals. During this period, many a young person today decides upon the ministry, social service, teaching, nursing, or some other of the more idealistic vocations in which the greater services can be rendered to mankind.

During that period of life, Hosea began to develop a second interest in addition to his farming. Even in the days before his marriage, it had occurred to him that he ought to take up the work of a prophet and attempt something similar to

HOSEA'S COURTSHIP

what Amos had done. The prophet of Tekoa had become a hero in the north. His words had found their way into every household in that part of the country. The ideals for which he stood had special appeal for Hosea. The possibility of his becoming a prophet was not a mere passing idea which flashed across the mind of this young farm lad. It was an inner urge that seemed to grow through the years.

It was a source of continuing regret that he had not been able to see Amos, and be a listener in at least one of his audiences. Oh, that he had been at Samaria, which was not far from home, when the shepherd-prophet was there! If only he had been able to see him just once, and have a talk with him!

Children

In the course of time, the first child, a son, was born into the home of Gomer and Hosea. Apparently this was one of the happiest moments in the life of that couple, and particularly Hosea. There was the question of a name. In those times the father supplied this for the child. In searching for a proper one, Hosea conceived the idea of combining the prophetic and domestic interests by giving this child what might be called a *prophetic name,* i.e., a name that would remind people concerning one of his prophecies. The child then would be a walking prophecy, spreading the message of Hosea wherever this son happened to be.

At that time there was ruling in Israel a dynasty of kings whom Hosea particularly disliked. He felt they were a bad influence upon the country. So he proceeded to denounce them in his initial prophetic attempts. A favorite among these was one in which he reminded people of the violence and bloodshed by which the ruling dynasty had come into power.

Jehu, an army captain, had staged a *coup d'etat* and seized the throne (II Kings 9-10). He was a cruel and merciless person. As he approached the capital in his chariot to assume control, he "drove furiously." The kings of Judah and Israel came out to greet the newcomer, but he killed both of them. He proceeded to the palace where he had the eunuchs throw Queen Jezebel out the window. Then, with his horses and chariot, he drove back and forth over her body until it was crushed and the horses and palace wall were splattered with blood. By this time he was hungry, and went into the palace for a feast. When the banqueting was over and he came out, the dogs had eaten the queen's body so completely, and carried off the bones, that he was unable to find anything left of her but skull, hands, and feet.

As those were days of polygamy, it was possible for a king to have many children. Strengthened by his first meal in the palace, Jehu proceeded against the sons of the dead king, and soon he had heads of king's sons by the basketful. These, seventy of them by count, he piled neatly in two heaps, one on each side of the city gate in Jezreel.

Then Jehu proceeded to a general carnage, killing all relatives of the previous monarch, and any who were connected in the slightest with the work of that dynasty. Even all prophets and priests, who had in any way co-operated with that ruler, were slain. When Jehu was on the way from Jezreel to Samaria, for the purpose of establishing his kingship there also, he met forty-two envoys coming from Judah. After asking them only a single question, he killed every one of these on the spot. At Samaria he carried on slaughter as widely as at Jezreel.

Jehu was a "religious" man, and so his benediction to all this bloodshed was to have an especially "holy" touch. The

cruel usurper made announcement that he was a Baal worshiper, and wanted all adherents of that cult in the nation to
gather in a large hall at Samaria on a certain day. The appointed time arrived, the worshipers assembled, and the Baal
priests, clothed in their vestments, were presenting the offerings. Suddenly Jehu's soldiers rushed in and slew every
person inside the temple. By this single act he eliminated all
religious opposition within the country. Amazing as it may
seem, all Jehu's deeds of violence and deceit were done in
the name of the *true religion.*

Inasmuch as Jehu's most terrble deeds had been perpetrated
at the city of Jezreel, Hosea decided to name his first child
Jezreel. This would help to keep in popular memory the outrage of the acts perpetrated there. Wherever the child Jezreel
would go, people would be reminded of his father's statements
concerning the carnage of Jezreel and how it was still calling
for revenge. The revolutionary character of Hosea's earliest
message is seen in the explanation which accompanied the
naming.

Call his name Jezreel;
For it will be only a little while
Until I avenge the blood of Jezreel upon the house of Jehu,
And bring the kingdom of the house of Israel to an end.

Hosea 1:4

As Hosea became more convinced concerning the importance of his message with regard to the Jehu dynasty, he
widened the scope of his activities. Apparently when he went
on marketing trips to Jezreel, and other nearby cities, he began
delivering short addresses at those places. Soon he was going
about talking to group after group, recalling to their memories
this succession of shocking events by which the reigning line

of kings had seized the throne, and of the treachery which had characterized that dynasty ever since.

In due season a second child was born, this time a girl. Following his earlier practice, Hosea named her after a favorite prophecy which he happened to be delivering at the time of her birth. So he called this child Lo-Ruhamah. This could be translated "She shall be shown no compassion," or simply "Uncompassionated."

In giving this name, Hosea was thinking of Israel and how the nation had become so corrupt and despicable. How could even God have regard for a people like that? The name given this second child symbolized an Israel which had cast aside its heritage, and had made itself so ugly that the deity no longer could love it. This time Hosea represented God as saying,

> Call her name Lo-Ruhamah (Uncompassionated);
> For never again will I show compassion
> Unto the house of Israel.
>
> *Hosea 1:6*

Assault upon the Priests

Ever since Priest Amaziah had silenced the prophet Amos at Bethel, and presumably had brought about his execution, that episode had rankled in the mind of Hosea. It had focused attention upon the shortcomings of the priestly class. That deed had built up within Hosea a distrust of the priesthood and caused him to be overobserving in respect to their failings. With the passing of each year, he became ever more critical of them.

Amos had been stopped when he came into direct encounter with Priest Amaziah. It is significant that Hosea began exactly where Amos had left off, by giving the priests a going over. The prophecies represented by the children's names, and what other speaking he may have done near home, were merely in the nature of a preliminary tryout. His real prophetic offensive began when he proceeded to expose, before the people, the hypocrisies and immoralities of the priesthood. It is evident that this prophet was not deficient in courage, or he would not have taken on such a large order.

Inasmuch as Hosea believed the laxity of the priesthood was the key to the low moral conditions of the times, he felt he must give early attention to them. Before a large audience in Samaria, perhaps comparable to the one where Amos made his first dramatic appearance, and possibly even on the same spot, Hosea rose to deliver his invective against the priests of that day. We can imagine that occasion when, in their presence, Hosea exposed these religious professionals before the people upon whom they had come to depend for their bounties.

Hosea began by describing, in pointed words, the sorry mess into which this lack of worthy religious leadership had landed the country.

> There is no fidelity, and no kindness,
>   And no Godly knowledge in the land.
> They swear falsely and deceive,
>   They murder and they steal,
> They commit adultery and are lawless,
>   And one bloody deed follows another.

> *Hosea 4:1-2*

Hosea reminded his audience that the priests were making no complaint against these evils, but were secretly, and at times openly, conniving in them. Those priests in reality did not want people to be good, for this would have cut off the flow of penance to them. So the priests "feasted upon" the sins of the people, and desired "them to increase their iniquities." Hosea proclaimed, before this entire audience, that he failed to find one upright priest in the whole lot of them.

The chief credential of the priesthood in that day seemed to be gluttony and harlotry. As long as they could have their food, their wine, and their women, the priests were happy. They had turned the glory of their office into a thing of disrepute. Hosea rebuked them by publicly announcing that the rank and file of the people were better than the priests. It is indeed a distressful hour for religion when its supposed leaders live on a lower level than the average of the people.

Hosea went into high gear as he became more specific with regard to the sins of the priests. Probably to dull its pointedness, the passage has been both disarranged and corrupted in our Bibles.

> Yet no one (of the priests) has made complaint,
> And no man (of them) has offered reproof.
> Not only are the priests like the people,
> The people are even better than the priests.
> Every one of them (the priests) has sinned against me,
> They have turned their glory into disgrace.
> They even feast upon the sin of my people,
> And desire them to increase their iniquities.
> They eat, but they are never satisfied;
> They patronize harlots, but have no offspring.

Hosea 4:4-10

Hosea also blamed the priests for encouraging primitive superstitions and taboos instead of exalted religion. The Israelites had come to worship wooden poles that were thought to contain deities. They also revered sacred trees in which gods were supposed to dwell. By going under the shadow of

these trees, people believed they were coming under the touch
of the divine. In fostering such primitive rites, the priests
were allowing religion to degenerate into magic. Hosea described the absurdity of this religious regression.

> My people seek oracles from wooden poles,
>   And trust rods to give them instructions.
> They sacrifice upon the mountain tops,
>   And upon the hills they burn incense,
> Beneath the oaks, poplars, and terebinths,
>   Because their shade is considered auspicious.

Hosea 4:12-13

Most tragic was the way in which the sexual looseness of
the priests had set the whole nation into the paths of personal
immorality. When groups of pilgrims came to the holy places,
the men at once would seek out the sacred prostitutes and
spend time in their company. The deserted women were left
to do the same with the "holy men," the priests of the temples.
Amos already had denounced this, but it apparently had
grown worse rather than better.

Religion should be the guardian of morality and the bul-
wark of the home. Here, however, the religion that was being
foisted on the people by the priests of Palestine was bringing
about the degradation of both. Brides were not remaining
faithful to their new husbands, even to the end of the seven-
day wedding festivities. Hosea could hardly blame them,
inasmuch as the men and priests acted the way they did.
To the people assembled that day, he gave a vivid description
of the prevailing conditions.

> I do not blame their daughters for playing the harlot,
>   And their young brides for committing adultery,

When the men themselves go aside in company with harlots,
And share their sacrifices with the sacred prostitutes.

Hosea 4:13-14

We can imagine the ringing climax with which Hosea, using *Ephraim* as a variant for *Israel*, represented God as saying,

Hear this, O priests!
  Give heed, O house of Israel! . . .
I have known Ephraim intimately,
  And Israel has not been hidden from me;
Therefore Israel's pride shall stare them in the face,
  The people of Ephraim shall stumble in their iniquity.

Hosea 5:1, 3, 5

Hosea was not so resourceful as Amos in working psychological techniques upon his audiences, but he was substantial and perhaps even more thorough in probing to the root of matters. This address, in which he fearlessly denounced the priesthood of Palestine in public, was a most daring and significant utterance. It gives one the flavor of the real Hosea.

International and Internal Crisis

As the international and domestic political scenes became increasingly agitated, they came to occupy the center of prophetic attention. The nation was beginning to become frightened at the prospects of foreign invasion, about which both Amos and Hosea had been warning. The remedy prescribed for the situation by these prophets was for the people of Israel to abandon their corruptions and immoralities, renew their devotion to right, and make the nation secure once more by strengthening its moral fibre.

It might have been expected that the political powers in

Israel would not choose such a wise way. They adopted the
expedient of foreign alliance. They began dickering with
both their enemies, Egypt and Assyria, sending enquiring em-
bassies to each. Soon the nation found itself mixed up in
a net of negotiations and counter-negotiations, alliances and
counter-alliances. Hosea warned them that such double-dealing could end only in ruin. He likened the Israelites to an
unintelligent dove in a cage, darting aimlessly from side to
side, attempting to escape.

> The Ephraimites are like a dove,
>   Simple, without intelligence;
> For they make overtures to Egypt,
>   They send embassies to Assyria.
> Therefore I will spread out my net over them,
>   And bring them down as a bird in the air.

Hosea 7:11-12

On another occasion Hosea employed even stronger language to impress upon the political leaders of the day the
potential disastrousness of their policies. Here he used the
figure of the lion, and God is represented as speaking.

> So Ephraim dispatches embassies to Assyria,
>   And sends diplomats to the great king;
> But he will not be able to heal you,
>   Nor can he cure you of your wounds.
>
> Therefore I will be as a lion unto Ephraim,
>   Even as a young lion to the house of Israel;
> I, even I, will tear in pieces and be gone,
>   I will carry off and there shall be none to rescue.

Hosea 5:13-14

It is amazing how the political mind is so often incapable of making intelligent choices. The wise words of Hosea were disregarded, and the powers in control continued trying to prop up the leaning nation by their foreign alliances. The double-dealing, and carrying of water on two shoulders, was what frightened Hosea most.

Eventually this matter of foreign alliances split Israel internally. Half the country wanted alliance with Egypt, and the other half, with Assyria. Over this controversy, the nation itself fell into turmoil. It was not necessary to wait for foreign attack. Israel was slipping down helplessly into the caldron of civil war.

This was only one chapter in the succession of tragedies that have befallen the nations. Only two centuries before, David and Solomon had built the Hebrew kingdom in Palestine to what was perhaps the greatest in the world at that time, with a sea empire extending as far as East Africa and India. By a long succession of unintelligent choices on the part of her rulers, that glory had vanished. Without even waiting for foreign conquest, Israel now was about to disintegrate into nothingness.

Why must people continue to be ruled by blind leaders, while the few prophets of vision are ignored, persecuted, or martyred? Why are nations so suicidal in their choices, and unintentionally hell-bent on destruction? These questions relate not only to the Israel of antiquity but should be pondered especially by the people of modern times in their ill-fated attempts at building a world of peace and brotherhood.

7

Man of Long-suffering Love

HOSEA SOON FOUND HIMSELF a hated individual. He was despised by the priests and all who continued to place confidence in them, or connive with them. He was abominated by the government, and all who were associated therewith, because of what he had said about the ruling dynasty. His political counsels, to make the nation secure and strong through right conduct, were spurned by practically all the people. His advice seemed to them entirely too nebulous. Politically speaking, he was being ground, as it were, between the upper and the nether millstones of the pro-Egyptian and pro-Assyrian parties as the nation became embroiled ever deeper in civil strife. Nevertheless, he was making a supreme attempt to turn his nation, even at the eleventh hour, into the pathway of independence and right. This seemed to him as offering the only possibility of assuring his nation a future.

Domestic Tragedy

As Hosea was getting into the full swing of his prophetic work, he was spending much time away from home. During that period, the world of Hosea crashed about him in an instant when he became aware one day that his wife had become unfaithful to him. No greater blow could have struck this

86

prophet. His high hopes for a happy married life had suddenly become shattered.

About this time a third child was born to Gomer, but Hosea was aware that it was not his. So he named this boy Lo-Ammi, which would be translated "Not-My-People." Even as the child was named, Hosea thought of the parallel between this infant, in whose conception he had no part, and the Israelite nation which was rapidly becoming apostate, worshiping primitive pagan deities and leaving God with no relationships with his "chosen people." So this too became a prophetic name, and the theme of one of his prophecies. As the name was given, Hosea represented God himself as saying,

> Call his name Lo-Ammi (Not-My-People);
> For you are not my people
> And I am not your God.

> *Hosea 1:9*

In spite of all that Gomer was doing, Hosea continued to love her with a passionate devotion. He pled and pled with her that she give up her wayward life. Yet, in spite of his noble attitude, she increasingly disregarded his love and devotion. She began to be away from home for days at a time, in company with other men. In spite of all this, Hosea continued to provide for her, purchase her clothing, and furnish her with money.

After several years of this had gone on, and all appeals on the part of her husband proved fruitless, he called upon the children to reason with her. Perhaps she might be made to consider if it came from her own offspring. He said to them,

> Plead with your mother — plead with her
> That she remove her whoredoms from before her face,

And her adulteries from between her breasts;
Lest I cause her to be stripped stark naked,
And expose her as on the day she was born.

Hosea 2:2-3

By this time Gomer had worked herself into such a sex-crazed condition that even these appeals of her own children proved fruitless. She merely replied,

I will go after my lovers,
Who give me my bread and my water;
My wool and my flax;
My oil and my drink.

Hosea 2:5

Concerning this statement by Gomer, Hosea added the pathetic remark,

And she no longer seemed to realize
That it was I — I who provided for her
Grain, and new wine, and fresh oil;
While with money I liberally supplied her.

Hosea 2:8

In spite of all her waywardness, Hosea could not bring himself to the point of using disciplinary measures against her. The accepted punishment for such a woman in those days, and continuing even into New Testament times (John 8:1-11), was that she should be delivered over to the people of the community who would strip her naked and pelt her to death with stones. Yet it was unthinkable to Hosea that he should resort to this solution.

There was the possibility of employing milder disciplines.

He might take away her clothing, so she could not go out, and confine her at home. He might take away all her luxuries, and feed her on the sparsest of diet, until such time as she would resolve to give up her adulterous ways. There is evidence that Hosea tried something like this, for he said,

> Therefore, I will act accordingly;
> By withholding my grain in its season,
> And my new wine at its appointed time;
> I will even take back my wool and my flax,
> Which should have clothed her nakedness.

Hosea 2:9

This type of discipline apparently achieved no lasting results. After each time, she soon slipped back into her old ways. In fact, things became constantly worse. Now she stayed away from home for long periods. Hosea was left alone at those times with care of home and children. By reason of this domestic necessity, his prophetic work had come to an end. He was needed more by his children.

Deep thoughts went through the mind of Hosea, left at home alone. Why was it that he should have had such a wife? This would have been bad enough for any man, but for a prophet to have a home situation like this was disastrous. She had completely undermined his ministry. Could it be that God had wanted him to marry this woman who had turned out to be an adulteress? After putting up with this situation for a half dozen or more years, Hosea found himself slipping into a mood of despair.

Spiritual Discovery

After repeated speculation, during his times of brooding, as to why he should have been subjected to such a lot, one day there came to him a thought which began to change his whole perspective. This prophet began to see that God himself was in the same situation. The deity, as it were, had become married to the nation of Israel. At Mount Sinai God had made his wedding covenant with her as his bride, when she had fled from bondage in the land of Egypt. The time of the wilderness wanderings, on the road to the promised land, was the honeymoon, with nothing to disturb their intimate relationships. Those may have been difficult days, but they held many happy experiences. The adversities they were called upon to endure, in the territories over which they were forced to pass, seemed only to increase the closeness of relationship between Israel and her God.

When the days arrived that the Hebrew people were firmly established in Palestine, it became a different story. As prosperity increased, the nation gradually came to depart from her God. Israel resorted more and more to worship of the Baals, and other types of idol cults, with their primitive and immoral rites. The Israelites even reverted to the ancient practice of human sacrifice, "passing their children through the fire" by laying them in the red hot arms of the god Moloch.

Yes, God and Hosea were in the same predicament. Each had chosen as his bride the one who seemed to be the best that was available at the time. Even so, the wife of each had turned out bad. Yet, in spite of prolonged apostasy and repeated provocation on the part of the respective wives, both God and Hosea continued to be loving devoted husbands.

These meditations proved to be a spiritual discovery, for they gave Hosea an insight into the heart of God. Apparently God was a loving deity, and long-suffering. If this had not

THE MOTHERLESS HOME

been so, he would have allowed his nation Israel to be destroyed long ago. This simple realization, that God is a God of love, was the greatest discovery in the Bible as regards the nature of the deity. It was Hosea who first glimpsed the truth that there is love at the heart of the universe.

The God at the beginning of the Bible was a God of caprice. He was notionate and could not be depended upon. When in a good mood, he was nice to people. If he felt otherwise, he could be more brutal and vindictive than any man ever dreamed of becoming.

Amos discovered that this idea of God was wrong. God was a God of justice. There was the principle of righteousness in the heart of God. He could be depended upon to do right at all times. People could be sure that God would reward the righteous and punish the wicked. This was justice.

Hosea now saw that there was a higher concept even than that of Amos. True, there is justice in the heart of God, but that justice is tempered by love. God may still punish the wicked, but it was becoming apparent to Hosea that the deity would not do such a thing until he had given opportunity after opportunity for repentance. Amos, in his quick reactions, conceived of God as rewarding or punishing automatically and immediately. Hosea saw that punishment is often almost interminably delayed, while every possible opportunity is allowed for repentance.

Hosea was much like Jesus, eight centuries later, who said you should not throw your brother over as hopeless until after you have given him 70 times 7 (490) chances to repent, and after each backsliding you have forgiven him. Hosea anticipated the concept that God is love. Many of the statements in the New Testament, which associate God with love, in reality echo the words and spirit of Hosea.

Even though love is the most powerful force in the world, and will win if it is possible for anything to do so, it sometimes fails. It had failed with Gomer, and it was failing for God in his dealings with the nation of Israel. When it has been tried to the limit, and has been found wanting, then something more drastic must be resorted to. With every possibility of her changing for the better exhausted, it had come to the point, in respect to Gomer, where further indulgence with her would only have made an intolerable situation worse. Her influence in the community was also to be considered.

It was a terrible struggle, but Hosea finally decided it was time that this shielding of his wife should come to an end. The moment had arrived when he felt he must deliver her over to the people, allow community sanctions to take their course, and let her be stoned to death. Reluctantly, but firmly, we hear him make this resolve.

> And now I will uncover her shame,
>   Before the eyes of her lovers;
> And no man shall rescue her from my hand,
>   For I will make all her mirth to cease. . . .
> So I will avenge upon her the days of the Baalim,
>   Unto whom she burned her incense;
> When, bedecking herself with her rings and jewels,
>   She went forth in search of her lovers,
>   While me she forgot.
>
> *Hosea 2:10-11a, 13*

What of God in relation to all this? The two situations had been going parallel. Was God also at the point of disowning his people Israel, and allowing catastrophe to overtake them? Hosea became convinced this was inevitable, and also long overdue. He did not say in specific words exactly what would happen to the nation in the hour of her chastisement.

Rather, the prophet expressed the resolve of God indirectly, in terms of what he would do to *the promised land* in which his people had been dwelling since the days of Moses.

> I will lay waste her vines and her fig trees,
>   Concerning whom she has boasted,
> "They are the price I have received,
>   Which my lovers have given to me."
> I will turn them even into a wilderness,
>   And the wild beasts shall devour them.

Hosea 2:12

The last half of Chapter 2 and all of Chapter 3 give an entirely different fate to Gomer by having her drift into slavery, and then be bought back by Hosea to live forever after in happiness. This is the view that is found in most books. Best present-day authorities, however, regard this as a section first inserted in the days of the exile, and therefore not written by Hosea.

It may seem this prophet was unduly cruel at the last. Perhaps the final disposition of Gomer should rather be considered as a cup of justice long overfilled. As we leave the episode, our attention should linger on the long-sufferingness of Hosea and his continuing love for Gomer, in spite of her actions, throughout those trying years.

Renewed Prophetic Activity

This period of spiritual illumination, with the discovery of long-suffering love at the heart of God, caused Hosea to feel urged toward renewed prophetic work. The fact that this love of God could not be trampled underfoot indefinitely, and was now at the point of exhaustion, needed announcement to a nation in potential peril. Time was running out. The hour of Israel's downfall was nearing. Hosea felt compelled to do everything in his power to save her, even at this late date. Now that his domestic situation had become stabilized, it was possible to leave home once more. Consequently he embarked upon the second phase of his prophetic activity.

As a result of what had happened at home, there was an element of pathos in the latter utterances of Hosea. They might even be described as parables of lost opportunity and despair. Since his marriage had ended as it did, and was unpleasant to think about, he began to relive the scenes of his boyhood, and found new joys in them. As he had discovered deeper significance in the events connected with his domestic life, Hosea also came to see analogies between some of his simple childhood experiences and the relationship between God and Israel.

He loved to recall one time when he went for a walk out in the hills and found a wild grape vine, laden with the most luscious fruit. What a happy lad he was, and how good the grapes tasted as he ate his fill of them! He concluded that God must have felt the same way when he first found Israel.

Hosea also remembered how, as a boy, his mouth had watered each year for the first ripe fig of the season, and how happy he was when at last he got a taste of it. He felt that God similarly had been overjoyed when he had finally found a nation, such as Israel, that was religiously mature.

Then the prophet painted the contrast between God's early satisfaction and later disappointment with his people.

> Like grapes in the wildwood,
>   I found Israel;
> Like the first fruit of the fig tree,
>   I regarded your fathers.

> But the glory of Ephraim
> Has taken flight like a bird;
> The womb has become barren,
> And the breasts, shriveled.

Hosea 9:10-11, 14

As he reminisced, Hosea also recalled a pet heifer which he had on the farm as a boy. He had trained it for all the tasks of farming. It was most unusual in its obedient response. It seemed to get joy out of doing what Hosea desired. He could see that Israel had been equally eager and happy in serving her God during the early days. Again, the obstinacy of the present came as an unpleasant contrast.

> Ephraim was a trained heifer,
> My favorite for threshing;
> And I caused the yoke to rest
> Upon her fair neck.
>
> I also harnessed Ephraim to plow,
> And Israel was accustomed to harrow;
> They sowed unto you for righteousness,
> They reaped according to lovingkindness.
>
> But you have plowed wickedness,
> You have harvested injustice;
> You have eaten the fruit of lying,
> You have drunk the cup of violence.
>
> So shall destruction descend upon your people,
> And all your fortresses shall be demolished;
> One of these mornings the king of Israel
> Shall indeed be utterly destroyed.

Hosea 10:11-15

Hosea also thought about the days of Israel's childhood when God led her out of Egypt. The prophet was reminded

of his own joys with his three children, how he had taught
them to walk and steadied them as they took their first falter-
ing steps. Hosea concluded that God must have gained equal
joy from Israel in her childhood, helping her to become established.

> When Israel was a child, I loved him;
> And from Egypt I called forth my son;
> I also taught Ephraim how to walk,
> Holding him up with my arms.
> With human bonds I drew him,
> Even with cords of love.

Hosea 11:1, 3a, 4a

Israel, or Ephraim as the nation was frequently called,
had become a "prodigal son." Hosea realized that the eventual
"wages of sin is death," for nations as well as individuals.
Israel had "sown the wind" and was about to "reap the whirl-
wind" (Hosea 8:7). Because such a fate seemed inescapable,
this prophet gave some indication in his final words as to the
devastation and atrocities that might be expected at the
capital city of Samaria when the Assyrian conquerors should
arrive.

> Samaria must suffer punishment,
> By the sword they shall fall;
> Their infants shall be dashed in pieces,
> And their pregnant women, ripped up.

Hosea 13:16

The Sequel

The pleading of Hosea, during those final years of his life,
was not listened to by the people of his country. They were

sure Israel was *the greatest nation in the world,* and that she would endure forever. God certainly would not let her down.

Among a callous citizenry, which did not want to hear the right, there was no room for a prophet such as Hosea. People looked upon him as a kill-joy, always disturbing their peace of mind. Why should they listen to such an alarmist? So the Israelites continued their joy ride down the rapids in spite of repeated warnings. Even though about to slip over the falls, they did not realize that there was the least danger ahead. They could be happy and carefree, even in their hour of impending destruction.

There is no way of determining whether Hosea died a natural death or was martyred. It is only known that he disappeared when civil war in Israel was at its worst. Whatever oppositions he encountered and whatever his fate, all later generations are indebted to this prophet who had such a tragic home life. His example of triumphing over suffering, rather than being crushed by it, is a source of inspiration for all who are tempted to give up in the face of adversity. His discovery of the fatherhood of God, the sonship of man, and the realization that God is a God of long-suffering love, establish Hosea in the front rank of the world's religious geniuses.

Isaiah

8

Prophetic Statesman
of Jerusalem

ALTHOUGH THE VOICES of Amos and Hosea had been silenced
by death, their words were remembered and passed on from
mouth to mouth. In many quarters of Palestine the memory
of these two prophets became increasingly revered by the
more thoughtful type of people. Their influence swept down
over the highlands of Ephraim into the Southern Kingdom.
In the regions of Jerusalem their messages began to find more
hospitable reception than had been true in the north country.

Man of Royalty

Our quest leads to the palace in Jerusalem where attention
becomes focused on a young man in the royal family. His
name was none other than Isaiah, who was to become one of
the most revered prophets. Jewish tradition asserts that he was
a nephew of King Amaziah, not to be confused with Priest
Amaziah with whom Amos had his disastrous encounter in
the north country. It is possible that Isaiah lived at the royal
palace. Whether or not this was his actual home, he undoubtedly was a frequent visitor at that marvelous structure
which had been built three centuries earlier by King Solomon
of costly stones and cedar from Lebanon (I Kings 3:1, 7:1-12;

9:10). It was a satisfaction to know that Solomon had lived
within those walls. His wisdom and keenness of observation
must have been a constant source of inspiration to Isaiah. In
those hallowed halls of state, Isaiah played as a boy and grew
to manhood.

The judgment hall may well have been the chief source of
attraction. There was the great throne, ornamented with
ivory brought from distant lands, and overlaid with gold.
On each side was a huge lion, cast in brass and possibly covered with gold. This judgment seat was approached by six
steps, of decreasing length as the throne was reached. On
each end of each step was a lion, also of brass and gold.
Mounted on the surrounding walls may well have been the
three hundred golden shields which King Solomon had made
(I Kings 10:17-20). It was indeed true that to all this
wonder "there was not the like made in any kingdom." As the
monarch sat on his throne, with the fourteen lions and the
ascending steps focusing attention on him, it was a most im-
posing sight. Isaiah was often a visitor in this throne room,
watching the king, with scepter in hand, sit in judgment upon
his suppliants.

Today children of the rich are often described as being
born with a silver spoon in their mouth. Isaiah was born with
a *golden* spoon in his mouth. All dishes, vessels, and utensils
in the palace were of solid gold. It was traditionally regarded
as beneath the dignity of Hebrew royalty to have anything
in the palace that was made of such a common thing as silver
(I Kings 10:21).

In those days, members of the royal family were placed
in charge of the various government services. Although
no one knows exactly what position Isaiah occupied, it is
certain he was active in the affairs of state.

It was like a bomb explosion in Jerusalem to have a prophet arise from such aristocratic circles. It had been easy for people to dismiss Amos by saying he was an illiterate mountaineer who knew nothing about affairs of the day; or Hosea, by reminding those who might be favorably inclined that he was only a hayseed from the farm. Here it was different. In Isaiah a prophet was arising from the peak of society. He was a man of wealth, education, social prestige, and government position. Inasmuch as he came from the highest circles of his day, people would not be able to discount him so easily.

The Prophetic Call

Most glorious of all the buildings in Jerusalem was Solomon's Temple, which was situated near the palace. This was one of the grandest structures of all time. King Solomon had built it of choice cedar and gold. It was "the joy of the whole earth" (Psalm 48:2). Extensive portions of the interior walls and doors were overlaid with gold. In the holy of holies the sacred ark was kept, and over it were the golden cherubim with their outstretched wings. There was also the great sea that rested on twelve large oxen of burnished brass.

This was such a revered holy place that all people longed to come there for pilgrimage and worship. Psalm Eighty-four shows how residents in the outlying regions of Palestine envied not only the priests and attendants, who could be in the temple all the time, but even the sparrows and swallows which nested there.

Inasmuch as Isaiah's dwelling was undoubtedly nearby, he was privileged to be in this magnificent shrine often. Spending time in its courts may have been his daily delight. Many were the inspiring hours of worship he participated in at that holy place, but there was one that outshone them all. That was

the service which changed the whole course of his life. It was
in the year that Uzziah died, and seems to have been the
coronation ceremony, when a new king was crowned.

As the young man Isaiah approached the temple on that
occasion, he went with a heavy heart. From the international
point of view, the times were critical. The dangers feared by
Amos and Hosea were rapidly materializing. The mighty
Assyrian power, far to the east, was showing increasing signs
of determination to conquer the west, including Palestine and
Egypt. Rumors from that quarter indicated that a great campaign was in preparation. Would this mean the end of Isaiah's
country?

While king, Uzziah had contracted leprosy and became
unable to perform certain functions of his office. Consequently
his son Jotham had been co-regent the last four years of his
father's life. As kings went, Uzziah had been quite acceptable.
He was not as good as some, but, what was more important,
he was far from being as bad as the average of them. Now
his son Jotham was about to be crowned. He would be made
to bear, from this moment on, the full responsibility of government. What a critical moment in which to ascend the
throne! Would Jotham be able to give the wise leadership
that would be needed for such troublous times? This was the
question in the mind of Isaiah as he entered the temple for
that coronation service.

He took his place and began looking around while waiting
for the festivities to begin. Before him was the matchless
throne, brought from the palace especially for this grand
occasion. On it Jotham would soon sit to receive his crown.
The brass serpent, or seraph, a choice curio which Moses had
made in the wilderness five centuries earlier, was on the front
wall above the throne. To right and left were places reserved

for the temple choirs. The altar of burnt incense was before the throne.

Soon the temple became alive with action at the coronation prelude. Jotham had now come forward and became seated on his throne. Following him was the coronation procession. Eventually people filled the temple. By this time the singers had come in and were stationed at their appointed locations (Isa. 6:1-3). The choirs were singing antiphonally, answering one another as they chanted,

> Holy, holy, holy, is the Lord of Hosts;
> The whole earth is full of his glory.

> *Isaiah 6:3*

Isaiah had never heard such wonderful music before. The thresholds of the doors and the windows of the temple vibrated at the singing, so powerful were its strains. By this time one of the priests had lit the altar of incense. As the fragrant smoke ascended, it hid the king on his throne and appeared to cut the brass serpent into a number of pieces. The curling and breaking strands of bluish white seemed to supply wings for these "seraphim" (Isa. 6:2, 4).

At this point in the service something happened to Isaiah which he had never experienced before. He seemed pulled out of himself. He was in such heights of adoration that he suddenly felt himself caught up into heaven, together with the temple and all who were in it.

Now he saw all things in a transformed light. This was no longer Jotham, seated on his throne awaiting his crown; it was none other than God himself. Those were not the Jerusalem musicians who were singing; they were the heavenly choirs of angels. This was no longer Solomon's Temple; it appeared to be the heavenly temple in which Isaiah was having this marvelous experience. There was no longer only one wingless brass seraph above the king; a whole group of seraphim with fleecy white wings were flying about over the head of the deity to protect him and to fly his errands. Isaiah was filled with awe as he beheld these things, and he was moved beyond measure.

His next reaction was a humbling experience. As Isaiah removed his eyes for a moment from the amazing heavenly vision which he was beholding, and looked at himself, he saw how inadequate he was by way of comparison. As a result, he felt all sinful and undone (Isa. 6:5).

By this time the high altar of burnt offering had become lit, and a priest was brandishing a piece of blazing wood which he was placing at another location. In his dreamy mood, Isaiah conceived that these burning coals were carried over to him especially by one of the seraphim, and that they touched his lips. Curiously enough, at that moment Isaiah felt purified. He seemed to be a new person, made holy by the service in which he had participated (Isa. 6:6-7).

Then Isaiah seemed to hear the voice of the Lord say, "Whom shall I send, and who will go for us?" Immediately this young man answered, "Here am I. Send me" (Isa. 6:8). This was the call of Isaiah, and by that experience the whole course of his life was to be changed.

As he left the temple that day, and went to his room, we can imagine that Isaiah was deep in thought. What should be the specific form of this service to which he had been called? That was not difficult to answer. He would do in the south of Palestine the same type of prophetic work which Amos and Hosea had carried on in the north.

His energies would be devoted primarily to two areas of

the national life that needed attention. Inasmuch as his people were in a critical situation internationally, his first consideration would be to help steer his country through those difficult times. After achieving this end, he would devote the remainder of his life to bettering the moral conditions in his nation, and eliminating corruption. So, in almost an instant, his whole life's work appeared clearly before him.

In light of the reaction against Amos and Hosea in the north, Isaiah had no illusions regarding the hostile reception he probably would receive. He knew he lived in a sluggish generation, when the eyes of most people were closed to the higher demands of life, when their ears were shut, when they were unable to think with their minds, when political life was degenerate, and when people seemed powerless to repent from their evil ways and change their manner of life (Isa. 6:9-10). He conceived that they would not be likely to heed his messages until some great catastrophe should overtake them. Perhaps then they would begin to consider his warnings (Isa. 6:11-12). Nevertheless, he felt forced to go out and do what he could.

During the course of Isaiah's life he was to profit by many other moments of worship, but none could compare with this. Even though the mystical ecstasy wore off somewhat with time, the influence of that sacred hour in the temple was to follow him all through his days. The inspiration of that service generated enough power to drive him out as a prophet and keep him going, against almost hopeless odds, for forty years. Such can be the power of worship.

International Crisis

Isaiah's first child was born shortly after his prophetic call, and he named this son Shear-jesheb, commonly miswritten

Shear-jashub (Isa. 7:3). This name meant "Only a Remnant shall be Left." Its point of reference was to the Northern Kingdom where the conflict between pro-Egyptian and pro-Assyrian parties was landing Israel in a disastrous civil war that would make her an easy prey to Assyrian conquest. It indicated that this "carrying water on two shoulders" would result in disaster for Israel. The name was also a warning to Judah lest she follow the same policy.

During the reign of King Menahem of Israel in the north (738-736 B.C.), the Assyrian armies of King Tiglath-pileser III, who was given the short nickname "Pul" in the Bible, finally arrived in Palestine, as Amos and Hosea had in a general way predicted, and began conquest of the Northern Kingdom. However, King Menahem bought off the Assyrian conqueror by agreeing to pay one thousand talents of silver (II Kings 15:19-22).

After ruling only two years, Menahem's son Pekahiah was slain by the pro-Egyptian party which then placed their man Pekah on the throne. Isaiah could see that such civil war would be suicidal for Palestine.

Pekah was an aggressive ruler in the Northern Kingdom of Israel. With the blessing of Egypt, he conceived the idea of forming a great western military coalition, of all countries in the regions of Palestine and Syria, for the purpose of stopping Assyria. Isaiah advised his Southern Kingdom of Judah not to join. He felt such a coalition, sponsored by Egypt, would fail, and would bring ruin particularly upon those small nations which would participate in it. As they would be only outposts for Egypt, they would be attacked first and would probably meet disaster. Convinced by his reasoning, the Southern Kingdom followed Isaiah's advice and decided to pursue an independent policy.

Pekah, however, refused to take "No" for an answer from the south. He therefore proceeded to lead the armies of north Israel against the Southern Kingdom of Judah in an attempt to force her into the coalition. Pekah even set up a puppet king, Tob-el ("God is Good"), who was to rule in Jerusalem after it should be conquered and forced into the alliance (Isa. 7:1-6).

King Ahaz, who had just been made king in Jerusalem, was frightened by this campaign of Israel and Syria against him (Isa. 7:1-2). Isaiah assured him these two countries were doomed because of their unwise procedures. He called them two burned-out "tails of smoking firebrands" (Isa. 7:4). The prophet pointed out that it would be impossible for such small countries to conquer the mighty Assyria. He gave to Tob-el the nickname Tab-eel ("Good for Nothing"), and insisted that Judah should continue following her policy of honorable independence.

When Isaiah called at the palace to congratulate Ahaz on the birth of a son, whom the king had piously named Immanuel ("God's on Our Side"), the prophet assured this monarch that "before that child should know to refuse the evil and choose the good" the two anti-Assyrian kingdoms of Israel and Syria would meet their doom. This meant that, in light of their international intrigues, Isaiah gave them at most but four or five years before they would be swallowed up by Assyria (Isa. 7:10-17).

As the invasion from the north gained headway, and after the armies of Syria and Israel had overrun much of Judah, including the Hebrew seaport of Elath on the Red Sea, they laid siege to the capital city. In spite of Isaiah's assurances that Jerusalem would be able to hold out, twenty-three-year-old King Ahaz became panicky and allowed himself to come under the influence of the party which, condemning Isaiah's policy of honorable independence, desired alliance with Assyria. So Ahaz appealed to Assyria for help against Israel and Syria, thus inviting the eastern power to annihilate the ten tribes of his fellow Hebrews. An alliance with that great nation was effected. To pay for it, Ahaz stripped from the palace and temple much of their silver and gold, sending these as a present to the Assyrian monarch (II Kings 16:5-8).

For five or six years the ship of state in Judah had been guided with relative safety through critical times as her rulers had followed the advices of Isaiah. Now that King Ahaz had made the great departure, and had plunged into world power politics, the prophet looked upon this as a most perilous choice.

At this time Isaiah had a second son born to him, and he gave that infant the name Maher-shalal-hash-baz, which meant "The spoil speeds, the prey hastens" (Isa. 8:3-4). Isaiah also constructed a large billboard at a prominent place in Jerusalem and painted the words Maher-shalal-hash-baz on it in man-sized letters, to make certain that all in the capital city would get this message (Isa. 8:1-2). The name signified that King Ahaz's mistakes had sealed the fate of his country. Becoming implicated with Assyria would bring disaster to Judah. This would come from the east as a great flood that would sweep over Palestine, destroying everything as it went (Isa. 8:5-8).

A partial fulfillment of the predictions made by Amos, Hosea, and Isaiah took place in 734 B.C. when King Tiglath-pileser of Assyria invaded the land of Israel and captured the northern part of Palestine which was called Galilee, the portion east of the Jordan River, and several cities of special military significance (II Kings 15:29-30). The people from these

THE PROPHET WARNS HIS KING

conquered areas were carried as captives to Assyria.

Two years later the Assyrians descended on the other chief party in this coalition, Syria, with its capital at Damascus. This country was quickly liquidated, as Isaiah had foreseen, and her populations were also carried away as captives.

After this there were about eight years of comparative quiet during which the portion of the Northern Kingdom that remained caught its breath. Considering Israel ripe for final conquest, the armies of Assyria returned in 724 B.C., swept through and laid waste all that remained of Israel's territory, and converged on the highly fortified capital of Samaria for a determined siege. This city-fortress was so adequately protected and provisioned that it was able to hold out for a three-year siege against these mightiest armies of that day. Eventually it fell in 722 or 721 B.C.

In accordance with usual Assyrian practice, Israel's captured populations also were carried as exile slaves, six hundred miles to the northeast where they were assigned to labor projects in the land of Assyria. The catastrophe which the prophets had feared, and concerning which they had lost no time in warning the nations of Israel and Judah, had now materialized with a vengeance in so far as Israel was concerned. This marked the end of the Northern Kingdom.

As these captive hordes proceeded on their terrible march to slavery, they must have wailed, "Oh, that we had listened to our prophets Amos, Hosea, and Isaiah! They were right." However, it was too late now to benefit from such a delayed repentance.

These prophets also had realized that the Israelites did not have sufficient moral fiber left to survive the rigors of bondage in a strange land. At this point their foresight proved true also. The ten tribes of Israel soon passed into extinction,

becoming lost among the many diverse populations of Mesopotamia. People have spoken ever since of the "ten lost
tribes."

The downfall of Israel, which was the most tragic event
in the history of Hebrew Palestine up to this time, ended the
first phase of Isaiah's ministry, in which he had devoted
most of his attention to political affairs. Inasmuch as there
was no indication Assyria had any immediate designs against
Judah, the Southern Kingdom settled down with the prospect
for some years of peace.

9

Higher Views on Religion

AFTER THE FALL OF ISRAEL, Isaiah changed his emphasis. Thereafter, he devoted attention chiefly to the religious and moral problems of his day. If the inner life of his nation could be raised to higher levels, he felt this would be his nation's strongest defense. By directing his efforts toward this end, he considered he was rendering his country the greatest possible service.

The Case of the Vineyard

Perhaps the first occasion for making this new emphasis was when he appeared in court and took the judges of Jerusalem by surprise. We can imagine the scene in an open square inside one of the city gates. The elders were seated there, hearing case after case which people in trouble were bringing before them for judgment.

It was a dramatic moment when Isaiah, the aristocratic man of royalty, stood before this legal array and brought a lawsuit. The presence in court of such a prominent person must in itself have almost overawed the judges.

The notableness of that moment was further increased because his suit was unusual in three ways. By phrasing his statement of the case in poetry, his presentation at once attracted attention. A further irregularity was that Isaiah did

114

not present his own litigation, for this purported to be his neighbor's case. Most curious of all, here was a man instituting suit against a vineyard, a strange type of lawsuit to bring before any court in any country. We probably would have seen a puzzled look on the faces of all who were present as Isaiah stated his case.

> Let me sing of my well-beloved
>   A song of my beloved concerning his vineyard.
> My well-beloved had a vineyard
>   In a very fruitful hill:
> And he plowed it carefully,
> And gathered out the stones thereof,
> And planted it with the choicest vines,
> And built a tower in the midst of it,
> And also hewed out a winepress therein.
> Then he waited for the time when it would produce grapes,
>   But — it brought forth wild grapes.

Isaiah 5:1-2

Then Isaiah called upon the judges for a decision, as he said,

> And now, O inhabitants of Jerusalem,
>   And men of Judah;
> Pass judgment, I beg of you,
>   Between me and my vineyard.

Isaiah 5:3

We can imagine the inquisitive spectators gathered around, looking at the legal authorities to see how they would handle this matter. Although many of these judges had been hearing disputes for years, they sat nonplused before this case. Even the oldest of them had never heard anything like it. What were they to do with it? How could they execute judgment against a vineyard? Courts were for settling disputes between people.

For a few moments the judges sat, in a quandary. Finally Isaiah brought an end to this silence. As he moved nearer the judges, all attention became centered on him. Then he did the unheard-of thing by unceremoniously taking this matter out of the judges' hands and passing sentence himself. The faces of these legal dignitaries must have appeared more perplexed than ever at seeing a plaintiff suddenly assume the role of judge. So much about these proceedings was unusual that everyone listened carefully to the judgment as Isaiah pronounced it. With voice sufficiently loud, he spoke so all spectators could hear.

> I will tell you what I will do to my vineyard:
> I will take away the hedge thereof,
>   And it shall be eaten up.
> I will break down the wall thereof,
>   And it shall be trodden down,
>   And I will lay it waste.
> It shall not be pruned nor hoed,
>   But there shall come up briars and thorns.
> I will even command the clouds,
>   That they rain no rain upon it.

Isaiah 5:5-6

It is possible to imagine the question running through the minds of the people, "Of course this is how one would proceed, but why make such an ado about it in court?" Before the end of that moment of silent suspense that followed his words, while the people were collecting their thoughts, Isaiah added,

> For the vineyard of the Lord of hosts
>   Is the house of Israel;
> And the men of Judah
>   Are his pleasant plant:

THE CASE AGAINST THE VINEYARD

And he looked for justice —
But behold — oppression;
For righteousness —
But behold — a moan.

Isaiah 5:7

By this explanation Isaiah indicated that he had not been presenting a real court case at all, but only a parable. These words resolved, for his puzzled audience, its inner meaning. The owner in question was none other than God himself. His vineyard, which produced the bad grapes, was the nation of Israel.

The masses were being crushed under the exploitation of the wealthy. These poor people were moaning and crying under the hardness of their lot. It was not a good picture for a nation's future. Countries which endure are built on freedom and the common welfare of all — not on oppression. When a nation becomes a hunting ground for exploiters, it might as well fold up, for it has reached its end.

This situation prevailed only because the judges were allowing bad conditions to exist. It is significant that Isaiah presented this parable of the vineyard, with its accompanying warning of impending national catastrophe, in court. There was a partially concealed sting in the prophet's procedure that day. It was an indirect but powerful rebuke to the whole judicial system of those times.

The Women's Club of Jerusalem

This prophet's most sensational appearance was before the Women's Club of Jerusalem. Perhaps they invited him, for he was a man of distinction. By having him as a speaker they would honor themselves and their club. However, he gave them stronger medicine than they had expected. We can imagine the wincing among these blue bloods of Jerusalem as he spoke.

> Because the daughters of Zion are haughty,
>   And walk with outstretched necks and wanton eyes,
> Tripping and mincing as they go,
>   And making a tinkling with their feet;
> Therefore the Lord will smite with a scab
>   The crown of the head of the daughters of Zion
> And the Lord will lay bare their secret parts.
>   And it shall come to pass that
> Instead of sweet perfumery — there shall be rottenness,
> Instead of a girdle — a rope,
> Instead of permanent waves — baldness,
> Instead of a robe — a girding of sackcloth,
> Instead of beauty — branding.
>
> *Isaiah 3:16-17, 24*

Isaiah was outspoken in addressing these wanton women whose chief stock in trade was sex appeal. Ordinarily rather quiet, he became wrought up as he spoke of their going about in a mincing way with little bells on their ankles, drawing attention to the suggestive parts of their anatomy. By their exploiting luxury and low morals, these society women were making their country morally rotten and ripe for conquest. Because of their important role in corrupting the life of that day, Isaiah was particularly vigorous in what he said to them.

As the prophet knew how things had worked themselves out at the fall of Samaria, it was not an idle dream when he told these women what would happen to them. With the arrival of invasion, they would find their rich apparel seized and sent back to the wives of the conquerors in Assyria. These once wealthy women of Jerusalem would find themselves in the naked line-up, soon the victims of venereal disease, with scabs from head to foot, together with baldness and the stench of their bodies. Those who would be lucky — if lucky it would be — to escape this fate, would be branded with the insignia of their new owners, clothed with coarse burlap, roped together in captive bands, and herded to their places of servitude in far-off lands. This was the message of Isaiah to the elite women of Jerusalem.

Undoubtedly they were greatly disappointed with their much announced speaker. It was not pleasant to hear such reprimands. It would have been far more delightful to have sat admiringly, listening to the recital of nice sounding platitudes with which they could all have been in agreement. Yet, even though he dealt with unpleasant matters, his words were phrased with such literary artistry that they could hardly have helped being effective. Although not invited back a second time, there can be no doubt but that the day when Isaiah appeared before the Women's Club of Jerusalem was long remembered.

Land-Grabbing

Throughout the centuries the matter of land distribution has been one of mankind's greatest problems. In new countries this is not a difficulty, but, when nations grow older, maladjustments tend to develop. Usually the upper classes buy up or appropriate the land for themselves while the masses lose the properties they may once have owned. With this comes poverty.

In early Palestinian society there was no reason for concern in this regard. Because people were anchored to the soil, there were practically no poor people. As the Hebrew monarchy grew older, the situation changed. By the time of Isaiah the land had become consolidated in great holdings. For the average Palestinian there was no such thing as private ownership. The landless gravitated to the cities where they were herded together in the squalor of slums.

Sometimes properties were acquired by violence. More often seizure was brought about through bribing judges to grant foreclosures in court for inability to repay debts at the moment of demand. Even when carried out by regular purchase, the result was an unhealthy monopolizing of the land. Isaiah was the first individual in the Bible to deal in a significant way with this problem of land-grabbing. His most pointed words were,

> Woe unto those
> > Who join house to house,
> > And add field to field
> Till there is no room,
> > And you are made to dwell propertyless
> > In the midst of the land.
> Of a truth, many houses shall be desolate,
> > Even great and fair, without inhabitant.

Isaiah 5:8, 9b

This factor of land monopoly is still one of the chief maladies over much of the modern world. As yet America is too new for the problem to be serious. However, corporation farming, chain farms, and the ever larger holdings by church and other tax-exempt charitable organizations are creating a situation of increasing concern. Inasmuch as our civilization is no longer dominantly agricultural but industrial, the most exact modern counterpart to the situation Isaiah faced lies in the monopoly control of industry. This, with its international cartels, already prevails in certain segments of trade and is far more alarming in most industrial countries today than the land situation. Socialist and communist societies also

incur blame at this point to the extent that they substitute
ownership by an oppressive and monopolistic state. Whatever
the form of government, when a civilization comes to the
point where a large portion of the citizenry own neither their
own homes nor the means of production, that is a sick civilization. Collectivism has its dangers, and Isaiah saw them. The
call of this prophet for decentralization could be a valuable
message for our present-day society.

Liquor

In the early days of Palestine, drunkenness was not much
of a factor, even though people had their vineyards. The
chief trouble began with the introduction of distilled liquors.
Amos had mentioned wine as an element in the luxurious
carousals of his day (Amos 2:8; 4:1; 6:6), but this was
only incidental in his descriptions. There also had grown up
two prohibitionist orders, the Nazarites and Rechabites, which
banned use of all wine and strong drink by their members.
It remained for Isaiah, however, to deliver a general broadside against the practice of drinking throughout the nation.
He was the first person in the Bible to call the public's attention to the increasing havoc which drink was causing.

> Woe unto those who excel at drinking wine,
>   And the men who are expert at mixing strong drinks.
> Woe unto those who rise early in the morning,
>   That they may follow strong drink,
> Who tarry late into the night,
>   Until wine inflames them.
> There is the harp and lute, the tabaret and pipe,
>   To accompany the wine at their feasts.
> But they give no consideration to the work of the Lord,
>   Nor do they discern the work of his hands.

Isaiah 5:22, 11-12

The evil of liquor was claiming as its victims people from ever-higher ranks in the social scale. In Isaiah's time the situation had developed to the point where prophets and priests were some of the chief addicts. The offensiveness of the habit was more apparent when it was observed how drink could make fools of these religious professionals. Isaiah had witnessed one occasion when the priests, in the stage of being sick from liquor, vomited over the table of shewbread, the Old Testament predecessor to the Christian communion table, while officiating at this most sacred rite.

> Even these also reel with wine,
>   And stagger with strong drink;
> Both priest and prophet reel with strong drink,
>   They are swallowed up of wine.
> They stagger with strong drink,
>   They err in vision,
>   They stumble in judgment;
> For all tables are full of vomit and filthiness,
>   So that no place is clean.

Isaiah 28:7-8

From Isaiah's day to this, drink has been a constantly increasing problem. As life grows more complex and mechanized, the greater becomes the potential menace of liquor. Even though others in the later portions of the Bible, and in the centuries from then to the present, have faced this issue, it must not be forgotten that Isaiah was the first to make a vigorous and widespread attack upon this problem. He went far toward sensitizing the conscience of mankind with regard to the mounting evil of drunkenness. Isaiah may therefore be looked upon as the founding patron of all temperance movements.

Concerning Worship

On a later occasion Isaiah discoursed on the subject of religion in an especially pointed manner at Solomon's Temple in Jerusalem. Worship at that magnificent shrine had meant much to Isaiah during the days of his youth and young manhood. As already observed, it was in the temple at one of its services that he had felt called to become a prophet. He had been deeply appreciative of the important contributions to the nation which the temple had rendered. Yet, in the course of his ministry, something had happened with regard to Isaiah's attitudes toward this place of worship.

Perhaps the temple was becoming corrupted during his days. Or was the change to be found in the growing sensitiveness of this prophet, so that he only gradually became aware of how superficial the services of religion really were? Probably both of these were important factors in his changing attitudes toward formal religious ritual. It had come to the point where the temple ceremonies, *as commonly observed,* were growing repulsive to him.

One day when Jerusalem was crowded with worshipers on the occasion of a major annual festival, Isaiah stood in an outer court of the temple and spoke to the assembled throngs. Comparing the capital of Judah to the moral stature of Sodom and Gomorrah was one of the most caustic rebukes the prophet could have administered. His representing God as disgusted with the temple ritual must have seemed no less astounding.

> Hear the word of the Lord,
>   You rulers of Sodom.
> Give ear to the law of our God,
>   You people of Gomorrah.

"What do I care for the multitude of your sacrifices?"
   Says the Lord;
"I have had my fill of the burnt offerings of rams,
   And the fat of fed beasts;
And I take no delight in the blood of bullocks,
   Or of lambs, or of he-goats.
When you come to appear before me,
   Who has required this at your hand —
   To trample my courts?
Bring no more vain oblations.
   Incense is an abomination unto me.
New moon and Sabbath, the calling of assemblies —
   I can't stand them — they are iniquitous —
   Even the solemn meetings.
My soul hates your new moons and appointed feasts,
   They are a source of trouble unto me;
   I am weary of having anything more to do with them.
And when you spread forth your hands,
   I will hide my eyes from you;
Yes, even when you make many prayers
   I will not hear,
   For your hands are full of blood."

Isaiah 1:10-15

Isaiah was not opposed to public worship and religious assemblies, with song and prayer. He was against such practices only when carried on by corrupt people in such a brazen manner that these observances became a travesty on religion. He had no hesitancy in confronting these callous worshipers with their record.

   Look, how the faithful city
      Has become as a harlot!
   She abounded with justice,
   And righteousness lodged in her;
      But now you are murderers.

> Your silver has become dross;
> Your wine, mixed with water.
> Your princes are lawless,
>   And companions of thieves;
> Every one of them loves bribes,
>   And they seek after graft.
> They deny justice to the orphans,
>   And refuse to hear cases brought by widows.

> *Isaiah 1:21-23*

Those were days when services of worship were crowded. There was such a rush at the temple that it amounted to "trampling" the "courts" of those sacred precincts. Most of the people who thronged that place were using religion only as a cloak to cover their sins, however, rather than as a source of inspiration for right living.

As the climax of his remarks, Isaiah gave one of the best statements in the Bible concerning the essence and fundamental duties of true religion which strives to avoid sin and possesses a social consciousness.

> Wash yourselves — make yourselves clean —
> Put away the evil of your doings from before my eyes.
> Cease to do evil, learn to do good,
> Seek justice, relieve the oppressed,
> Judge the fatherless, plead for the widow.

> *Isaiah 1:16-17*

This construing of religion as a matter of living, rather than merely performing easy rituals, was not appreciated in certain quarters. The priesthood and temple authorities, who were dependent for their maintenance upon keeping up the old shallow types of false religion, resented Isaiah's remarks. You can imagine them going back to their appointed stations, saying, "Isaiah will have to pay for this."

To a Backsliding Nation

During the latter part of Isaiah's life his attention was drawn again primarily to political matters. This was particularly true in the tragic year of 701 B.C. Up to that time King Hezekiah had been following Isaiah's international policy of honorable independence. However, like King Pekah in the Northern Kingdom twenty-five years earlier, Hezekiah eventually came under the influence of the more aggressive pro-Egyptian party and was led to adopt their more tangible program of security. Ignoring Isaiah's pleadings, Hezekiah entered into a secret military alliance with Egypt, purchased large quantities of war materials from that country, and turned Judah into an advance camp against Assyria. King Hezekiah was unable to see that he was following the same path which had brought ruin to Israel (II Kings 18:7).

Faced with this situation of hostility, the armies of the east descended on Judah in 701 B.C. and captured all outlying towns and cities, with only Jerusalem left. At that point Hezekiah begged for terms. The sum designated was "three hundred talents of silver and thirty talents of gold." The silver was taken by the king from the vessels and treasures of the temple and palace. The gold was obtained by cutting off the overlays with which the temple doors and pillars were partly covered (II Kings 18:13-16).

After this payment, Hezekiah apparently, against Isaiah's emphatic warnings, continued conspiring with Egypt against Assyria. When this was discovered by the Assyrians, they descended upon Jerusalem with the idea of making an end of

it (II Kings 18:17-19:34). The siege was set and the
capital city seemed doomed. Then it seems that a plague developed in the Assyrian camp and thousands of their soldiers
died in a few days. Those who had not yet contracted it fled
in fright and returned to their own country (II Kings 19:35-
37). Thus Jerusalem was saved, but only by a hair's breadth.

Although a "remnant" of Judah remained, this defeat was
a major catastrophe for the Southern Kingdom. During the
siege the population of the capital had been decimated by
hunger. Now that the city had almost miraculously been
spared, Isaiah expected the people would be chastened and
repentant. He hoped they would desert their sinfulness and
turn to better ways of living.

Instead, they seemed to do just the reverse. They descended
to a new low by stooping to racketeering and black market
operations, with new forms of crime and exploitation. In his
old age Isaiah was pained beyond measure by this turn of
events. His final message to the citizens of his country
shows his great disappointment. These people may have been
of the genus *Homo sapiens,* but when it came to realistic
political thought or discerning things spiritual, he labeled
them duller than oxen.

> Hear, O heavens!
> And give ear, O earth!
>   For the Lord has spoken.
> "I have nourished and brought up children,
>   And they have rebelled against me.
> The ox knows his owner,
>   And the donkey, his master's crib;
> But Israel does not know —
>   My people do not comprehend."
>
> *Isaiah 1:2-3*

The Prophet's Fate

These last addresses were more than the corrupt forces of Jerusalem would tolerate. Isaiah was meddling in their affairs. It seemed to them he should have known better than to keep on with this agitating. He was threatening their livelihood, and such a person must be silenced. Business was business. They could be excused for trying to make their way of life secure for the future. Even though he was an old man, they felt forced to take matters into their own hands. This prophet's trouble-making voice could be allowed in Jerusalem no longer. Isaiah must go.

Jewish tradition tells how he was supposedly martyred. His executers apparently had some remaining twinges of conscience, and hesitated to face the prophet as they committed this act. It might have been a trying experience to see such a saintly old man suffer. They solved the problem by getting a large hollow log. They slipped him into it, and then proceeded to saw the log in two. That was the end of the prophet Isaiah.

After getting rid of him, the capital city seemed to rest more comfortably. With no continuing voice to disturb their consciences, the people of Jerusalem settled down again to the joys of self-satisfaction and complacency.

It must be remembered that during the forty years of his ministry, Isaiah's counsels on international policies were usually followed. Only when they were forsaken did catastrophe for Judah result.

It was easy to silence the voice of Isaiah, but his spirit was to go marching on. His greatest service lay in inspiring a long line of prophets — thirteen in number — who were to follow him in the Southern Kingdom. As with most prophets, he has influenced later generations more than his own.

Perhaps the breadth of his insights and interests was the most remarkable aspect about Isaiah. Although a man of wealth, aristocracy, and royalty, he was in reality a commoner. He had a regard for the common people, and a devotion to them. In these attitudes he possessed something of the democratic spirit in an age when this was yet largely unknown.

Micah

IO

The Paul Revere of Judah

IN CONSIDERING MICAH, it is necessary to retrace our steps somewhat, for his work took place during Isaiah's later ministry. By contrast with the dates 739-700 B.C. for Isaiah, Micah's public activity covered the latter part of this period, 715-700 B.C. Even though Micah was the younger contemporary of Isaiah, and they were working in the same country and at the same time, there is no evidence that they ever met each other. This may be accounted for largely by the fact that they came from opposite poles of society, and also by the distance between their homes.

The small town where Micah was born and grew up was located on the southwest border of Palestine. Its name was Mareshah, and was situated in a region called the Shephelah. This was a territory of foothills between the highlands of central Judah and the level coastal plain that was occupied by the Philistines. It was also practically on the border of Egypt, for this was one of the last towns in Hebrew Palestine on the highway which led toward the land of the Nile.

Because of its location on the frontier, near an international boundary, Mareshah was one of the first points to be invaded in any attack from the southwest. The residents of this village were subject to the fears which commonly prevailed in border communities during those days when war was more or less of an annual occurrence. One of the first acts of King Hezekiah, who began ruling as Micah started his prophetic work, was to wage war on the Philistine cities in the regions of Mareshah (II Kings 18:8). This international anxiety and war consciousness which prevailed in Micah's environment played a considerable role in determining his concerns. The peace of Mareshah, and surrounding communities, was of deep concern to this prophet.

The village of Mareshah was not a pretentious place. If it had not been for Micah, even the name might not have survived. Nothing is known concerning his parentage, home, early life, or decision to become a prophet. He simply appeared "out of the blue." Indications point to the fact he was an artisan, or "laboring man" as we would say.

His utterances show that the influence of Hosea and Isaiah had swept down over the highlands and valleys of Judah, even into this remote place. Nevertheless, Micah was influenced most by Amos who had lived not many miles away and whose words were still echoing and re-echoing among those hills of southern Palestine. In Micah was to become blended the spirit of his three prophetic predecessors.

Naked and Wailing

The ministry of Micah began in a mood of distress, over the increasing corruption in his nation. As he saw it, the ten northern tribes of Israel had developed a depraved manner of life. Samaria, their capital, was the center from which a host of iniquities had proceeded. Those blighting influences had spread from the cities of the north until they had brought moral perversion into even the most inaccessible places in the southern land of Judah. Although the Northern Kingdom had fallen some seven years before Micah began his work, he

could see how the corrosive influences which had come from
that source were about to bring destruction to his own people.

Micah compared this plague of iniquity, that was sweeping
his country, to a disastrous flood moving down over the
highlands of Ephraim. This deluge of ungodliness was now
threatening to engulf the Southern Kingdom and bring about
its ruin.

> What is the transgression of Jacob?
>   Is it not Samaria?
> And what is the sin of Judah?
>   Is it not Jerusalem?
>
> On account of this I lament and wail,
>   I go about stripped and naked;
> I make a wailing like the jackals,
>   And a lamentation like the ostriches.
>
> For her infection is incurable.
>   It has spread even unto Judah;
> It reaches unto the gate of my people,
>   Even unto Jerusalem.
>
> *Micah 1:5, 8-9*

As Micah journeyed among the cities of Palestine, giving
these words of wailing, he followed the manner of dress used
by the prophet Elijah some two centuries earlier. Like that
picturesque character, Micah went about "stripped and naked."
This meant that he wore no clothing except a loincloth. Probably he adopted this spectacular appearance to attract the
curious crowds so that all people might get his message.

Micah proceeded on a desperate march through the
countryside, villages, and cities of Judah, wailing over the
dire condition into which his people had gotten themselves.
He probably uttered this same message thousands of times,

wherever groups were gathered, whether few or many in number. He tried to awaken the people from their moral slumbers.

To a generation that was eating, drinking, and making merry, with no thought of impending danger, the prophet's warnings seemed absurd. His wailings sounded to these listless people as strange as the cries of jackals on distant hills in the darkness, or like the moaning of ostriches. Yet he did his best to make the Palestinians aware that the heart of their country was rotting away with moral decay.

Forerunner of Paul Revere

The time of international crisis, long anticipated by Isaiah and more recently by Micah, finally arrived. In 711 B.C. Assyria was preparing for a major western campaign, the first since the fall of the Northern Kingdom in 722 B.C. News of these plans apparently leaked out and spread to the west. It appears that Micah was in Jerusalem when he heard the report.

He immediately got busy and did for his countrymen what Paul Revere was to do centuries later in America. As Paul Revere rode his horse from Boston toward Concord, awakening the farmers of the New England countryside and announcing that the British were coming, the prophet Micah went from village to village, as he proceeded hurriedly toward Mareshah, warning the cities and villages concerning the approach of the Assyrians.

For each location he devised a couplet in which the name of the village played special significance. Sometimes it was a pun, which is indicated here by Hebrew transliteration in parentheses. In other instances he reversed the meaning of the town's name. In each settlement he seems to have repeated the couplets spoken in the former places. So he had a growing

THE CRY OF ALARM

poem as he proceeded on his way. By the time he came home
to Mareshah, and delivered the completed warning to his
fellow townsmen, it was a production of considerable length.
It does not mean so much to us because we cannot appreciate the full significance of the names or places. Nevertheless,
it is possible to imagine something of the stir he created between Jerusalem and Mareshah on that fateful day in 711 B.C.

In Gath (*gath*) — keep your silence (*taggithu*).
At Tear-town (*bku*) — repress your weeping (*tbku*).
Roll yourselves in the dust (*'aphar*), O people of Dust-town
    (*'aphrah*).
Take you to flight, O inhabitants of Fair-view (*shphyr*);
    Lest you be stripped (*shphur*) naked, and ashamed.
Soon the inhabitants of Go-out-town (*tsa'anan*),
    Shall go out (*yats'ah*) no longer.
At Isolated-town there shall be wailing,
    Because he will take your territory for his camp site.
For the name of Halah-letob (*She has entreated for good*)
    Shall be changed to Yoshebeth-maroth (*She shall dwell in bitter-
      ness*)
    When calamity comes down from the Lord
    To the gates of Jerusalem.
Hitch the chariot to the swift steed (*larekesh*),
    O inhabitants of Lachish (*lakiysh*);
    You who were the beginning of sin to the daughter of Zion,
    For the transgressions of Israel have been found in you.
Therefore, give your parting gifts
    At Gift-town in the region of Gath.
The houses of Deceit-town (*achzib*)
    Shall be for a deceptive one (*achzab*),
    Even for the king of Assyria.
I will yet bring the conqueror (*yoresh*) upon you,
    O inhabitant of Mareshah (*moreshah*).
Once more the glory of Israel shall come
    Even unto Adullam.
Make yourselves bald, and cut off your hair
    Because of the children in which you delight;

Enlarge your baldness as the eagle,
For they are as good as gone into captivity from you.

Micah 1:10-16

Although this projected Assyrian campaign toward the west was carried out in 711 B.C., it did not get far. Practically its whole force was spent on the Philistine city of Ashdod. Apparently it took a siege lasting all summer before the invaders were able to capture this military objective (Isa. 20:1). This meant that Micah's country of Judah would be allowed to continue for some time longer.

To the Jerusalem Men of Wealth

The Assyrian menace subsided to such an extent that Judah was to live in peace for almost another decade. With the passing of that crisis, Micah apparently discarded his sensational appearance and again dressed as other men. Inasmuch as foreign affairs were no longer such a pertinent issue, he began to concentrate on the social maladies of his country. This prophet was continually haunted by the immorality of his countrymen. In this phase of his public work, he dealt heavy blows against the forces of corruption.

One of Micah's most startling experiences occurred in the midst of an address delivered in Jerusalem before an audience that was well sprinkled with blue bloods. Many of these people had degenerated into spending their nights devising plans to despoil their fellows, and their daytime hours were occupied in executing these plots. In facing those who were responsible for such deplorable conditions, Micah was fearless.

Woe unto those who plan wicked schemes
And devise evil upon their beds;

At break of day, they carry them out,
  Being powerful enough to do so.
They covet fields and seize them,
  Even houses, and take possession of them;
They exploit an individual and his household,
  A man and all his property.
Therefore thus the Lord has spoken:
"Behold I am devising against this family a calamity,
  From which you shall not remove your necks;
Then you shall no longer walk in haughtiness,
  For it will be a time of tragedy."

Micah 2:1-3

Certain of his hearers, who smarted under these condemnations and resented the way he was exposing them before all the people, decided this type of prophesying must stop. So they cried out from the audience, "Stop your prophesying." Another shouted, "They shall not prophesy before these people." A third indignant person yelled out, "All he does is offer reproaches" (Mic. 2:6). This occasion, when Micah's audience blew up on him, was one of the most exciting experiences in the annals of the prophets.

Even though things had gotten out of control temporarily, Micah was able to regain mastery of the situation quickly. He reminded his listeners that he had bad words only for bad people. Even if the shoe did pinch, they had better wear it. Thereupon he proceeded with renewed vigor to denounce the civil violence, racketeering, and exploitation of which these prominent families were guilty.

Do I not have good words
  For those who walk in uprightness?
But of late my people are risen up as an enemy;
  You strip the garments from harmless people,
From those who go about their ways peacefully,
  Even from veterans returning after war.

You cast out the women of my people
  From the homes which are their delight;
From their young children you take away,
  My glory for all time to come.
Rise up, and get you away,
  For you will not have long to stay here,
Because corruption is bringing ruin upon you,
  And the destruction thereof shall be grievous.

Micah 2:7-10

Most notable in these remarks was Micah's account of the reception the Jerusalem people accorded the veterans of those days. Instead of giving parades, honors, and pensions, they waylaid the returning soldiers and stole even what few belongings they had brought from the front. The practice of foreclosing on the homes of widows, driving them and their children out to shift as best they could, was equally ruthless.

Micah ended with the announcement that such corrupt people were no longer worthy to continue occupying the Holy Land. God, as they thought, had given it to them centuries earlier. However, they had failed him. Now they might as well be up and gone, for it was not to remain their heritage. This land, "flowing with milk and honey," was about to pass into the hands of people who might be more deserving, and might go farther in ordering it according to principles of right.

The Drunken Pretender

Micah always received a hostile reception from the powers in control and the people of influence. They refused to have anything to do with him, or even hear his utterances if they could help it. It was interesting to see the type of person to whom they would listen. Apparently on one occasion the prophet observed a good example of this.

When Micah possibly was forbidden to speak, and was ushered unceremoniously out of that audience, there came into the same group a drunken pretender. This drink-crazed specimen of humanity proceeded to inform the people that he would gladly be their prophet. He would tell them what they wanted to hear. The only condition on their part would be that they should keep him supplied with drinks.

Elated at the prospect of having one who would tell them what they liked to hear, they took him in with open arms and proclaimed this lying impostor the prophet of the people. We can hear the scorn in the voice of Micah as he told about it.

> If a man walks in the spirit,
>   And in falsehood dispenses lies, saying,
> "I will prophesy to you for wine and strong drink";
>   Even he is accepted as the prophet of this people.
>
> *Micah 2:11*

This episode dramatized a problem that is ever present through the ages. Shall the members of the congregation determine what the preacher may say? Do the occupants of the pew have a right to hear from the pulpit only platitudes and nice bits of nothing which please and soothe? Is it their right to be spared listening to anything disturbing within the sacred precincts? Or is it the duty of the pulpit to arouse and agitate, serving as a divine X ray that purges the moral cancers from the worshipers?

In almost every age there are certain vested interests which will not tolerate an outspoken voice such as that of Micah. Out of the degeneracy and corruption which they may help produce, there are certain people who make great profits, and they will not give these up without a struggle. Because for them it seems a matter of life or death, they exert every effort

to keep the prophet from the pulpit. Corrupt groups usually
do not lack money. As the power of finance is rather invincible, it is frequently able to stampede the people into getting rid of the true prophet.

Anti-prophetic interests usually work hard to place in the
pulpit a minister who is willing to compromise slightly with
evil, at least to the extent of treating their shortcomings with
silence. They want one who is not overly critical about
personal conduct, and will condemn "sin" but not "sins."
They like a "spiritual" leader who will tickle the ears and
please. They prefer a minister who shares somewhat in their
lesser vices. This gives them a more comfortable feeling. It
serves to crown their corruptions with a halo of sanctity. Instead of leaving the morning service pained at heart over their
shortcomings, and resolving to do better, worshipers can go
home from hearing such a minister on Sunday with untroubled
conscience, feeling they have had a heavenly experience and
saying, "Wasn't that a wonderful sermon?" So, from Micah's
day to the present, there hangs over many a pulpit an invisible
sign which reads, "No minister with the spirit of the prophets
need apply."

Against Misleaders and Despoilers

The episode of the drunken pretender apparently placed
Micah in a fighting mood. He showed his greatest courage
when he took on the four major classes of prominent people
in Judah for what was to prove the major speech of his life.

Presumably the occasion was one of the national festivals,
on a day when the political phase of the celebration was taking
place. The scene can be imagined in the open square between
the royal palace and the temple. Most of the prominent
people of Judah were there. Reviewing the names in that

audience would have been a veritable *Who's Who* of the Southern Kingdom. Micah's intrusion into the program as an uninvited speaker was a source of embarrassment to those in charge of the ceremonies, but he addressed them with such forcefulness that they seemed powerless to stop him.

First, he exposed government officials and the business interests that were in league with them. The rulers had been ordained to establish law, order, justice, and serve the general welfare. Instead, they were despoiling the people. Without mincing words, Micah proceeded to call them what they were — virtually a bunch of bloody butchers.

> Listen, I pray you, O chief men of Jacob,
>   And rulers of the house of Israel.
> Is it not for you to know justice,
>   You haters of good and lovers of evil;
> Who pluck off their skin from upon them,
>   And their flesh from off their bones;
> Who even devour the flesh of my people?
> They strip the skin from their bodies,
>   And their bones they cleave asunder;
> They chop them in pieces as for a kettle,
>   Even as flesh in the midst of a caldron.
>
> Then they cry out unto the Lord,
>   But he will not answer them;
> He will even hide his face from them,
>   According as they have corrupted their deeds.
>
> *Micah 3:1-4*

These caustic remarks had been occasioned by Micah's visit to the slaughterhouse. There he had seen the butchers skin their victims, cut up the flesh with a knife, break the bones with a cleaver, and throw the chunks into the caldron to be boiled and eaten. All this was carried on in a thoughtless manner, without any apparent concern, just as part of the day's work.

This procedure reminded Micah of what the upper classes of his country were doing by way of despoiling the masses. They were ruthless in bringing ruin to their victims, even though human beings. The slaughterer killed his animals before he skinned them. The Hebrew overlords, as it were, skinned their people alive. They regarded this as an essential in their system of completely free enterprise. These people proposed to have no interference of any type in the carrying out of their business plans. They resented Micah because he was undermining their way of life.

One of the most amazing religious phenomena to Micah was the effrontery with which such people went to the place of worship and, without any apparent twinges of conscience, joined sanctimoniously in the services. How could they be so brazen after spending a week in which they had brought financial and physical ruin to their fellow men? It seemed clear to Micah how God must regard such pretentious actions by the *pillars* of the temple. This brand of religion, praying to God on the holy day and then preying on their fellows the rest of the week, was a mockery.

After delivering this devastating broadside to the rulers and business magnates, Micah directed his second volley against the guild or school prophets to whom prophecy had become a lucrative profession. By the time of Micah there were thousands of these prophets in Palestine. Willing to sanction anything which would please their patrons in government and high finance, and thus assure the continuance of their own support, these prophets had degenerated into conniving with the forces of evil.

Micah was the first of the great prophets to attack this

growing multitude of false prophets in a vigorous manner. On this occasion he took them on lonehanded, and exposed them before their clientele. To bring upon his head the wrath of all these prophets, together with the government officials, was no light undertaking for any individual. Nevertheless, Micah went ahead and denounced them.

> Thus the Lord has spoken concerning the prophets
>   Who have become the misleaders of my people;
> When they munch with their teeth,
>   They call out "Peace";
> But whoever does not put into their mouths,
>   They even declare holy war against him.
>
> Therefore visionless night shall descend upon you,
>   And darkness, so you will be unable to predict.
> Then the sun shall set upon the prophets,
>   And the day shall grow black upon them.
> The seers also shall be put to shame,
>   And the diviners shall be confounded.
> They shall cover their faces, every one of them,
>   Because there will be no response from the Lord.

Micah 3:5-7

In a contrasting interlude of four lines, Micah declared how he, a true prophet, was speaking by the spirit of God. This gave him power and courage to declare to the people the sins of that generation. He was no mere yes man for the powers that were then in control.

> But as for me, I am filled with
>   Power, and justice, and might;
> To declare unto Jacob his transgressions,
>   And unto Israel, his sins.

Micah 3:8

While taking the major influential groups of Palestine into the range of his reproofs, Micah thought to make the rounds complete by not omitting any. Accordingly, he included even judges and priests in a third stanza.

> Pray, listen to this, O heads of the house of Jacob,
>   And those who bear rule in the house of Israel;
> Who abhor justice,
>   And pervert all equity;
> Who build Zion with blood,
>   And Jerusalem with iniquity.
>
> Her head men render judgment for bribes,
>   Her priests give instruction for gain,
> And her prophets divine for money.
>   Yet they lean upon the Lord, saying,
> "Is not the Lord in the midst of us?
>   Misfortune shall not come upon us."

Micah 3:9-11

Micah felt certain that a city which was built upon oppression and bloodshed could not endure. It mattered not how many times the wishful prophets, in their assumed piousness, shouted that "the Lord was in the midst" of them and that "no misfortune could befall" them. With Amos, Micah was convinced that justice was the only sure foundation upon which an enduring nation could be built, and here Jerusalem was found wanting.

As he gave his final stanza, the prophet apparently was thinking about the ruined site of the northern capital. Because Jerusalem was treading the fateful pathway of wickedness down which Samaria had descended, Micah could not help but fear that Jerusalem would soon join her as a twin city in destruction.

> Therefore, on account of you,
> Zion shall be plowed as a field,
> And Jerusalem shall become a heap of ruins,
> And the temple mount, but a bare hill in a forest.

Micah 3:12

Reformation

The combined work of Isaiah and Micah produced some visible results, for King Hezekiah carried through a religious reformation (II Kings 18:1-8). By order of the king, pagan altars and cult paraphernalia were destroyed all over Judah. Idols, which had long been worshiped, were demolished. The wrath of the reformers even descended upon the old brass serpent which had been made five centuries earlier by Moses himself, who had commended its worship to the Hebrew people. Although this "seraph" was treasured as one of the choice relics of Hebrew religion, and occupied a position only second to the ark in Solomon's Temple, King Hezekiah had it destroyed, because it was a religious image. This was the first general reformation on record among the people of Palestine.

Apparently the influence of Micah was an important factor in bringing about this reform. As the "elders of the land" looked backward a century later in the days of Jeremiah, they gave Micah all credit for having caused King Hezekiah to "fear the Lord and entreat the favor of the Lord" (Jer. 26:17-19). These elders were also certain that the sparing of Jerusalem from destruction by the Assyrian armies in the crisis of 701 B.C. was due to the measure of repentance which had been brought about at the instigation of the prophet Micah.

King Hezekiah also deserved much credit. Speaking of the prophetic movement as a youth movement, it may be significant that Hezekiah was only twenty-five years old at his accession. If he had not come to the throne until ten or twenty years later, it is likely he would have lacked the courage to put through such a sweeping reformation.

The chief debit in the situation was that this ruler did not have backing for his good purposes among the influential classes. Consequently, most of his good work was soon undone by them. This is all the more reason why King Hezekiah, who formed a trio with Isaiah and Micah in the cause of right and justice, should be appreciated. We can understand how this prophetically minded king was given the epitaph of which any ruler might well be envious.

> He trusted in the Lord, the God of Israel,
> So that after him there was none like him
> Among all the kings of Judah,
> Nor among those who were before him;
> For he kept close to the Lord,
> He departed not from following him,
> But kept his commandments
> Which the Lord had commanded Moses.
> And the Lord was with him.
> Whithersoever he went forth, he prospered.
>
> *II Kings 18:5-7*

Appraisal and Foregleams

Micah was the prophet of the common man, the friend of the poor. He did his part to set in motion those attitudes and lines of thought which have developed into our welfare movements, social agencies, and other institutions of a benevolent nature. Even the modern labor movement may be indebted, far more than it realizes, to this artisan of Mareshah who proclaimed that every segment of society must be free from exploitation and have a fair opportunity to develop.

From Micah's time to ours, there has been a human chain

of religious leaders who have kept alive his message that there is good in even the lowest classes of people, and that they must be salvaged. In this succession of apostles to the poor were the prophet Zephaniah, the authors of the Psalms, John the Baptist, Jesus, Saint Francis, and John Wesley, to mention only a few. When Wesley echoed and re-echoed in his sermons "the poor are the Christians," he was continuing the spirit of Micah.

We are left to wish that more of Micah's writings had survived, for most of the material in Chapters 4-7 is by later writers. From the book of Jeremiah (Jer. 26:18-19) we learn that Micah was not martyred, nor is there any evidence that he was ever imprisoned. This may indicate a personality of unusual power. When proper estimates are given, it seems apparent that Micah holds a well-deserved place among the big four of the eighth-century prophets.

Although Amos, Hosea, Isaiah, and Micah were not all living during all those years, all four did their work between 750 and 700 B.C. All four could have been seen within a radius of relatively few miles. This period of fifty years may be called the golden age of Hebrew prophecy, for then it possessed the virility of a new movement.

As in most periods of degeneracy, the people in those times were proud of their prejudices and treasured their corruptions. Yet, even though their generation could not think of giving up its choice sins, those religious leaders made an amazing impact upon their own and later ages. Looking back in retrospect, it is apparent that those four individuals have shown themselves men of courage such as has seldom been equaled in the annals of heroism. As these eighth-century prophets recede from view, one is left with the feeling they were spiritual giants.

Jeremiah

II

God's Rebel

THE EIGHTH-CENTURY PROPHETS had pushed forward the front lines of progress in religion more rapidly than perhaps any previous age had ever witnessed. Yet the masses of people failed to fall in line with the quickened pace. After Amos, Hosea, Isaiah, and Micah had passed from the scene, there came an actual moral retreat, with desolate times for the residents of Palestine.

Such regressions are rather typical in the course of history. Throughout the centuries life has frequently been an alternation between progress and retreat. The law of physics that "every action produces an equal and opposite reaction" holds true also to an embarrassing degree in human trends. Therefore it is perhaps not a matter of surprise to find that the amazing religious advance achieved by the eighth-century prophets was soon completely undone.

After the passing of seventy distressful and prophetless years, the good elements in the life of the Southern Kingdom began to stage a comeback as another group of prophets responded to the cause of right. Like those of the previous century, they were heroic and able to command public attention. These are commonly called the seventh-century prophets, and were three in number — Zephaniah, Nahum, and Jeremiah. Instead of considering all of them, as was done with those of the eighth century, only one prophet is selected here for special treatment. There can be no question but that Jeremiah is the logical choice, for he greatly outshone the other two.

Tragedy at Nob

Much in the personality and views of Jeremiah can be understood only by looking at his remote ancestry. Of key importance was a catastrophe which overtook the people of his village years before, in the days when that settlement was called by the name of Nob and was located a half mile nearer to Jerusalem.

This story goes back to the early days of the Hebrew monarchy. It begins when David, as a young man, was in flight from King Saul who had tried on many occasions to kill him. Even though the clever lad David had always escaped, he decided it was not safe to stay longer within range of a king so crazed as Saul. David therefore fled to the isolated woodland and cave regions of Palestine. A number of young men, who also had incurred the wrath of the king, accompanied him.

As they came to this small Israelite village of Nob, David and his young men were desperately hungry. Accordingly, he went into the little temple there and begged for some bread. As the priest in charge was about to put fresh communion upon the altar, he gave the old bread, which he was removing, to David and his men.

David also asked for arms to equip himself for battle. The priest granted this request also, giving him the sword of Goliath which had been kept near the altar as a curio ever since

David had slain the giant. Cheered by this kindness of Ahimelech, the high priest of Nob, David and his men went on their way (I Sam. 21:1-9).

An Edomite herdsman named Doeg, who happened to witness this transaction, went at once and told King Saul about it. Saul was furious when he heard this news, and construed such kindness to David as treason against the king by the priests of Nob, for Nob was a village of priests. He immediately summoned eighty-five of them to the palace for questioning. Not satisfied with their replies, the king commanded them to be slain; however, the military guards refused to carry out such an outrageous order. As Doeg, the witness against them, was still there, Saul commanded him to do the deed. Presumably in the royal palace, or just outside, this Edomite herdsman slew these eighty-five men of Nob, all clad in their priestly garments.

The insane rage of King Saul had only begun to burn. At once he sent a section of his army to Nob and spread devastation throughout the village. He had all inhabitants of the place killed. It mattered not whether they were civilians, priests, women, children, or infants — all of them Saul "smote with the edge of the sword." His rage was so great against anything savoring of Nob that he even killed all the oxen, all the donkeys, all the sheep, all other animals, and life of any kind that was found about the place (I Sam. 22:7-23).

All this vindictiveness and bloodshed was because one man, Ahimelech, the chief priest at Nob, had befriended David. In doing so, Ahimelech had not even been conscious of committing any wrong. The person to blame in this situation was David. To get food and armor in his desperation, David had lied to the priest, telling him he was on an errand for the king. Because of his rage, Saul had been in no mood to make investigation and find out facts. This cruel and bloody deed, of destroying a whole village for the supposed sin of its leader, was expected to mark the end of an episode.

However, that triumph at Nob was partly spoiled for King Saul because one person from the village escaped, Abiathar, a son of Ahimelech. The relation of this story to the prophet under consideration is that Jeremiah was descended from Ahimelech, the high priest of Nob, through this son Abiathar who alone escaped that tragedy of injustice.

A Rebel Ancestry

Apparently Abiathar was but a youth in his late teens or early twenties at the time Nob was destroyed. In desperation, he sought out David and joined that company of "outlaws" whom Saul was trying to slay. By this time there were four hundred such men with David, and soon six hundred (I Sam. 22:2, 20-23; 23:13). Abiathar became the priest to this group.

All through the hardships which David and his men endured, and the hairbreadth escapes when Saul's army almost captured them, Abiathar was loyal to David. When Saul was killed in battle and David was made king, Abiathar became the new monarch's personal priest and the religious adviser to the nation. Throughout the forty years of David's kingship, Abiathar was the religious pillar of his rule.

To assist Abiathar as his duties increased, another priest named Zadok was appointed to help him (II Sam. 20:25). As Zadok proved to be an ambitious and jealous-minded person, a cleavage between him and Abiathar soon developed. While David was alive and active, peace was preserved, but, at the close of that monarch's reign, an open break occurred between these two priests.

When the moment of David's death drew near, Priest Abiathar prepared, as a matter of course, to anoint Adonijah, the oldest living son of David, as the new king. This presumably was David's intention when still of sound mind. Everyone admitted that Adonijah was "a very goodly man" (I Kings 1:6).

Zadok and a group of his followers, however, organized a conspiracy to place Solomon, one of the youngest sons, upon the throne. They played up David's love for Solomon's mother Bathsheba, even though it was a tainted love. Presumably by undue influence on his deathbed, with Bathsheba weeping over his shoulders and begging him to display this last show of love for her, Zadok and his group succeeded in getting David to agree that Solomon should be king. In a hurried service they anointed him at once, even before David had died (I Kings 1; 2:15).

Priest Abiathar apparently resented this underhanded trick, especially the exerting of undue influence upon a dying ruler who was probably mentally deranged. Abiathar may well have voiced openly his opinion regarding such a procedure. The result was that he became hated by the new king. Even though Abiathar had been the leading priest of David's reign, Solomon had him defrocked and banished from Jerusalem. The king even pronounced him "worthy of death," but spared his life because of the regard which David had had for him. Although Abiathar was put on probation, Solomon indicated this ex-priest might be killed at a later time (I Kings 2:26-27).

In disgrace, so far as the kingdom of Solomon was concerned, Abiathar returned to his boyhood home at Nob. He found it still only a heap of ruins, as left by King Saul. A little north of this wasted town, Abiathar was able to locate a knoll of land which had belonged to his father. On that site he built himself a home.

The belief that priests ought to remain unmarried, which arose later in certain parts of Christendom, had not yet developed at this time. Consequently, one is not surprised to learn of Abiathar's having a family. At that place he, and his sons after him, continued to live. The number of his descendants gradually grew to the point that their homes became a village, and it was named Anathoth. Its residents resumed the priestly role, the vocation of Abiathar and their more remote ancestors. So, in the course of time, Anathoth, like the settlement of Nob before it, became a village of priests. It was into the home of one of these, the good priest Hilkiah (Jer. 1:1), that Jeremiah was born.

By reason of his ancestry, parentage, and place of birth, Jeremiah as a growing boy was subject to all the undercurrents which had been set in motion by the events of previous years. Lights and shadows over his boyhood came from that name which was most frequently on the lips of Anathoth people in those days — their revered ancestor Abiathar.

Even though the happenings relating to Abiathar had occurred almost four centuries earlier, we can imagine that they were so often rehearsed in Anathoth that they seemed to the boy Jeremiah as if they had happened only yesterday. By hearing constantly concerning those outrages which had been committed by King Saul and King Solomon against Abiathar and his people, the conscience and sense of justice within this growing lad became sensitized in an unusual manner at an early age. The recollection of that tragedy at Nob burned in his memory.

The statements of Micah and Isaiah indicate that, by the

seventh century, the Zadokite priests at the capital had forfeited the honor of their calling and had become a corrupt lot. By contrast, the priesthood at Anathoth seems to have remained honorable. Four centuries of pressure from Jerusalem had made them a more disciplined and honorable group. In light of the earlier origins of their priesthood, and their greater worthiness, the men of Anathoth felt they were a surviving true priesthood. It was no accident of history that the prophet Jeremiah, who was to become one of the greatest in the Hebrew tradition, should have arisen from that small group of upright people at Anathoth who, through the years, usually had been on the side of the unpopular right, and had been called upon to suffer much persecution.

Jeremiah's lot was made more difficult because he was born at a time when wickedness was in the saddle and allegiance to right was regarded as rebellion. In light of the continuing echoes of the Abiathar story and the rivalry between the priesthoods of these two communities, we can see how Jeremiah grew up at Anathoth in an atmosphere that was regarded, by the political and religious authorities in Jerusalem, as saturated with the odor of treason. According to their standards, Jeremiah had rebel blood flowing in his veins.

Prophetic Influences

From the point of view of geographical position, Anathoth occupied a central location in the prophetic arena. This village was within the triangle formed by the homes of Amos, Hosea, and Micah. The scene where Isaiah carried on his activities was only three miles to the southwest. As a boy Jeremiah was probably a frequent visitor at the scenes of Isaiah's activity in Jerusalem. The old home of the prophet

Samuel was only three miles to the northwest of Anathoth, and the traditions regarding that "Man of God" were well known over that whole region. The places where Elijah and Elisha did their work were located to the immediate north, in the highlands of Ephraim, and to the east along the Jordan River. By reason of its central location, in the midst of the territory where all these earlier prophets had lived and worked, their influences converged in a remarkable way on Anathoth.

Even within the line of priests at that place there was something of the prophetic spirit and heroism. They seem to have been almost as much prophets as priests. The background of this village was perhaps the major factor in causing the recollections of the prophets to be treasured there. Because all the "great" prophets were also nonconformists, and had been popularly regarded as rebels, their memories had found an unusually appreciative abiding place in that spirit of understanding which prevailed in Anathoth. Possibly the priests at that village had come to spend some of their time collecting and reducing the utterances of the prophets to writing.

As he was growing up, Jeremiah probably heard not only the stories of his own priestly ancestors but also tales concerning the heroic adventures of the prophets. These may have been the nursery rhymes on which he was lulled to sleep. There seems to have been something about his nature which made them of particular appeal to him. Throughout boyhood, and into young manhood, contemplating the deeds of these spiritual heroes of Israel may have been his special delight.

Manasseh the Terrible

The immediate background of deep shadows, against which the work of this prophet must be viewed, was provided by the *dark age* of Palestine into which Jeremiah was born.

Hezekiah, rated the best king in Hebrew history, was followed by Manasseh, who became the worst of all Judah's twenty-one rulers. Strange as it may seem, these two kings were father and son.

On second thought, it is perhaps not so remarkable that such a thing should have happened. Manasseh was one of those occasional youths who *scorned the old man* and felt that whatever his father had done was wrong. So, at every point, he set out to do the opposite. This accounts partially for how the worst reign in Hebrew history could follow immediately after the best.

Manasseh was only twelve years old at his accession, and what could have been expected of such a boy in coping with the political complexities of a nation? He was immediately dominated by unscrupulous advisers, and became the easy tool of that corrupt royalty and upper-class group in Jerusalem whom the prophet Micah had denounced so mercilessly. By gaining control of Manasseh, the members of this clique won the upper hand and proceeded to remake Jerusalem according to their perverted likings. As the helpless victim of his advisers, Manasseh soon found himself mired in a morass of corruption.

The Hebrew heritage of high religion, which had been won through centuries of devoted effort on the part of Israel's leaders, was now all junked in a few years. Manasseh's reign introduced a new age of paganism such as the Hebrews had given their lives to fight against when they first came into Palestine. Primitive and immoral practices, which had survived in neighboring countries, were now borrowed and made to replace the more worthy rites which had become sacred in Judah. Manasseh even went so far as to fill Solomon's Temple with idol images. In the open courts outside, he placed altars of the astrological cults which he had brought into the country. The adherents of these worshiped the moon, stars, and planets at night, accompanied by immoral debauches. Manasseh stooped to primitive levels and reverted to the superstitious practices of magic and divination. The fortuneteller and sorcerer came to replace the prophet.

Many of these crude religious rites and primitive beliefs had been making inroads on Hebrew religion through the years in isolated quarters, or had continued to exist as an undertow with a retarding effect upon the advancing religion of Israel. At this point the tragedy of Manasseh's work lay in staging an about-face in which the former pagan undertow suddenly became the mainstream.

This development was most apparent in the matter of human sacrifice, which Manasseh also reintroduced. He even set the precedent for the nation by offering up his own son. Others followed his example and soon it became popular for parents to "pass their children through the fire." This was done in the Valley of Hinnom, on the southwest side of Jerusalem. There they heated the iron image of the pagan god Moloch until it was red hot, and then they lay their children in his outstretched arms.

As early as the time of Abraham the Hebrew people had practically freed themselves from this barbaric ancient practice. Through the centuries an occasional Hebrew had slipped into sacrificing a son or daughter in a moment of desperation. Even Manasseh's grandfather, King Ahaz, had sacrificed one of his sons when Jerusalem seemed hopelessly besieged (II Kings 16:3). The disservice of Manasseh, at this point, lay in making into the rule of the day what had formerly been the rare exception.

The record of those vile doings of King Manasseh is pre-

served in II Kings 21:1-9. The passage comes to a climax
with the verdict, "And Manasseh seduced them to do that
which was evil, more than did the nations whom the Lord
destroyed before the people of Israel." Through the work of
this misguided man, and those associated with him, religious
progress in Palestine had been turned back in one generation
by more than a thousand years.

Prophetic Interlude

The forces of righteousness in Jerusalem did not accept
these developments without protest. They spoke out, but there
was not a chance for them to succeed in stopping the downward trends. All who attempted this were liquidated. So a
prophetic underground movement gradually developed during
those bitter days. How extensive it was, who its adherents
were, or how they contrived to deliver their protests to King
Manasseh must remain a prophetic secret. Fortunately, one
of their ultimatums to this monarch has been preserved. We
can imagine the expression on King Manasseh's face as he
read it.

And the Lord spoke by his servants, the prophets, saying:
"Because Manasseh, King of Judah, has done these abominations,
And has done more wickedly than the Amorites did before him,
And has made Judah also to sin with his idols;
Therefore thus says the Lord, the God of Israel:
'Behold I am about to bring such calamity upon Jerusalem and
    Judah
    That whosoever hears of it, both his ears shall tingle.
I will stretch over Jerusalem the line of Samaria,
    And the plummet of the house of Ahab;
I will even wipe Jerusalem as one wipes a dish,
    Turning it over and wiping it clean on both sides.
And I will cast off the remnant of my inheritance,
    And deliver them into the hand of their enemies;

So, they shall become a prey,
And a spoil to all their enemies;
Because they have done that which is evil in my sight,
And have provoked me to anger.' "

II Kings 21:10-15

In spite of an occasional voice such as this from the underground, those years under Manasseh were a time of prophetic famine during which the work of the Lord found practically no advocates in public. As time progressed, Manasseh took extreme measures against any who raised a voice in criticism. He eventually became barbaric in his violence against those whom he even suspected. The record of those distressful years, when all prophetic voices were silenced by the sword, is summarized in the short epitaph, "Manasseh shed innocent blood very much, till he had filled Jerusalem from one end to the other" (II Kings 21:16).

To prolong matters, Manasseh's son Amon, who reigned after him, was almost equally bad. Between the two of them, they occupied the throne in Jerusalem for half a century, fifty-seven years to be exact. This prophetless era in Judah extended even beyond the actual reigning time of these two terrible kings, and was about seventy years in total length. The immediate dark background of shadows, against which any new prophetic awakening must be viewed, is found in the record of that period during which terror reigned in Judah, when the Hebrew religious heritage was plundered, and there was a general return to paganism.

The figure of Manasseh undoubtedly cast its shadow over Jeremiah's early years in a remarkably vivid manner. Even though that king had died during Jeremiah's childhood, it must have seemed to him as if that bloodthirsty tyrant were still alive. The memory of Manasseh was a haunting presence and source of fright to this boy of Anathoth throughout his growing years, intruding itself often into his consciousness. In his home he likely heard an unending succession of sordid stories about that barbaric ruler. Even the sleep of Jeremiah may have been disturbed by bad dreams in which he saw that cruel man carrying on new tortures, with himself at times the victim. The very name Manasseh probably made Jeremiah cringe with fear, as the European Jewish child of the late thirties and early forties of the twentieth century was made to shudder at mention of the name Hitler.

When Judah was scourged during those years, and all voices of right were silenced in the capital, the spirit of true religion seems to have continued on rather quietly in the outlying town of Anathoth. It was fortunate for the welfare of the nation that, in the days when Judah returned to paganism, there remained such a group, which could serve as a righteous remnant, by which the fires of real religion might again be kindled. Palestine was in sore need of someone who would give his life for the purpose of fighting those disastrous trends which King Manasseh and King Amon had championed.

"Only a Child"

Decision to take up a special type of public service was not made suddenly by Jeremiah. The resolves, which had been growing upon him through the years of boyhood and youth, gradually began to take on definite form. Increasingly he felt the voice of duty urging him to recall his generation to standards of right, and do for his people what the eighth-century prophets had done for their times.

Yet, this seemed an impossible task because Jeremiah had so few years to his credit. At the time these ideas were growing upon him, he was probably younger than any of the prophets before him. It is certain that Jeremiah could not have been older than in his twenties. Quite possibly he was still in his teens. He lamented his immaturity, and that he was not fitted, by more ripened age, for the tasks which seemed to call him. He cried out, "Ah, Lord God! Behold I do not know how to speak, for I am but a child" (Jer. 1:6). How could a person so young have any influence over a great nation? To try it would be only foolhardy and hopeless.

Doing the type of work which Jeremiah was contemplating would have been hazardous even for a middle-aged person of prestige. At best, the vocation of a prophet was a perilous undertaking. It amounted to forfeiting all hope of comfort, and meant risking one's life.

Jeremiah had no illusions in this regard. He saw dark clouds on the horizon. He knew that, if he should throw himself into this ministry with vigor, he must expect ill treatment. To realize this required no special revelation. It was simply a matter of observing what had happened to earlier prophets. He knew that, when under attack, the forces of evil can be relied upon to fight desperately.

This was the main reason Jeremiah hesitated to take up prophetic work, and protested so vigorously against it. Why should he be required to forfeit his life? Why should he give up the prospect of comfort for years of turmoil and strife, in which abuses would be heaped upon him? Why should he invite upon himself a life of suffering?

Nevertheless, in spite of his attempts to dismiss the whole matter, there was working within him a divine compulsion which would not take "No" for an answer. It seemed that an overshadowing presence was beckoning him on. He was powerless to resist it. In trying to escape this mission, he was losing even what little peace of mind he had possessed.

There was a burning within his bones that would not let him rest.

Those were times of heart searching. Someone would need to take risks in the pursuit of good if the downward trends of that day were to be reversed. Someone must be willing to make sacrifices. Apparently this lot, which held portents of being unpleasant in many ways, was to fall upon him.

Jeremiah eventually came to the conclusion that there was no other way. He must become a prophet. It was a commitment which he could no longer shirk. All of his vigorous protests were of no avail. At last he became resigned to taking up this matter of prophetic service, and giving his whole life to it. This final decision was made in the year 626 B.C. (Jer. 1:2).

For a time Jeremiah felt some uncertainty. He did not consider himself able for the tasks ahead. This had been another reason why he had tried to avoid being a prophet in the first place. The more he thought over his new resolve, the more he came to recognize that this increasing urge, which had come to dominate his life, was the voice of God. Now he went one step farther and gained the faith to believe that, with God's help, he would eventually prevail (Jer. 1:19).

The Unfolding Task

Looking back upon his early years, following these days of decision, the thought began to grow on Jeremiah that God had called him to be a prophet in early childhood. In the course of time he projected his call back even farther to the time of birth, then to the moment of conception, and eventually he came to feel that, even before that time, he had already existed as a prophet in the purposes of God (Jer. 1:5).

With the deepening of these conclusions, there grew upon

Jeremiah the increasing assurance that this was the task for which God had brought him into the world. This belief gave to him a confidence and poised courage which none of the other prophets ever quite achieved. So he went forth with the resolve that he would wage his prophetic campaign

> Against the whole land,
> Against the kings of Judah,
> Against the princes thereof,
> Against the priests thereof,
> And against the people of the land.

Jeremiah 1:18

From the beginning, Jeremiah was conscious that there are two phases to prophetic work. One is destructive and the other constructive. It is frequently wiser to tear down old tottering structures and build anew, rather than try to patch and prop. Jeremiah felt the same was true with regard to the social, religious, and political institutions of life.

The first phase of his work was therefore to tear down and discard that which was unworthy. It took a man of determined courage to face the task of demolishing and clearing away the degenerate manners of life which had been set up during the seventy prophetless years. Yet, this was required in order that he might clear the way for his constructive task of restoring the worthy institutions and beliefs of Israel's more noble past. Although Jeremiah eventually hoped to conserve, he first appeared on the scene of action as a revolutionary.

There was also an international aspect to his call. He was the first of the prophets to conceive that he had a world mission, with a message for all nations. He seemed to hear the voice of God saying to him:

See, this day I have set you
Over the nations and over the kingdoms;
To pluck up and to break down,
To destroy and to overthrow,
To build and to plant.

Jeremiah 1:10

It has been an amazing story to see how this fearful youth became transformed, by the events and thoughts of the years, into a young man of iron. He became, as it were, "a fortified city, and an iron pillar, and brazen walls" (Jer. 1:18). It took such a person to face the residue of paganism left by the kings Manasseh and Amon. Jeremiah, who had become tempered by God's fire, was that man.

12

Preacher of New Awakenings

THERE WAS HARDLY A PERSON in the regions of Jerusalem
who escaped Jeremiah's prophetic touch, for he gave his
heart-searching messages to all classes. He addressed kings,
paupers, princes, residents of the slums, old men, children,
young men, the middle classes, and every other group that
might be mentioned. In the course of his rounds, Jeremiah's
voice was heard at practically every place, from playground
to palace. By working among all segments of society, he succeeded in raising the whole moral and spiritual tone of his
country's civilization.

Searching for a Man

This prophet had an unusual ability at dramatizing his
messages. This is illustrated by the time he went to Jerusalem
and carried on a strange search. After entering the walled
city through one of its gates, he began hunting in every corner
and cranny of the capital. His strange actions attracted people's attention immediately. Wherever he went they gathered
about him. We can imagine them saying to each other, "Has
that man lost something? What is he looking for?"

Those who were bold enough to ask Jeremiah what he had
lost were told in a matter of fact manner that he had not lost

anything. Thereupon we can hear them saying, "Well, what are you hunting for then?" The prophet replied that he was trying to "find a man," but he was having no luck. He was beginning to conclude that Jerusalem was a city without men.

Then a questioner conceivably retorted, "What's the matter with you? Are you blind or are you crazy?" If we had been there we probably would have heard Jeremiah reply, in a tone of only the most casual concern, "Oh, you mistake me. I meant that I am searching for a real man. I mean a man 'who does justly and seeks truth,' but I haven't found even one in all Jerusalem" (Jer. 5:1).

He seemed not to care whether people gathered around him. He appeared so absorbed in his search that he hardly noticed them, and seldom took time to answer their questions. The few replies he gave must have been scarcely audible, even to those who were nearest him. He likely prolonged this dramatic episode for a number of days by continuing his search through all the streets, alleyways, and public squares of the capital city.

This unconventional approach to his mission contrasted with the common procedure among prophets. They usually spoke impassioned utterances at prominent places to large audiences, and shouted to make certain of being heard. On this particular occasion Jeremiah chose a course of action which seemed exactly the reverse. Although his method of procedure may have seemed trivial, it apparently was effective. Because it was spectacular in its unspectacularness, it had more possibilities of attracting attention than the usual prophetic approach.

By the time his searching was over, and he returned to Anathoth, every man, woman, and child in Jerusalem must have known about those strange actions of Jeremiah on that occasion. The news concerning his unusual procedures in the capital city soon spread over all the land of Judah. Even in the most inaccessible regions it probably was a subject for general conversation. The question on the lips of everyone was, "Is the prophet's charge justified?" Jeremiah had chosen an effective method. He was stimulating the people of Palestine to do their own preaching. This proved far better than if he had tried to do all their thinking for them.

In the remark of Jeremiah, concerning his searching of Jerusalem, there was an implied rebuke that was indeed severe. The prophet's statement suggested that God would pardon the city if he could find only one person who was devoted to justice and truth. This was a veiled reference to a similar search, a thousand years earlier, in the two cities which were considered the most wicked of all time, Sodom and Gomorrah. God was represented as having promised Abraham that he would save these cities if he could find ten righteous people in them (Gen. 18:22-33). In the case of Jerusalem, the situation had grown so bad that Jeremiah would have been pleasantly surprised if he had been able to find even one good person among her residents.

Did this mean that the prophet was accusing Jerusalem of being more wicked than Sodom and Gomorrah? Apparently so! Isaiah had proclaimed that the people of Jerusalem were as bad as the residents of those ancient cities (Isa. 1:10). Jeremiah went him one better by declaring, in the seemingly innocuous manner of subtle suggestion, that the people of Jerusalem had degenerated to the point where they were ten times worse than those two cities of perverts had ever been.

Essentially the same drama was re-enacted at a considerably

later time in Greece when Diogenes went about the streets of Athens by day with a lighted lantern — searching, searching, searching. When people asked this old philosopher what he was looking for, he replied, "An honest man." No one knows whether this was an original idea with Diogenes or whether he was consciously re-enacting in Athens what the prophet Jeremiah had done in Jerusalem some two centuries earlier.

When we stage a manhunt today it is usually for criminals. Perhaps it would be better to begin looking around, as did Jeremiah and Diogenes, for the really good men who may yet be able to save our cities, our nations, and our civilization.

The Potter's Wheel

There was a more optimistic note in the perspective of Jeremiah than had been true with the prophets before him. Not the least of the experiences which gave him this hope was a visit one day to the house of a potter (Jer. 18:1-5). With absorbing interest Jeremiah watched the master potter at work. After preparing a chunk of clay to proper consistency, he placed it on the potter's wheel. By treading with his feet, he proceeded to revolve it at high speed. Now the master workman began to use his hands, forming the clay into shape. Gradually a beautiful vase took form.

When Jeremiah was at the point of marveling at this accomplishment, something suddenly went wrong. In an instant, the vessel had become warped and spoiled. Jeremiah was saddened over the way in which a creation of such beauty could so quickly be destroyed.

This, however, was not to be the end of the story. He

noticed the potter squeeze the marred vessel together until it became once more only a ball of clay, as at the first. Then he placed this on his potter's wheel, and once more proceeded as he had done before. Jeremiah stood amazed at seeing created before his eyes a vase even more beautiful than the one that had been spoiled. This time it was not marred, and would survive as a work of art for the use of future generations.

As the prophet was walking to his home that day, he suddenly thought, "That lump of clay, and the vases made from it, suggested a parable of Israel." God, the great master potter, had taken Israel, the clay, and had tried to mold it. During the days of Moses, the wilderness wanderings, the judges, and the monarchy, it seemed that God had been successful. It appeared that Israel was at the point of being the choicest of the nations, and the first to attain anything comparable to spiritual maturity.

Then, under Manasseh, all had crashed. The fondest expectations of God, the great master potter, for his people Israel had been completely shattered. All hope seemed gone.

Nevertheless, as the Jerusalem potter proceeded to form his clay again into an even more beautiful vessel than the one which had become spoiled, Jeremiah had gained the faith to believe that the same type of transformation would occur with his people. The new Israel which would emerge, following the spiritual and moral collapse in the Manasseh-Amon period, would be vastly more wonderful and worthy than even the best of the old Israel which had preceded that dark period.

This story, of his observations at the house of the potter and his meditations upon them, was built by Jeremiah into

Jeremiah at the Potter's Stall

a sermon which was one of the most significant of his ministry. It was a masterful presentation, probably delivered many times, and must have exerted much influence in raising the spirits of Jerusalem people.

Jeremiah was at all times a man of hope. He had faith in God. He had love for his fellow men. In his days, however, the most needed of these qualities was hope. The parable of the potter's vessel, with its promise of a second chance, did much to inspire hope for the future in him and in his people.

In Time of Drought

Jeremiah was a poet. At times he achieved superb effects. One of his best poems was a dirge in four stanzas, composed when a devastating drought had brought ruin to Palestine. He used this as the beginning of a sermon which he preached at that time. It is noted for the passionate concern which lies behind it, and the power of description which it displays.

Judah is in mourning,
    And the gates thereof languish;
They sit in black upon the ground,
    And the cry of Jerusalem has gone up.

Their nobles send their little ones for water,
    They come to the cisterns, and find no water;
They return with their vessels empty,
    They are disappointed, confounded, and cover their heads.

Since the ground has become cracked,
    Because of no rain in the land,
The plowmen are put to shame,
    They cover their heads.

Also the doe casts her young in the field,
    And forsakes it because there is no grass.

Even the wild asses stand on the bare heights,
   They pant for air like jackals,
Their eyes fail, because there is no grass.

Jeremiah 14:2-6

Counselor to Kings

The prophet Jeremiah was a regular caller at the royal palace. Bringing his influence to bear constantly upon the leaders of government was one of his greatest services to the people. He was counselor to the last five kings of Judah. The monarchs following King Josiah, who ruled when Jeremiah began his work, were a degenerate lot. Occasionally they sought out the prophet, but usually he came and imposed his counsels upon them. Jeremiah's vigor in confronting kings is illustrated by his words to the renegade, King Jehoiakim.

Woe unto him who builds his house by unrighteousness,
   And his chambers by injustice;
Who uses his neighbor's service without wages,
   And gives him not his hire.

Who says "I will build me a wide house
   And spacious chambers,
Making in it large windows and panels of cedar,
   And painting it with vermilion."

Do you expect to reign by excelling in cedar?
   Did not your father eat and drink
And do justice and righteousness?
   Then it went well with him.

But your eyes and your heart
   Are used only for your coveting,
For shedding the blood of the innocent,
   And for oppressing and doing violence.

Therefore thus says the Lord concerning
Jehoiakim, the son of Josiah, king of Judah:
"They shall not lament for him, saying,
'Ah, my brother!' or 'Ah, my beloved!'
They shall not lament for him, saying,
'Ah, Lord!' or 'Ah, his glory!'
He shall be buried with the burial of an ass,
Dragged forth, and cast outside the gates of Jerusalem."

Jeremiah 22:13-15, 17-19

The Preacher

Jeremiah was the first real *preacher* in the Bible. One of his most notable sermons (Jer. 19) was delivered at Topheth in the Valley of Hinnom. This was located outside the walls, on the southwest side of Jerusalem. At that place were carried on human sacrifices and those extreme immoralities which were not tolerated inside Jerusalem, even in the depraved times of Manasseh.

On a certain day Jeremiah lured a company of elders and priests down into that den of iniquity. There he gave a powerful sermon on how Judah would inevitably meet her destruction if such perversions were to continue. He had taken a large water jar with him, and, all the time he was preaching, this earthen vessel was held in his hands. When Jeremiah reached the climax of his sermon, he suddenly dashed the jar to the pavement where it crashed into hundreds of pieces. He said the country of Judah was about to be broken in a similar manner.

By using such vivid techniques, Jeremiah made his speeches unusually impressive. He was a dramatic preacher in the best sense of the term. Instead of basing his remarks on some passage from a book, he frequently used *action texts* as a means of stating his point. As a result, people could not forget his messages. He knew how to use illustrations effectively, and they made his sermons memorable.

Preaching, side by side with teaching, has formed one of the two chief pillars of organized religion throughout the centuries. Whenever we go to church or synagogue, and hear a thought-provoking sermon, we should breathe a prayer of thanks for the contribution of the prophet Jeremiah in this regard. He was not only a pioneer in this field but, in spite of the passing of time, probably remains the most notable preacher in the whole Judeo-Christian tradition.

13

The Great Reform

ONE OF THE GREATEST CONTRIBUTIONS to his age lay in
Jeremiah's work as a reformer. Within this prophet there
was an innate passion for remaking the life of his country
according to more noble patterns. Through all his acts this
man of Anathoth exerted a renovating effect upon the
life of his day. He went farther than this, however, by devising
an elaborate program of constructive change, and instituting
definite action. Through this approach Jeremiah succeeded in
bringing about the greatest national reformation in the history
of the Hebrew people.

There was one earlier precedent for a widespread movement
of purification. Micah and Isaiah had caused King Hezekiah
to carry through a reform almost a century earlier. Nevertheless, the reconditioning of the religious and national life in
Palestine, as inspired by Jeremiah, was far more sweeping.

The Mystery of the Book

This second reformation in Israelite history was well
planned by Jeremiah. He apparently met in secret with a
group of prophets and priests in Jerusalem over a period of
several years, during which they formulated their program.
They eventually wrote this on a scroll, the type of *book* in
use during those days. When completed, this document, now

the book of Deuteronomy in our Bibles, was placed in the collection box located at the temple door. This was part of their plan to keep the authorship secret, for they feared the political administration might liquidate them if it should become known that they had written it.

When the time came for repairing the temple, and the collection box was opened to see if enough money had accumulated, the officials were amazed to find this scroll. Inasmuch as it purported to have been written by Moses, they stood in awe of it. This manuscript was taken in turn to various religious authorities, and all of them pronounced it genuine (II Kings 22:3-8, 14-17).

Reinforced by these opinions, the temple leaders took this document to King Josiah. He had been reigning since the age of eight and was a young man of twenty-six years at the time. When the newly found scroll was read to him, he became frightened at hearing its vigorous demands. The king came down from his throne, tore his clothes, and wept over the severe punishments pronounced in the book upon those who should disobey its precepts (II Kings 22:3, 9-20).

King Josiah immediately proclaimed a national emergency, and summoned all the people of Judah to Jerusalem. As they assembled, we could have seen immense crowds gathered before the temple. Then the king came and took his place, standing on the top step, beside the pillar, on one side of the front entrance. The impressiveness of the scene was increased by the fact he was flanked on the temple steps by priests, in all their regalia; and prophets, probably including Jeremiah. Before them stood the citizens of Judah and Jerusalem, from the poorest to the most prominent and wealthy.

The king was carrying a scroll of considerable size in his

hand. Soon he raised it before him and, when the people became quieted, he himself began to read. This manuscript of Deuteronomy, which had its first reading in public on that occasion, was not so long as the book is now, for a number of chapters were added later. Even so, it was a long scroll and under normal circumstances there would have been many tired legs in that vast audience. Popular excitement over the contents of Deuteronomy was so great, however, that people apparently continued to stand there, without realizing their tiredness, until the king had completed the reading.

Then Josiah raised his hand to heaven and solemnly swore to God that he would see to it, as king, that all the prescriptions of this law would be put into effect among the people throughout his land. Then the priests and prophets about him took the same covenant. After that, the audience followed by making their vows and giving assent to the demands of this newly discovered law. That was one of the first constitutional conventions in history, where the citizens had a voice in saying whether they approved the laws by which they were to be governed (II Kings 23:1-3).

House Cleaning in Jerusalem

Before that audience could start to leave, things began to happen. A national house cleaning was begun immediately, and right where they were — in the temple. The king commanded Hilkiah the high priest, the priests next to him in order, and the temple porters to remove the pagan paraphernalia which had accumulated there during the years of kings Manasseh and Amon. These attendants obeyed at once and went into the temple. It was not long before they began to come out with the altars and images which had been used in worshiping foreign deities. All the cult articles and vessels employed in venerating those idols were also brought out. This was indeed a day of cleansing the temple.

Prominent among the images removed were those of the god Baal and his wife, the goddess Asherah, or Ashtoreth, as it was sometimes spelled. These were sex deities. She was the special patron of female fertility. The immoral religious rites, which had grown up in Palestine among the Canaanites and by now had intruded themselves into the practice of the Hebrews, had been inspired largely by this Baal-Asherah religion. On this occasion the reformers took special delight in clearing this cult's religious prostitutes, or sodomites, from the rooms which had been especially set aside for them in the temple (II Kings 23:4, 6-7).

By this time the priests were proceeding to dismantle the altars and images of the lunar, planetary, and stellar deities which were located in the temple courts. The horses and chariots, which had been placed near the entrance to the temple, were likewise destroyed because of being used in worshiping the sun. King Josiah himself seized the initiative and broke in pieces the altars which his predecessor Manasseh had constructed in the two courts of the temple (II Kings 23:11-12).

After this holy structure and its immediate environs were cleared of everything which savored of King Manasseh's heathen importations, the priests and representatives of the king carried their campaign all over Jerusalem and its suburbs. They went down into the Valley of Hinnom, southwest of the city, and destroyed the place called Topheth where the rites of human sacrifice had been carried on. King Josiah purged his own home, removing from the palace all vestiges of foreign religious intrusions, including the roof shrines which had been placed there by previous kings.

Throughout Jerusalem all pagan shrines were demolished.
Places where non-Israelite deities had been worshiped on
the hills about Jerusalem since the days of King Solomon
were now desecrated and destroyed. Even such types of
people as the fortunetellers, wizards, and astrologers were
taken care of so they could no longer continue their arts
(II Kings 23:10, 12-14, 24-25).

It was an exciting day in Jerusalem when all these things
happened in a few hours, with such rapidness that the assembled throngs could hardly keep track of what was
transpiring. At first the people were straining to see what
was going to be done with those "sacred" articles and relics
which were removed from temple, palace, and shrines throughout the city. Where were the demolition squads taking these
things?

That question was soon answered. Headed by the king,
those who carried these objects proceeded to the east gate of
the city. The crowds of people rushed after them, wanting to
see what would happen next. This concourse then proceeded
down into the Kidron Valley, just east of Jerusalem. There
all the removed objects were placed on a great pile and burned
(II Kings 23:4, 6). We can imagine load after load being
brought and cast into that fire.

The reformers were re-enacting the scene which had occurred when Moses burned the golden calf at the foot of
Mount Sinai six centuries earlier (Exodus 32:1-20). The
difference was that here, instead of only a single idol, there
were perhaps hundreds of images, of many types, which were
being burned in the fires of Kidron. In the eyes of those who
were leading the activities that day, every one of these objects
had a heathenish significance as bad as that which Moses had
attributed to Aaron's golden calf. For all people who dis-

paraged the degeneracy of the Manasseh-Amon period, it was a happy moment to see the accumulated relics of Judah's great regression burning before their very eyes. Around that pyre in the fields of Kidron the residents of Judah and Jerusalem stood watching the symbols of their pagan civilization go up in smoke.

House Cleaning in the Provinces

After the job in Jerusalem was completed, King Josiah and his destructionists set their attention upon the outlying districts. If Palestine was to be made safe for the religion of Israel, Josiah felt they must make a clean sweep everywhere. Under the king's personal direction, his men went all over Palestine breaking down altars, burning shrines, and demolishing images. He desecrated their places of worship so they could never be used again. When local priests resisted, they were often mercilessly slain. The king would not tolerate any interference with his program (II Kings 23:5, 8, 15-20).

As the "reform" spread through the cities and villages of Palestine, it took on an added role. This stemmed from a decision made by the original small group of priests and prophets who formulated the Deuteronomic program. They looked upon the native Israelite altars, where the Hebrew god Yahweh was worshiped in the villages and cities outside Jerusalem, as so saturated with the Manasseh spirit that they too had become hopelessly corrupt. This was regarded as the situation even in the places where no idol deities were revered. Consequently, Jeremiah and his group came to the conclusion that all shrines in the outlying cities and villages of Palestine should be abandoned. It would be much easier to watch the ritual, and keep it pure, if sacrificial worship were confined to Jerusalem.

Although such a provision had been included in the Deuteronomic law, Jeremiah apparently assumed that this step would be brought about gradually and peaceably. The Jerusalem priests chose differently. With their selfishness coming to the fore, they seized this as an opportunity to eliminate all competition in other areas of the country, and gain for themselves a monopoly in Jerusalem. Accordingly, they decided to press for fulfillment of this program at once, by using force and violence.

To this end these agents of the king and priests went all over Judah in their enforcement crusade, destroying in the outlying regions not only all objects associated with foreign cults but also all native Hebrew shrines and altars where Israelite ritual was carried on. Like the heathen shrines, the sites of these former places of Hebrew worship were also desecrated so they could never be used again. Those who executed this program even tried to take the priests of these places by force to Jerusalem (II Kings 23:8). This was all done in the interests of establishing Jerusalem as the one and only place of sacrifice.

Spotlight on Anathoth

The net results of this phase in the Deuteronomic program can be appreciated best by observing its impact on Anathoth, which was a close second to Jerusalem in priestly importance. As has already been pointed out, these priesthoods of Anathoth and Jerusalem were located only three miles apart, and had been rivals for centuries. Jeremiah looked upon this traditional antagonism as absurd. Would not the cause of religion be strengthened by eliminating this rivalry?

This was attempted in the Deuteronomic program which Jeremiah and his co-workers had sponsored. One phase in the plan of reform was that the old enmity between these two places should be ended by uniting the two opposing priesthoods and having them work together in a spirit of co-operation. Inasmuch as Jerusalem was the population center of Palestine, and already had a magnificent place of worship in Solomon's Temple, there could be no doubt but that the projected merger of priestly effort should be centered around that famed place of worship. The priests of Anathoth, and other outlying shrines, would be brought to Solomon's Temple, where they would be given preferable financial treatment (Deut. 18:6-8). Thus a great religious unification at Jerusalem was to be brought about. This was the first movement for the union of diverse religious groups in the Bible.

This plan looked attractive on paper, and seemed good to the authors of Deuteronomy; however, it did not work out so nicely in practice. With the spirit of independence, which had been flowing in their veins ever since the days of Abiathar, the Anathoth people did not take kindly to the Deuteronomic plan in so far as its provisions regarding worship were concerned. For such a strategic priestly village to refuse co-operation in this venture of religious consolidation was a severe blow to King Josiah, who was executing the new arrangement. Their refusal was also a great disappointment to the Zadokite priests, who were expecting to profit highly by gaining an ecclesiastical monopoly for their shrine at Solomon's Temple in Jerusalem.

No details are available as to how the king proceeded against the Anathoth people. Although not using such measure of violence as King Saul had employed against their ancestors on the adjoining hill of Nob four centuries earlier, resort was probably made to measures that were unduly severe. The enforcement officers may have thought that the Anathoth people needed to be taught a lesson. In light of the procedures at other places (II Kings 23:15-20), the ruthless executors of this program probably demolished the altars and destroyed the little shrine at Anathoth.

In harmony with the priestly reaction at other "padlocked" places of worship, the men of Anathoth resented especially these radical methods which were resorted to in enforcing the Deuteronomic program. These priests became infuriated at what had happened in their town. They refused to go up to Jerusalem and join their efforts with the Zadokite priests, whom they did not respect. In no mood to surrender their cause, these descendants of Abiathar presumably repaired, as best they could, the damages to their little temple, and continued their ministrations at Anathoth in defiance of the Deuteronomic plan (II Kings 23:9).

The fatal mistake in implementing the Deuteronomic proposals was made when the representatives of King Josiah, who were charged with enforcement throughout Judah, construed the unification program as obligatory rather than permissive. By following the advices of the Jerusalem priests and proceeding to put the program into effect by force, great antagonism was created. Their brutality in seeking their ends did much to defeat the purpose of the reform and bring it into disrepute in the outlying regions. This was intolerance with a vengeance, and could not be called worthy. It has been described here in some detail because this was the key to much of Jeremiah's subsequent unpopularity outside Jerusalem.

The Birth of Judaism

For the most part, the occurrences just described were only the outer visible acts executed through force by king, government officials, and ecclesiastical hierarchy. That was the priestly side of the Deuteronomic program. The manner in which the plan of reform was sabotaged by these interests must not blind us to the great number of unquestionably constructive changes which were introduced by reason of Jeremiah's influence.

The valuable part of the Deuteronomic movement consisted in the prophetic side of it, i.e., the enactment into law of the high principles which had been proclaimed by the eighth-century prophets. Along that line, this newly instituted code established significant alterations and refinements throughout many phases in the fundamental structure of Hebrew life, thought, and institutions. This great change began to take place at the time of the reform, which was 620 B.C. (II Kings 22:3).

That year became the most strategic point in Hebrew religious history. Before 620 B.C. one should speak of *the Hebrew religion* or *the religion of Israel*. Thereafter the term *Judaism* is used. In reality these were two different religions. Judaism was as superior to the earlier religion of Israel as the standards of the prophets were higher than the level of life during the days of the monarchy. The influence of the prophet Jeremiah was of key significance in transforming those early primitive types of Hebrew religion into this much more worthy later form. It must not be forgotten that, as the inspiring force behind these developments, Jeremiah became *the father of Judaism*.

By contrast with the priests' enforcing their side of the code at once, the prophetic part of the Deuteronomic system was brought into observance voluntarily and only gradually. General compliance was not achieved until some four or five centuries later. In the long run, however, the prophetic gains proved far more substantial.

Passover

It would take a whole book to treat adequately the many beneficial transformations which were initiated under the guidance of Jeremiah. Space can be taken here to point out only two of the fundamental changes which this prophet succeeded in bringing about by means of his legislation.

The system of religious feasts observed by the Hebrews up to this time had been borrowed from their Canaanite neighbors in Palestine. These were essentially Baal festivals. They were seasonal nature feasts, and in observing them it was difficult to avoid worshiping nature deities.

Jeremiah and his colleagues thought this intimate association of their festal system with Baalism was unfortunate, and was retarding Hebrew religious development. So they decided to cut these connections. This was done by revising the rituals and reinterpreting the significance of the feasts. A typical example of what they did in this regard is observed in their reconstruction of the annual spring festival. They reinterpreted this in terms of the most strategic event in Hebrew history, the exodus of the Hebrews from their years of slavery in the land of Egypt. Thus the annual spring nature festival became *the Passover,* an annual historical feast in memory of that great escape of the Hebrews from bondage. The new purpose was to give adequate recognition to the power which an intimate trust in God had given their people throughout the centuries, and to reactivate that faith each year.

After King Josiah had completed his program of action throughout Palestine, this lure of the Passover caught his imagination. As the last of his acts, he summoned the people of Judah to Jerusalem for a national festival celebrating the conclusion of the reform. The high light of that occasion consisted in observing the Passover. Latest scholarly opinion leads to the conclusion that this religious festival was introduced by these reformers. This was therefore the first celebration of the Passover to be held among the Jewish people (II Kings 23:21-23).

Through the centuries since Jeremiah's time, observance of the Passover has become one of the most sacred rites of the Jewish people. Even the Christian Easter is an outgrowth of it and the Christian counterpart to it. The connection of Jeremiah with these feasts has been largely forgotten. If we wish to give credit where credit is due, we should give recognition each spring to the way in which this prophet set a higher religious level for the feasts of his time. A prayer of special thanks for the work of Jeremiah should be made by every Jew and Christian as they celebrate Passover and Easter.

Sabbath

Another, and far greater, contribution made by Jeremiah and his group concerned the keeping of weekly holy days. It has usually been thought that the observance of a weekly day of rest goes back to the beginning of the Bible. This is not true. Even the law of Moses has been misconstrued, and should be translated "Remember the holy day, to keep it sacred" (Exodus 20:8). What follows this simple law is elaboration, added at least six centuries later (Exodus 20: 9-11). In the days of Moses, there were no regular holy days. His law provided that whenever a holy day was proclaimed, it should be properly observed.

After the Hebrews had established themselves in Palestine, they began revering the new moon. This is how a regular day of worship once a month developed. Later they added to this a recognition of the full moon. In the days of Jeremiah this was the situation, with two regular holy days each month. In other words, there was a holy day every fourteen days. The Hebrews had become moon worshipers, and had in many respects forgotten the idea of a higher God.

In the Deuteronomic reform, provision was made for eliminating those stated days of moon worship as a survival of paganism. In place of such lunar festivals, on the first and fifteenth days of each month, the Deuteronomic reformers substituted a wholly new system of Sabbaths. These were held on the seventh, fourteenth, twenty-first, and twenty-eighth days of the month.

As people are always slow to change their religious customs and adopt anything new, a large portion of the people ignored this newly commanded observance which was to occur every seventh day. Most of them continued to observe, if at all, the old moon worship twice a month. To take off four days a month for worship and rest seemed to the residents of Palestine as cutting too deeply into their opportunities for work and money making.

On a certain Sabbath, when Jeremiah went to the temple for worship, he was amazed at the disturbances that were going on. It may have been a time of unusual commercial activity, in preparation for taking care of the pilgrims at one of the feasts. Loads of food and other supplies were moving in every direction as part of this feverish commotion. The merchants were united in their purpose to trap the last coin of every unwary pilgrim.

The temple covered a considerable area in the southeastern part of Jerusalem, and was surrounded by courts and quadrangles. It was a great temptation for people to pass through the temple, rather than around it. On this particular morning, men with cargoes on their backs, leading heavily laden donkeys, were going through the temple areas. Such turmoil made it impossible for worshipers to carry on their devotions with any degree of quietness and satisfaction.

Finally Jeremiah took his place at the gate of the temple and delivered his notable sermon on Sabbath observance (Jer. 17:19-27). With power he commanded the people to stop using the temple for a thoroughfare.

> Give ear to the word of the Lord,
>   You kings of Judah, and all Judah,
> And all the inhabitants of Jerusalem
>   Who enter in by these gates.
> Thus the Lord has spoken:
> "Take heed unto yourselves.
> And bear no burden on the Sabbath day,
>   Nor bring any in by the gates of Jerusalem;
> Neither carry a burden out of your houses on the Sabbath day,
>   Nor shall you do work of any kind;
> But you shall hallow the Sabbath day,
>   As I commanded your ancestors."

Jeremiah 17:20-22

Even the merchants who were transporting their wares must have paused long enough to hear at least part of what this prophet had to say. He assured these residents of Jerusalem that if they observed the Sabbath prescriptions properly

Then kings shall enter in by the gates of this city,
And princes, sitting upon the throne of David;
Even the men of Judah and the inhabitants of Jerusalem,
They and their princes, riding in chariots and on horses,
And this city shall remain forever.

Jeremiah 17:25

Supported by his original followers in the Deuteronomic reform, Jeremiah gave to the world the institution of a weekly holy day in which people cease from their ordinary labors. He was not narrow and legalistic, like the later Pharisees, in the matter of its observance. He only insisted that it be set aside as different from other days, devoted to worship, rest, and doing good.

This custom, which Jeremiah pioneered in establishing in that little country of Judah, has spread through the centuries until today it is established over much of the nearer Orient and practically all of the Western world. The followers of Mohammed have their observance on Friday. The Jewish Sabbath is on Saturday. The Christians have their holy day on Sunday. Even though there is this diversity, all three families of religions are united in following the practice which Jeremiah and his group first originated.

Wherever the Sabbath has been observed, its adherents have shown added vigor because of this periodic rest from which they have profited. By setting aside one day in each week for the people of a given area to assemble together, this holy day has served to build community feeling among those who participate. Through the Sabbath's offering of special time for worship, prayer, song, and instruction, the religious life of mankind, with its higher morality, has been especially nurtured during the centuries. This, and the other good influences which have radiated from the observance of a holy day each week, have perhaps done more than has ever been realized to bring the great developments and progress in the Western world. Again, a major portion of this tribute belongs to Jeremiah.

Passover and Sabbath were only two of the ways in which this prophet and his followers modified the religious institutions of their day and directed them into more noble channels. Changes for the better in personal morality and inner living are not so easy to trace, but it may be assumed that Jeremiah's influence has become no less effective in these areas. This was all achieved by establishing as the basic law of his people the book of Deuteronomy, which made a synthesis of the teachings and principles which the eighth-century prophets had proclaimed, and by placing it at the center of Judaism. This is how the prophet Jeremiah came to deserve the title "father of Judaism."

Although Moses is generally revered as the great Hebrew lawgiver, reappraisal is necessary at this point also. Moses gave the ten commandments (Exodus 20:1-22) and presumably Samuel wrote the Code of the Covenant (Exodus 20:23-23:33). Deuteronomy, which appeared during Jeremiah's time, was therefore the first great codification of Hebrew law. The much larger and composite Priests' Code, in the latter half of Exodus, Leviticus, and the first half of Numbers, was not produced until almost two hundred years later than the time of Deuteronomy. So it may even be warranted to call Jeremiah the major lawgiver of the Hebrew people.

The Great Reformer

Through his preaching, his emphasis on Sabbath observance, and his general work as a reformer, Jeremiah became perhaps the most strategic person, during ancient times, in developing the institutions of our religious tradition. He was not only a talker and preacher of reform. He participated in devising a practical program and helped put it into effect. The significance of his reforming role is greatly increased by the realization that his efforts were spread over a period of more than forty years. By contrast with the ruthless methods of the priests in trying to gain their ends at once, Jeremiah exerted a constant pressure for good throughout those years. When all factors are taken into consideration, the verdict seems assured that Jeremiah holds undisputed place as the greatest preacher-reformer in the Bible.

14

Target of Persecutions

Up to this point attention has been devoted chiefly to the accomplishments of Jeremiah. Significant as these were, there was another side to the picture. In most ages the reformer, who tackles the forces of evil and accomplishes things, is badly treated. In this Jeremiah was no exception. Persecution was heaped upon him more constantly and more severely than upon any other individual in the prophetic succession. This was partly because he was caught in the backwash of that pagan movement set up by Manasseh and Amon.

Portents of Trouble

Because of his premonitions regarding adversities lying ahead, this young man came to the conclusion very early that he ought not to marry. It would not be treating a wife fairly if he should subject her to the ordeals through which he feared he would be called to pass. Also, he did not feel that he should have children, for they would inevitably be made to share in his daily trials. It would not be right to victimize little ones in that way. Furthermore, he did not wish to bring children into the world at a time when they would be made to serve only as fertilizer for the fields (Jer. 16:1-4), or *cannon fodder* as we would say. So Jeremiah

197

remained, throughout his days, a man without the joys of home or family.

Not having a household of his own, in a sense he adopted the people of the nation as his family. He was deeply concerned for their welfare. As he thought of the international dangers in the midst of which Judah was carrying on her precarious existence, he was pained beyond measure. At times he could have poured forth his soul in weeping. It seemed so certain to him that the residents of his country would soon be forced to join other exiled peoples in the regions of Babylonia that he could already hear, as it were, their moanings in that distant land. At one especially discouraging moment he expressed his deep grief over what seemed to lie ahead. In uttering his lament, he spoke of Jerusalem as "the daughter of my people."

> Oh, that I could comfort myself against sorrow!
>   My heart is faint within me.
> Behold the voice of the cry of the daughter of my people
>   From a land that is very far off.
>
> For the hurt of the daughter of my people am I hurt;
>   I mourn — dismay has taken hold on me.
> Is there no balm in Gilead?
>   Is there no physician there?
>
> Oh, that my head were waters,
>   And my eyes were a fountain of tears,
> That I might weep day and night
>   For the slain of the daughter of my people!

Jeremiah 8:18-19, 21-22; 9:1

Because Jeremiah was so persistent and intense in his attacks on all people of evil intent, he brought the full force of their concerted wrath upon himself. This also fell upon all who were in any way associated with the prophet. Soon his former associates avoided being seen with him, and no longer wanted to be known as *a friend of Jeremiah*. This left him increasingly in a state of isolation. Without home, without family, and without friendships, he went about his work a lonely person. This was the predicament of a prophet who had moved far ahead of the stage at which the people in his times were living.

Conspiracy at Anathoth

It would hardly have been expected that the first bitter opposition to Jeremiah should have arisen among the people with whom he had been born and reared. Yet this is exactly what happened. As Jeremiah returned to his ancestral home, some seven years after taking up his prophetic work, he found himself in the midst of a veritable hornet's nest. From one of his old friends he was amazed to learn that the residents of Anathoth were plotting to take his life (Jer. 11: 18-23). This was hard to accept from the people of his own home town. When Jeremiah heard this he was deeply moved, and said,

> And I was like a gentle lamb
> That is led to the slaughter,
> And I never suspected that
> They had plotted devices against me, saying,
> "Let us destroy the tree with its fruit,
> And let us cut him off from the land of the living,
> That his name may be remembered no more."

Jeremiah 11:19

The antagonism of those villagers to Jeremiah had arisen over the great reform. These fellow townsmen, who had been deeply wronged, held Jeremiah, as the chief sponsor of the

Deuteronomic movement, personally responsible for all the priestly and governmental excesses in that rash program of forced compliance. Among the individuals who had become the special victims of those proceedings, the feeling against Jeremiah had become bitter at Anathoth. They blamed this prophet for trying to sell out his own home town. The businessmen especially resented what he had brought about. Anathoth was dependent for its existence on the pilgrim trade. The merchants looked upon the reform program as an attempt to take away their business and means of livelihood.

Undoubtedly the more irresponsible and extreme elements in the Anathoth population were responsible for devising this plot. Nevertheless, most Anathoth people seem to have joined in this hysteria against the prophet who had come from their midst.

Did they fear when it came actually to taking Jeremiah's life? Or did he return to Jerusalem when he discovered the feeling in Anathoth? At any rate, they did not come to the point of executing their plot and killing him. They concluded the matter on that occasion by warning him that if he should continue his prophetic work, they would take his life. Thus Jeremiah became permanently estranged from his former friends and relatives. His loneliness was increased by the fact that after this he was virtually in a state of banishment from his home town and no longer dared return, under threat of death.

There is an amazing parallel between this occurrence and the initial plot on the life of Jesus some five centuries later. With the prophet of Galilee it also occurred on the first visit to his home town following the beginning of his ministry. After preaching one sermon in their midst, the people of Nazareth took Jesus to the top of a cliff and were about to cast

him over to his death when something in the power of his
personality and goodness overcame them. On that occasion
Jesus pointed out that the community in which a prophet is
born and grows up is the last place he may expect honor
(Luke 4:16-30). This was putting it mildly. The experiences
of both Jeremiah and Jesus showed that a prophet is likely
to meet his first threat of death in his own home town.

A Whispering Campaign

The movement of opposition against Jeremiah rapidly
widened. Although for different reasons from those which
were urged at Anathoth, various elements in Jerusalem also
formed their conspiracies against him. He was too vigorous
in denouncing the wickedness which he found there. He had
trampled on the toes of certain influential interests at the capital, and they were beginning to make life miserable for him.

If we had been there, we could have seen Jeremiah struggling one day in prayer over this predicament into which
he had gotten himself (Jer. 17:14-18). He reminded God
that he had not desired this woeful day. He had not wanted
to become a prophet. It had been virtually forced upon him.
And now look at the trials he was made to endure! That prayer
ended with the words,

> Be not a terror unto me.
>   Be a refuge unto me in time of calamity.
> Let my persecutors be put to shame, and not me.
>   Let them be dismayed rather than myself.
> Bring upon them the day of calamity,
>   And break them until they are twice crushed.

Jeremiah 17:17-18

A whispering campaign was inaugurated against Jeremiah by priests, judges, and prophets to discredit him. They said,

> Come, and let us devise scandal about Jeremiah. . . .
> Come, and let us smite him with the tongue,
> And let us not listen to any of his words.
>
> *Jeremiah 18:18*

This was used as a more effective way of nullifying his influence than killing him. Certain of his enemies were aware that martyrdom is likely to dramatize the victim's cause rather than kill it. They thought it better to stigmatize Jeremiah, destroy his reputation, and, when wholly discredited, let him go at large. Then people would no longer listen to his utterances.

Other opponents, who were more impatient, began devising plots to kill him. Again we see Jeremiah on his knees in prayer over this development (Jer. 18:19-23), only praying at greater length and with deeper passion for release from the predicament caused by these people who were planning to destroy him.

> Give heed unto me, O Lord,
> And hear what my opponents are saying.
> Shall good be recompensed with evil?
> Seeing they have dug a pit for my soul.
> Remember how I stood before you
> To speak good on their behalf,
> To turn away your wrath from them.
>
> But they have dug a pit to take me,
> And have hidden snares for my feet.
> Surely you have become aware, O Lord,
> Of their whole plan to kill me.
>
> *Jeremiah 18:19-20, 22-23*

We can perhaps understand how this prophet, with only good purposes in view, felt upon seeing his evil-minded opponents discrediting and wrecking his whole ministry, and about to bring an end to it. To see such selfish designs prevail was almost more than any upright person could endure. To Jeremiah's credit it is to be said that, with the passing of time, he became more mellowed in his attitudes toward his persecutors, and even achieved a measure of sympathy for them.

In the Stocks

In spite of all these means which were used to discredit Jeremiah, he became ever more powerful in his preaching. His address concerning his observations at the house of the potter (Jer. 18:1-17), and the sermon in which he broke the water jar (Jer. 19:1-15), attained a new high level in effectiveness. The latter was a sermon in two parts. The first portion was delivered in the Valley of Hinnom, just outside the wall of Jerusalem, where the bottle was smashed into many pieces as a parable of what would happen to Judah. Then he brought his audience up to the temple and concluded his remarks in the "court of the Lord's house."

Unfortunately for Jeremiah, Pashur, the chief officer of the temple, joined the audience and listened to what Jeremiah was saying. Pashur took pride in being the son of a priest, and was apparently a very officious person. It had been reported to him that, in a previous sermon, the prophet had called this temple "a den of robbers" (Jer. 7:11). Only a few days before in his Sabbath sermon, Pashur was informed, Jeremiah had *meddled* into the financial aspects of the temple procedures (Jer. 17:19-27). Pashur resented these criticisms of the temple administration as a personal attack upon him-

self, and he was not going to let that pass. On this occasion
Pashur had come in person to seek more accusations against
the prophet, and he soon found them.

After Pashur had heard all he could tolerate, he walked
over to Jeremiah and gave the prophet a beating. This was
a new type of benediction with which to close a sermon. This
act of flogging the prophet was done before all the people to
whom Jeremiah had been preaching. Then Pashur took his
victim to the north gate of the temple as the excited audience
followed to see what would happen. There Pashur placed
the prophet in the stocks.

The torture of languishing in stocks is something which no
one can appreciate who has not experienced it. Even a
half hour in such a forced unnatural position seems as ages.
On this occasion Jeremiah was made to endure that strained
tension for what seemed an endless period of almost twenty-
four hours (Jer. 20:1-3a).

The most aggravating part of this experience lay in being
made a laughingstock and spectacle of ridicule. This labeled
him as a criminal before all Jerusalem. The presence of a
man in the stocks called out the worst passions in the populace.
They were accustomed to jeer and hoot at such a one. He
would become a rallying point for all the hoodlums in the
city. The antagonists of Jeremiah encouraged such elements
to go there so they could tease and torment the prophet. His
enemies probably gathered from all parts of Jerusalem to see
this sight and make fun of him. They undoubtedly brought
along their supplies of rotten vegetables and eggs, and pelted
him with them as they passed by. Urged on by their elders, it
was a thrilling experience for the children of the city as they
joined in making sport of Jeremiah. We can imagine how he
looked by the time of evening on that fateful day.

JEREMIAH IN THE STOCKS

Leaving him in the stocks overnight was a special measure of reproach. To be unable to sleep would have been sufficient punishment. To endure the agony of the stocks during those lonely hours, when other people in Jerusalem were resting in comfort, would have tried the sanity of any person.

We can imagine something of Jeremiah's thoughts during the long hours of darkness. That the wicked men should be going about their ways or enjoying peaceful sleep, while the man of God was thus confined and tortured, seemed difficult for him to understand. Although a night of terror, it was also a time of such deep and moving thought as he had never experienced before.

On the following day Pashur came and released Jeremiah from the stocks. He hoped the prophet would be so intimidated by this experience that he would henceforth remain silent. However, it worked just the opposite way. The torture of that night brought to Jeremiah a new realization concerning the evil of the forces against him, and fired this man of God with a determination to go forth and confront them with even greater vigor.

No sooner had Pashur released Jeremiah than the prophet proceeded to deliver a sermon, far more severe than the one for which he had been placed in the stocks (Jer. 20:3b-6). Most of his remarks were about the future of Judah. We are interested especially in the part where he attacked Pashur personally and told him what he thought of him. Jeremiah exposed this temple official in the presence of the many people who happened to be in the courts of that holy place at the moment.

> The Lord has not called your name Pashur (Safety),
>   But Magor-missabib (Terror on Every Side).
> For thus the Lord has spoken:

"Behold I will make you a terror to yourself,
    And unto all of your friends;
They also shall fall by the sword of their enemies,
    And your eyes shall behold it.

"And you, Pashur, and all who dwell in your house
    Shall go forth into captivity;
You shall come even unto Babylon,
    There you shall die and be buried;
You, and all your friends
    Unto whom you have prophesied falsely."

Jeremiah 20:3-4, 6

Perhaps Pashur did not consider that he dared place Jeremiah in the stocks immediately again. Or, he may have felt it would be futile to do so. It is conceivable he thought Jeremiah might change his mind and quiet down after thinking this episode over. At any rate, he let the prophet go.

Meditations on Persecution

Back in his room Jeremiah was too wrought up to rest. Although physically exhausted, he was mentally agitated over this experience. The hours spent in recuperation were some of the most troubled moments of his life. As he opened his heart to God in prayer (Jer. 20:7-18), he reviewed the way he had been treated since becoming a prophet.

I have become but a laughingstock all day long,
    Everyone mocks me.
For as often as I speak and cry out,
    Announcing violence and destruction;
Even though the word of the Lord is in me,
    I am reproached and derided all the day.

For I have heard the defaming of many,
    With terror on every side, saying,

"Denounce!" and "Let us denounce him!"
All my friends watch for my downfall, saying,
"Perhaps he can be enticed, so we can prevail against him;
Then we shall take our revenge upon him."

Jeremiah 20:7-8, 10

Such soul-moving experiences and times of loneliness were by no means unique with Jeremiah. Apparently they were more or less typical of all the prophets. It only happens that in the book of Jeremiah the inner heart-searchings of a prophet are described in some detail. This is because he was the first prophet who produced his own book, and could therefore record some of his deep emotional experiences.

On another occasion, when troubled over how the country was being victimized by false prophets, Jeremiah again expressed vividly his inner turmoil.

My heart within me is broken,
 And all my bones shake;
I am like a man who is drunken,
 Even like one overcome with wine;
On account of the Lord,
 And because of his holy words.
"Is not my word like a fire," says the Lord?
"And like a hammer that breaks the rock in pieces?"

Jeremiah 23:9, 29

This type of dynamic religion, which is "like a hammer that breaks the rock in pieces," is so powerful that few individuals have been able to meet its demands. One difference between the prophets and other people was that these seers of Israel were able to develop within themselves religion of such high intensity.

15

King Jehoiakim and the Book

JEREMIAH REACHED A PEAK OF UNPOPULARITY during the reign of Jehoiakim (608-597 B.C.). This son of the good King Josiah was a great disappointment to the prophet. Jehoiakim was almost as inferior to his father Josiah as Manasseh had been to Hezekiah. Direct and indirect clashes with King Jehoiakim made that one of the most hectic times in all Jeremiah's ministry. Everything described in this chapter took place during those years.

Victim of the Mob

One day while the prophet was preaching before the temple, he told how the evil ways which were being condoned at that time would result in Solomon's Temple's being laid in ruins as completely as the ancient sanctuary at Shiloh. Also, Jerusalem itself would become "a curse to all the nations of the earth" (Jer. 26:1-6).

Apparently some people in that audience had not listened carefully enough to sense the proper distinctions. They had failed to note that Jeremiah said this was the disaster which their low manner of life inevitably would bring upon them. In their superficial understanding, certain of those people left that scene and at once began spreading over the capital city *the news* that Jeremiah was about to lead a subversive

movement whose aim was to overthrow his government, de-
molish the temple, and annihilate Jerusalem.

This proved a good excuse for the anti-Jeremiah forces
in Jerusalem. They immediately formed a mob composed of
priests, prophets, ordinary people, and the rabble of the city.
Their purpose was to "get" Jeremiah. They descended upon
him, laid hold on him, and it appeared they were going to
lynch him immediately.

This plot was spoiled when a group of princes, who heard
the commotion, came from the royal palace in the nick of time
and halted the procedures. Although the priests and prophets
who led the mob explained that Jeremiah was worthy of
death, this did not convince the princes.

Always resourceful in utilizing every opportunity to the
limit, Jeremiah made use of this altercation between the
princes and the leaders of that mob as an occasion to speak
forth and give a supplement to his sermon (Jer. 26:7-12). He
faced the mob fearlessly and addressed them with amazing
poise.

> Therefore now, amend your ways and your doings,
>   And obey the voice of the Lord, your God;
> Then the Lord will repent him of the doom
>   Which he has pronounced against you.
>
> But as for me, behold I am in your hands.
>   Do with me as seems good and right to you.
> Only, know for a certainty, that if you put me to death
>   You shall bring innocent blood upon yourselves,
>   And upon this city, and upon its inhabitants;
> For, of a truth, the Lord has sent me unto you
>   To speak all these words in your ears.

Jeremiah 26:13-15

This scene shows how Jeremiah had some friends at the palace in the persons of those princes who were secretly working for him. In this instance they used their influence to block his execution. Also this scene shows what a masterful person Jeremiah was becoming, even in the face of a threat to his life. He spoke with a composure which would not have been possible for him several years earlier.

Jeremiah won the day again. The princes gave pronouncement that he was not worthy of death. They reminded the mob of the similar prophecy by Micah, and how the people of those times did not subject that prophet to death. On this occasion the princes virtually joined Jeremiah in pleading for national repentance, so the threatened doom could be avoided (Jer. 26:16-20). His continuing life and ministry was only by sufferance of the fact he had developed a number of these friends at court who were convinced that his policies were wise. Consequently they were passively and semi-actively protecting him (Jer. 26:24). This was one of the happiest achievements in the later life of Jeremiah.

Impasse with King Jehoiakim

For some time opposition against this prophet had been mounting, especially among most people from the influential circles in Jerusalem. This was particularly true with regard to the king and royal family. Jeremiah was merciless in denouncing King Jehoiakim for his unrighteousness and the injustices he was perpetrating in the course of his ruling (Jer. 22:13-19). He condemned the king for using his office for personal advantage, building a wonderful palace and laying by a personal fortune at the expense of unpaid labor. Jeremiah pointed out to the people how their king was excelling only at coveting, shedding innocent blood, oppressing, and doing violence. The prophet also reminded Jehoiakim that he would go to an unmourned grave. In fact, he would have no grave at all, for Jeremiah ended that speech by saying that Jehoiakim would

> . . . be buried with the burial of an ass,
> Dragged forth, and cast outside the gates of Jerusalem.

Jeremiah 22:19

When Jeremiah thus denounced Jehoiakim to his face, and exposed his misrule before the people, it was more than this king could tolerate. So he took away Jeremiah's freedom of movement. All the prophet said about this experience was "I am shut up; I cannot go into the house of the Lord" (Jer. 36:5). This hardly seemed a jail experience but more like being prohibited from leaving his rooming quarters. Was it a means of punishment for his past activities? Or was it to prevent him from doing further prophesying?

Writing a Book

Whatever the exact reason for this confinement, Jeremiah was the type of person who would not be defeated, even by such restraints. The thought occurred to him that he might improve his time by writing a book. His plan was to record on a scroll all the prophecies he had spoken to the people of Jerusalem and Judah since the day he became a prophet. He had begun his work in 626 B.C. and now it was 604 B.C. (Jer. 1:2 cf. 36:1). This meant that he would attempt to recall from memory all the speeches he had delivered during the previous twenty-two years (Jer. 36:2).

Jeremiah's main purpose in this plan was to keep his influence active in the outside world during this time when he was confined. It would be a means of by-passing this edict of censorship upon his speaking. Also, he perhaps rationalized the situation by concluding that this might not be such an unfortunate development after all. Perhaps if the highly controversial factor of his own personality were removed as an issue, and the messages were read by another party, there might be more possibility of favorable popular response (Jer. 36:3, 7).

In those days, writing was a specialized art and there is no evidence that Jeremiah possessed this ability. So he hired a scribe by the name of Baruch, and sent him to buy a scroll. Then Jeremiah began dictating his utterances to this newly employed scribe who wrote them on the scroll. It was a laborious task. It took weeks, and perhaps months, before this project was brought to completion (Jer. 36:4).

In the year 603 B.C., when "all the people in Jerusalem and all the people that came from the cities of Judah to Jerusalem" had gathered for the great fast day (Jer. 36:9), Jeremiah saw his opportunity. Even though he could not go to the temple and address the crowds in person, as was his custom, he did the next best by sending his scribe. Jeremiah commanded Baruch to stand in the temple and read the scroll to the people assembled at the celebration.

Baruch was obedient, and read this first edition of Jeremiah's book before the pilgrims in a room by the new gate of the temple (Jer. 36:6, 8-10). Micaiah, grandson of Shaphan the scribe, was in the audience and heard this first reading of Jeremiah's manuscript. In those days the publishing of a new book, or scroll, was little less than a sensation. After the reading was concluded, Micaiah hastened to the palace. Finding his father, four other temple officials, and a group of princes, he proceeded to tell them regarding the things he had heard from the book (Jer. 36:11-13).

They were at once so interested in seeing the volume that they sent one of their number to find Baruch and bring both him and the scroll to them. Baruch was soon located and was taken to this scribal chamber in the palace. After examining the manuscript, they requested that he sit down and read it to them. This he did. As the writing of such an extensive book by dictation was an unheard-of procedure, they plied Baruch with questions as to how he had produced it (Jer. 36: 14-18).

Those who were present in that small group found themselves impressed with the contents of the document. This indicates that not all the temple authorities and men of royalty were unresponsive to Jeremiah's messages. Because so many of its prescriptions were not being observed, the members of that company were struck with fear as the book was read to them (Jer. 36:16). This was one of the most receptive groups in all the ministry of Jeremiah.

These men considered this writing so important that they wished the king could hear it read also. Yet, knowing Jehoiakim as they did, they had their suspicions that this material would not commend itself to him. Fearing he might go into a rage over it and kill both Baruch and Jeremiah, this company advised Baruch that it might be best if both he and Jeremiah should go into some place of hiding where they could not be found (Jer. 36:19).

Then the princes summoned their courage, went to the royal chambers, and sought an audience with the king. This was granted, and they proceeded to tell him about this wonderful new book and its contents. The king seemed interested and requested that the scroll be brought and read to him. Jehudi,

JEHOIAKIM BURNS JEREMIAH'S SCROLL OF PROPHECIES

one of the group, went to the temple, brought the scroll from the place they had hidden it, and proceeded to read it before the king and his princes (Jer. 36:20-21).

It was wintertime and King Jehoiakim was sitting in his audience chamber beside a burning brazier. Not more than three or four columns of the text had been read when the king reached over and took it angrily from Jehudi's hand. Using his penknife, this ruler began to cut off pieces from the papyrus scroll and throw them into the burning brazier. Three of the company made vigorous protest to Jehoiakim, begging him to spare the scroll. The king ignored these pleas, continuing to cut off and cast into the fire piece after piece, until the entire scroll was burned (Jer. 36:22-25). This was one of the first book-burnings in recorded history.

In addition, the king sent three of his officers to arrest Jeremiah and Baruch, and bring them to the palace. These two could not be found, however, for they had taken the advice of the princes (Jer. 36:26). So the lives of prophet and scribe were preserved for the time being.

We can imagine the happiness of Jeremiah when Baruch had returned from the temple and had told of the interesting response to the reading, and how the princes seemed so receptive.

Now this mounting hope was all shattered in an instant when word arrived, by a secret informer, that the king had burned the scroll and presumably would like to do the same with its co-authors. Think of it! All their labor of weeks and months gone up into smoke in a few moments!

The Second Edition

Jeremiah was one of those invincible persons who could not be intimidated and was not subject to defeat. He im-

mediately thought of writing another book. He would re-
dictate everything which had gone into the volume that had
been burned, but he would add much new material to it. He
was happy in his expectation of how much better and larger
the second edition of his collected prophecies would be (Jer.
36: 27-28).

Now that Baruch, as well as Jeremiah, had come under
the wrath of the king, they were drawn together by their
mutual misery. In their hiding they provided company for
each other. Their secret couriers apparently furnished them
with supplies and food. A new scroll was secured, and the
prophet with his scribe proceeded anew at their task of dictating and writing (Jer. 36:32).

Among the supplementary materials, which were added in
the second edition, was one that he took special satisfaction
to include. It was a vigorous denunciation against King
Jehoiakim, a worthy companion piece to the one in Jeremiah
22:13-19.

> Therefore thus says the Lord
> Concerning Jehoiakim, king of Judah:
> "He shall not have any descendant
> To sit upon the throne of David.
> His dead body shall be cast away,
> To heat by day, and frost by night.
> So I will punish both him, and his children,
> And his servants for their iniquity.
> I will even bring upon them,
> And upon all the inhabitants of Jerusalem,
> And upon the men of Judah
> All the calamity against which I warned them,
> And yet they did not hearken."

Jeremiah 36:30-31

Nothing is stated as to how this second edition of the prophecies was used. There is no evidence that it was read in public. Jeremiah may have feared that, if that were done, it would go the way of the first book. Perhaps it was preserved in a place of safety until the day when passionate feelings would be calmed and the authorities would be more considerate. If so, it perhaps was never read to the people of that generation in public. This second edition, with some later supplements, is essentially the book of the prophet Jeremiah as we have it in our Bibles today.

The production of this book was an epochal event in the annals of prophecy. This was presumably the first time a prophet had assumed any responsibility for reducing his oral speeches to written form. Those who preceded Jeremiah were not writing prophets. They were so concerned with the issues and struggles of the present that they never thought of preserving their productions for the future. Nothing of their utterances has survived except those few portions which interested people were able to record from memory and collect in the generations immediately after the respective prophets lived. This new departure of Jeremiah is notable as the first time in the Bible that a religious leader resorted to the written word by producing an edition of his own works for wider circulation.

Baruch, the Discouraged

Baruch had no concept of what he was getting into when he hired out as scribe to Jeremiah. When, by a chain of circumstances, he suddenly found himself marked for death by the king, and forced into hiding, it was almost more than he could endure. After all, he was not a partner of Jeremiah. He was only his hired scribe. So why should he be made to suffer? While under house arrest or in hiding, during the time they were preparing the scrolls, in an especially blue moment Baruch poured forth his grief.

> Woe is me now!
> For the Lord has added sorrow to my pain;
> I am weary with my groaning,
> And I find no rest.
>
> *Jeremiah 45:3*

To have only one companion left, and have that one lament day after day because of his plight, was difficult for the prophet to bear. Jeremiah tried to comfort Baruch and convince him that he would be better off in the long run by remaining as scribe (Jer. 45:1-5). Apparently Jeremiah succeeded in this. In spite of the hardships already involved, and likely to be met up with even more in the future, Baruch remained loyal to Jeremiah and deserves credit for having continued as a faithful companion to the end of the prophet's days (Jer. 43:1-6).

Tempted to Quit

Jeremiah himself had thought on more than one occasion of stopping his prophetic work. What was the use of one man's making himself so miserable in the face of a whole nation ganged up against him? Apparently he did stop several times, thinking on each occasion that he was through for good. Yet there was something "as it were a burning fire shut up in his bones" which would not let him rest. This flame of the spirit burned within him until he could no longer contain himself, or continue to repress it. To relieve a self that was bursting with truth for need of an outlet, he was each time forced to go forth anew, proclaiming again the messages of his God.

Jeremiah was of all men most miserable. When he gave forth his messages he got into trouble and was abused by the people. When he refrained from speaking he was even more distressed, for he found himself being consumed by these fires of truth that were seeking expression. It seemed that whatever he did, he found himself in a state of agitation. It was either persecution from without or turmoil within. He seemed to be ground between these two millstones. A perpetual divine discontent within him, caused by passion for righteousness, was doing this to the prophet from Anathoth. Yet humanity would continue to degenerate, and would never be remade, except for the work of men like Jeremiah who are willing to sacrifice everything, including comfort and even life itself, for the cause of right and progress.

Assyria on the March

During the ten years from 600 to 590 B.C. foreign policy occupied foremost consideration in Palestine. The chief question was, "What should be Judah's relationship to the great world power, Assyria?" This was a major issue which each generation had faced for more than a hundred years, but it was becoming more acute now. Three possibilities were open. Judah could try to maintain her independence. She could ally herself with Assyria. Or she could fight Assyria, either alone or in coalition with other nations. The prophets had consistently chosen the first of these possibilities as offering greatest safety for a small isolated non-military state such as Judah.

In the days of Jeremiah, Assyria seized the initiative. In an extensive western campaign by King Nebuchadnezzar in 600 B.C., Judah was overrun. King Jehoiakim was forced to acknowledge vassalage and pay tribute. The victorious armies then swept on to Egypt and administered stinging defeat there. Thus Nebuchadnezzar became supreme from the Nile to the Euphrates (II Kings 24:1, 7).

Inasmuch as it would clearly have been suicide for a little country such as Judah to resist Assyria, Jeremiah departed from general prophetic policy, and even his own former position, by insisting that Judah must be resigned to being a loyal vassal of Assyria during the foreseeable future. The more loyal she was in that vassalage, the better she would fare. It was only a matter of good common sense. There was no use trying to do the impossible and attempt to win independence now. As a statesman of keen insight, Jeremiah could see that such an attempt would probably bring catastrophe to Judah.

Yet this was exactly the choice which King Jehoiakim made. Turning his back on all realism, he rebelled against Assyria in 597 B.C. (II Kings 24:1). The decisive answer soon came from the east. Nebuchadnezzar's armies returned and bottled up Jerusalem. King Jehoiakim died just before the enemy arrived, and this left his eighteen-year-old son, the new king, Jehoiachin, to cope with this desperate situation and reap the vengeance which his father should have borne.

Jerusalem was quickly taken. The conquerors stripped the temple and palace of all their overlays and vessels of gold. Most of the prominent and economically useful residents of Judah were carried away as captives. These included all soldiers, royalty, artisans, smiths, priests, and people of wealth. Ten thousand such persons from Judah were herded together and transported to a life of servitude in distant Babylonia. In the country districts only peasant farmers were left to till the land, and in Jerusalem, only the poor (II Kings 24:2-16). This was how King Jehoiakim had landed his country in ruin.

16

Imprisoned, But Yet Free

BEFORE THE ASSYRIANS RETIRED from Palestine on the occasion of their decisive victory in 597 B.C., they set up twenty-one-year-old Zedekiah as ruler in Jerusalem (II Kings 24: 17-18). He was a brother of the late King Jehoiakim and a son of the late Josiah, the great reforming king. Zedekiah ruled for eleven years as the last king of the Hebrew people.

From the very start of his reign, Zedekiah had difficulty in keeping the independence movement under restraint. Presumably a majority of the people in Palestine would have been willing to hazard rebellion at any time. Because he would not act along this line, Zedekiah was subjected to severe criticism. Nevertheless, for the first nine years of his reign he followed Jeremiah's policy, even at the cost of making himself almost as unpopular as the prophet with whose advices he was in harmony. At least, the nation continued to endure. This in itself should have been regarded as a vindication of the king's and prophet's strategy.

On one occasion, it seemed certain that this policy would be abandoned. The foreign ministers of Edom, Moab, Ammon, Tyre, and Zidon were meeting at Jerusalem to conclude an alliance for purposes of joint rebellion against Babylon. Jeremiah lost no opportunity to impress upon these people that they were playing with dynamite. In desperation he sent back home with each minister an ox yoke as a gift to his respective king, and with it the urgent request that he should not rebel but should continue to wear the yoke of Babylon (Jer. 27:1-11). He also made a special appeal to King Zedekiah to continue living at peace with the Babylonian world power (Jer. 27:12-22).

Encounter with the Prophets

The few great independent prophets and the many prophets of the schools had always been on opposing sides. This opposition was even more clearly drawn in the days of Jeremiah. These *majority prophets* of the schools formed the hotbed of revolution. They pressed the king constantly to rebel against Babylonia and win independence for Judah. By contrast, Jeremiah offered the only strong voice in opposition, calling for continuance of peaceful submission to Babylon as the only policy which could provide any future for his people.

The influence of Jeremiah at the capital was given a severe jolt when Hananiah of Gibeon, one of the most prominent school prophets of that day, appeared at Jerusalem in 593 B.C. on a patriotic *speaking* tour. Hananiah was the special champion of the independence movement. A large crowd assembled before the temple in Jerusalem to hear him. In an impassioned address, radiant with optimism, he predicted that Judah soon would be free. He asserted that Babylon would be overthrown in less than two years time (Jer. 28:1-4).

As soon as Jeremiah saw the trend of Hananiah's remarks, he ran quickly to his room to get one of his ox yokes. He arrived back at the audience as Hananiah was concluding his address. Carrying his yoke, Jeremiah worked his way through the throng until he stood directly before the orator.

As this popular *patriotic* speaker concluded his words, at-

tention became centered on Jeremiah who at the moment
was in the strange process of putting his ox yoke about his
neck. By this curious action Jeremiah at once stole the
show. Thereupon he proceeded to give his version of things,
which was quite opposite to what the people had been hearing
from Hananiah (Jer. 28:5-9). Jeremiah boldly asserted that
Hananiah was a misguided person, and that his advice was
wrong. Jeremiah appealed for Palestine to continue, without
protest, wearing the yoke laid upon her by the king of Babylon. This was equivalent to saying that the time for revolt had
not yet come. In this way Jeremiah undermined the advices
given by one of the most prominent and popularly acclaimed
leaders in Palestine.

This made Hananiah angry. He rushed over to Jeremiah,
broke the yoke from his neck, and demolished it. He said
the power of Babylonia would be destroyed just as easily
(Jer. 28:10-11). The quick-witted Jeremiah came back
and said virtually, "All right, you may perhaps break the
yoke of wood. But if you do, you shall be made to wear a
yoke of iron" (Jer. 28:12-17). These were the words of a
clearheaded analyst who could see the eventualities of Hananiah's shortsighted policy and told the people what they needed
to hear concerning it. His words nullified the message of this
popular prophet who had been uttering what the people
wanted to hear. As this dramatic meeting came to its conclusion, Jeremiah spoke some pungent words to Hananiah.

> Hear now Hananiah! The Lord has not sent you,
>   But you have caused this people to trust in a lie. . . .
> This very year you shall die,
>   Because you have spoken rebellion against the Lord.

Jeremiah 28:15-16

After this episode, Jeremiah went at once to a nearby blacksmith shop and had the smith forge him a yoke of iron. Soon he was back at the temple again, wearing the new yoke about his neck. This iron yoke was a warning to all the people regarding the dire consequences of their proposed rebellion. It was his graphic way of reminding them that they should not try to gain independence at that inopportune moment. If they should try to break "the wooden yoke," which represented the mild measures of control to which they were then subjected, Babylonia would become indignant at the people of Judah and fasten upon them "a yoke of iron," with rigid controls and grievous bondage. By a foolhardy attempt to defeat Babylonia, the Palestinians could only inflict upon themselves a much more bitter servitude. Jeremiah may have continued to wear this iron yoke for a number of days to keep all the people of Jerusalem reminded that they had better be satisfied with their present lot, and not indulge in plans for revolt.

In the Guardhouse

The time came when King Zedekiah felt forced to choose finally between the two sides. On the one hand, he could follow the extreme minority counsel of the one free-lance prophet, and a few princes, who advised continuing the peaceful submission of Palestine to Babylonia, with payment of tribute. Or he could adopt the advice given by Hananiah and the hundreds of trained school prophets, as well as the masses of the people, who wanted to pursue a policy of independence and resistance to Babylonia. We can understand how the king was puzzled in this situation.

According to the democratic principle that the voice of the majority is the voice of God, and is always right, it seemed increasingly clear to the king that the prophet Jeremiah must be wrong. Zedekiah forgot that a majority can be trusted only when it is an enlightened majority and the mass of prophets at that time, in spite of their schooling, did not come in that class.

King Zedekiah finally made his choice. It amounted to changing sides, for he had been following the policy of Jeremiah rather halfheartedly for nine years. He decided he would try the opposite method, for a time at least. So he rebelled against Babylonia early in the year 588 B.C.

On the tenth month of the same year, the armies of Nebuchadnezzar of Babylon appeared before Jerusalem, constructed forts, and began laying siege to the city (II Kings 24:20-25:1). All this time Jeremiah was telling the people that it would be suicide for the city to resist. He was advising the residents of the capital to ignore the unwise decisions of their government and go over to the Babylonian side.

By reason of these activities, the king decided that this prophet could not be left at large any longer. So Zedekiah placed Jeremiah in ward in the guardhouse of the palace (Jer. 32:1-5).

As the siege progressed, food became scarce. Blackmarketers abounded and prices became unreasonably high. This inflation grew into a general panic. As the situation became desperate, there was wild selling of property in order to buy food. All faith in the future began to vanish.

At this time one of Jeremiah's cousins came frantically to the guardhouse one day and wanted to sell his property in Anathoth. He had lost faith that it ever would be worth anything again. By contrast, Jeremiah still had faith in the future and bought the field for seventeen silver shekels. The deed was signed, sealed, and witnessed there in the guardhouse.

Then it was given to Baruch to place in a jar for safe keeping (Jer. 32:6-15).

Strange as it may seem, when everyone else was losing faith, Jeremiah retained his. He regarded his king and nation as having made a deplorable mistake. Nevertheless, he had faith to believe that even the calamity which this decision was inviting would not be the end of his country. Although Judah would meet bitter defeat, houses, fields, and vineyards soon would be bought and sold again in Palestine. In the hour of Judah's crisis, Jeremiah appeared as the prophet of hope for the long-range future.

Even though the residents of Jerusalem should be carried into captivity, he was certain they would return in due time and re-establish themselves in Palestine. This purchase of land in Anathoth was a material demonstration concerning Jeremiah's confidence in the future of his country (Jer. 32: 16-34:5). It was an act of faith.

In a private conference with the king during this crisis of war, Jeremiah had prevailed on Zedekiah to make a decree freeing all Hebrew slaves in Jerusalem (Jer. 34:6-10). This too was another step toward a more progressive future.

Temporary Freedom

The Babylonian troops broke the siege of Jerusalem long enough to pursue the Egyptian armies into that country and defeat them (Jer. 37:5). The people of Jerusalem breathed a sigh of relief, thinking the crisis was over. Jeremiah was released from the guardhouse and given his freedom. The former owners repented of having liberated their slaves, and began to force them back again into servitude (Jer. 34:11, 16).

As this lull settled over Jerusalem, King Zedekiah sent two of his representatives to seek out Jeremiah and inquire as to what the future might hold in store for Judah. Again Jeremiah shattered the new false sense of security in Jerusalem by announcing that the Babylonian armies would soon return and that the tragedies ahead, as the city would be starved into submission and burned, would be much more terrible than anything they had yet experienced (Jer. 37:1-10). He also chided the people for re-enslaving those who had been freed, thus failing to observe the law of Deuteronomy (Jer. 34:12-22).

The prophet thought he would use his new freedom by going out to Anathoth and looking over the property which he had bought during the previous siege.

In the Dungeonhouse

As Jeremiah was going out the north gate of Jerusalem, a guard accused him of intending to desert to the Babylonians and arrested him. Jeremiah protested, but without avail. He was taken by force and brought before certain princes who apparently believed the charge and flogged the prophet. Then he was placed in a solitary cell in a dungeon under the house of Jonathan the scribe. In this dread prison Jeremiah was held for many days (Jer. 37:11-16). No sooner was he placed there than the Babylonian armies returned, encircled Jerusalem, and the siege was on once more.

Even though, due to popular pressure, Zedekiah had ceased to follow Jeremiah's advices, the king apparently had a hunch that his critic was right. To discover Jeremiah's views, the king had sought him out at various times, usually in secret. Now the prophet was summoned from the dungeonhouse and was brought to the palace where King Zedekiah in person consulted with him at length as to the outcome of the siege.

Jeremiah replied, as formerly, that the city would be taken and the king captured (Jer. 37:17).

The prophet used this opportunity for presenting a personal appeal to the king, protesting especially against this imprisonment. Jeremiah asked why it was that the king was permitting the mass of prophets, who were misleading the people and bringing ruin on the nation, to go free while he, who was able to discern the truth, was made to suffer one prison experience after another. He begged that he should not be sent back to that terrible dungeon cell, lest he die.

In the Court of the Guard

The king had mercy upon Jeremiah and arranged to have this prophet transferred to a more respectable prison, called the court of the guard. He also provided that Jeremiah should have a loaf of bread each day so long as there should be food in the city (Jer. 37:18-21).

Four of the leading men in Jerusalem protested against such luxury for Jeremiah in his imprisonment, inasmuch as they were sure he was a traitor of the worst sort. They reminded the king of how Jeremiah had prophesied that the city would be taken and destroyed, and how he had been mistaken in this prediction. They called Zedekiah's attention also to the way the prophet had urged that the people of Jerusalem should desert to the Babylonian side, and a considerable number had followed his advice. These four complained especially because Jeremiah was demoralizing the defenses of Jerusalem. In light of all these considerations, they demanded that this traitor be put to death. King Zedekiah, who did not have sufficient backbone and could be swayed by any group which could reach his ear, told them the prophet was in their hands and they could do with him as they pleased (Jer. 38:1-5).

The Deep Watery Dungeon

Apparently, because they did not wish to take time for executing the deed at once, they took Jeremiah from the court of the guard and let him down by ropes into a deep underground cistern that had been hollowed out of the solid limestone rock. It was empty except for three or four feet of soft watery mud in the bottom. Jeremiah sank into this mire and there he stuck, unable to move. We can imagine how he must have felt in that dank place, far down under Jerusalem, without food and with no drink except the mud about him (Jer. 38:6).

During those hours of desolate loneliness he was able, for the first time in his life, to enter with some depth into the emotions of Joseph in his similar experience, more than a thousand years earlier. Jeremiah probably thought of how that boy must have felt when he was cast into the deep dry well and then was apparently deserted by his hateful brothers (Gen. 37:18-28).

After Jeremiah had languished for some time in the watery dungeon, a certain servant of the king took mercy on him. This Ebed-melech was a Negro from Africa. Feeling outraged by such treatment of the prophet, this servant went to the king and presented an appeal in person, saying, "My Lord the King, these men have wrought evil in all that they have done to Jeremiah the prophet, whom they have cast into the dungeon; for he is likely to die in the place where he is because of the famine, for there is no more bread in the city" (Jer. 38:7-9).

This weak king, who lacked stability and tended to capitulate to those who happened to be speaking with him at the moment, again reversed himself. He gave Ebed-melech permission to assemble a group of men and rescue Jeremiah from the dungeon. This Ethiopian's concern was evident in his care that the prophet should not be injured while being rescued. With the rope this servant let down a bunch of rags. He told Jeremiah to put these under his arms so the rope would not cut him. When the prophet had the rags and rope in place, the men raised him up. Thus Jeremiah again saw the light of day (Jer. 38:10-13).

At the crucifixion of Jesus, six centuries later, it took a Negro from Cyrene in Africa to bear the cross of Jesus up the hill on which that tragic event was to take place. So it was in Jeremiah's time. Here it was also a Negro who appreciated the prophet and had pity on him.

Back in the Guardhouse

Jeremiah was not freed, but was returned to the "court of the guard" where he had been imprisoned on an earlier occasion (Jer. 38:13). Here he existed without food during the final days of the siege. At one time during that period the king in secret sought him out for advice concerning what should be done in that crisis. Jeremiah was hesitant to comply for two reasons. He feared Zedekiah would kill him if he should tell the truth. Also, he reminded the king that the prophetic advice probably would not be followed even if it were offered. So what was the use of giving it?

In response to this hesitancy on the part of Jeremiah, the king gave him a positive commitment in order to get him to speak. Even though offering no assurance that he would follow Jeremiah's counsel, the king at least promised not to kill him (Jer. 38:14-16).

Encouraged by this assurance, and Zedekiah's continued begging for the prophet's advice, Jeremiah decided to lay before the king the truth as he saw it. Inasmuch as defeat appeared inevitable to Jeremiah, he advised immediate surrender. By bringing this terrible siege to an end at once, many lives would be saved, not only among the military defenders of the city but also among the civilians who were dying of starvation. If the defenders were to hold out until the bitter end, the Babylonians would be much more cruel to their captives, and undoubtedly would burn the city (Jer. 38: 17-23).

The king charged Jeremiah strictly that he should keep this meeting a secret. Zedekiah apparently was rather inclined toward Jeremiah's views but was afraid of the extreme *fight to the finish* sentiment in the city. The king always feared he would do the unpopular thing and be killed himself (Jer. 38:24-27). Once more he ignored the lone prophet's advice and followed the insistence of the many who asserted that God would never allow his holy city to be destroyed.

Surrender

After a siege of two years, the situation in Jerusalem became unspeakable. The agonies of those starving for lack of food, and burning up because there was no water, were ghastly to behold. Eventually the defense capitulated, the enemy made a breach in the wall, and the city rather unofficially surrendered.

During the night after Jerusalem was taken, the king and his army slipped out by a secret gateway and fled. The Babylonians soon discovered this escape and followed them. On the plains about Jericho these fleeing soldiers and royalty were captured and marched to the camp of King Nebuchadnezzar at Riblah. There the great Babylonian conqueror in person executed judgment upon them as war criminals. While King Zedekiah was forced to stand watching, Nebuchadnezzar, presumably with his own hands, slew all the sons of King Zedekiah and all the nobles of Judah. In order that this sight of his dying sons and advisers might be with him as a lasting vision to torture him throughout the rest of his days, the Babylonians then put out Zedekiah's eyes. This Judean king, whom the Babylonians regarded as a double-crosser, was now bound in fetters and prepared for transport to Babylon. We can imagine how often, through those sightless years of torture and terrible memories, Zedekiah must have wished he had followed the advice of the prophet Jeremiah (Jer. 39:1-7).

That Jerusalem might never be a turncoat capital and center of insurrection again, the Babylonians stripped it of its valuables and burned the entire city, including palace and temple. It was a sad day when that famous structure, and the ark which it housed, went up in flames. Probably a number of early Israelite books collected there were also burned. In order that this capital of Judah should forever be eliminated as a source of trouble, even the walls were broken down.

Before Jerusalem was burned, Jeremiah had been removed from the court of the guard and had been carried off with the other captives to Riblah. There he was bound with them in chains. Practically all the people of Jerusalem and Judah were herded together in a concentration camp, awaiting the moment when they would be marched as captives to Babylon where they would suffer the lot of an enslaved people. Only the poor rural dwellers throughout the land of Judah were allowed to remain so that the farms and vineyards might be kept in order. There was a bit of irony in seeing this land of Palestine being divided up among the dispossessed while their former exploiters went into captivity and slavery (Jer. 39:8-10). This also was in harmony with the predictions of the prophets, especially Isaiah and Zephaniah.

The Babylonians heard how, through the years, the prophet Jeremiah had constantly advised tribute payment and the continuing of alliance with Babylonia. They also learned that, during the siege, he had insistently recommended immediate surrender. Interested especially in his welfare, they made search for Jeremiah and eventually found him at Riblah. They removed his chains and proceeded to treat him with respect, giving him whatever he desired. They promised him a place of honor if he should wish to go with the others to Babylon. On the other hand, if he preferred, he would be allowed to remain in Palestine, residing wherever he might choose. They practically left with him the keys to the country (Jer. 40:1-4).

Apparently Jeremiah had only one special request to make of the Babylonians, that his scribe Baruch be allowed to remain with him. This was cheerfully granted. As might have been expected, Jeremiah chose to return to his beloved country. He decided to cast his lot with Gedaliah, the governor, who established his headquarters at Mizpah (Jer. 39:14; 40:5-6). The prophet would take up his abode at this potential capital of the new Palestine which he hoped would come into being. As Jeremiah left the Babylonian hosts at Riblah, their captain of the guard gave him a supply of food and a parting present.

With the Remnant

After the Babylonians had departed with their captives, it began to appear that the remnant at Mizpah would again

EXILED! THE DESTRUCTION OF THE HOLY CITY

enjoy peace under their new governor. Gradually the refugees, who had fled to surrounding countries at the time of the siege, returned and re-established themselves in Palestine. However, there was an especially vicious character by the name of Ishmael in the group, a member of the former royal family. Ambitious for the governorship, he slew Gedaliah, all the Babylonian garrison that was left in the land, and hundreds of Jews whom he suspected might be sympathetic with Gedaliah. He filled a large dungeon with the corpses of those whose lives he took during this thrust for power.

Ishmael was eventually driven out of the country, and fled across the Jordan into the land of Ammon. Even so, the fatal damage had already been done. The small community which remained in Palestine had become almost completely disintegrated through bloodshed and civil strife (Jer. 40:7-41:15).

The bewildered few who survived this tragedy were afraid that Ishmael would return at any time and bring more bloodshed. They also feared the wrath of the Babylonians when they should learn that their garrison had been slaughtered. So this remnant moved for possible safety to the southern border of Palestine. Even there they were afraid. An increasing number of them insisted on fleeing to Egypt where it was believed they might find a place of true safety (Jer. 41:16-18).

This puzzled group of about a hundred people finally appealed to Jeremiah for advice. They promised to follow the counsel he would give them (Jer. 42:1-6). It took the prophet ten days to reach a conclusion. After having considered every possibility, he felt certain as to the correct decision. He told the remnant to remain in Palestine and they would be secure. By fleeing to Egypt they would again place themselves in the path of the advancing Babylonian armies, because Egypt was next on the list for further conquest. By fleeing there, they would be forced to undergo another siege like that of Jerusalem. As new immigrants, they would receive no consideration even from the Egyptians. So he predicted that all who should go to Egypt would die by sword, by famine, or by pestilence (Jer. 42:7-22).

Kidnaped to Egypt

In spite of their promise to follow his advice, the group not only disregarded Jeremiah's counsels but also accused him of being a quack prophet. They gathered together all the Jews who were left in Palestine and proceeded on their happy way toward Egypt. Jeremiah presumably was taken with them by force. This brought to an end even the remnant of the Jews in Palestine. Unrealistic political thinking had been the curse of these people. When they had a person such as Jeremiah who could see clearly the trends of the times, they refused to follow his advice. Jeremiah had a passionate love for Palestine and we can imagine his sorrow as he was kidnaped and carried as a virtual exile into the land of Egypt (Jer. 43:1-7).

There they settled in four different localities, at Migdol, Tahpanhes, Memphis, and Pathros (Jer. 44:1). Jeremiah was at Tahpanhes and even continued his prophetic work at that place. One day he took the Jews of that settlement to the royal palace which was located there. In harmony with his love for acting out his prophecies, he took mortar and brick and constructed a small masonry platform before the gate of Pharaoh's regional palace. We can imagine the curiosity of the group as he was making this structure. When it was completed, Jeremiah announced to his audience that the king of Babylon would set his throne on this base when his conquest of Egypt would be completed. This was another hint to his fellow exiles as to the adversity they might expect in Egypt (Jer. 43:8-13).

His last recorded utterance to these refugees concerned the preservation of their religious traditions (Jer. 44:1-30). As soon as they arrived in the land of the Nile they began to desert the religion of Israel and take on the primitive forms of idolatry practiced in Egypt. Worship of the female goddess, called the queen of heaven, seemed to attract them especially. Distressed by this religious apostasy, Jeremiah went to all four settlements, pleading with the Jews to retain their unique heritage of Israelite religion with its exalted spiritual worship. Seemingly bent on destruction, they gave no attention to his pleadings or his warnings. Yet he did his duty by them to the end.

Before the time of Moses the Hebrews were also in Egypt, in a condition of progressive slavery, until they were ground down so completely that all their religious heritage and traditions had become forgotten. They were but a miserable lot of depressed humanity when Moses came among them. Now the glory of David, Solomon, and the prophets was all being forgotten. The residue of Israel was voluntarily settling down again into a place where they would meet a national extinction as complete as before the time of Moses. All the progress of the centuries was becoming undone.

The Curtain Falls

Jerusalem was destroyed in 586 B.C. and the refugees, with their kidnaped Jeremiah, fled to Egypt perhaps six months or a year later. Jeremiah carried on with them in Egypt for perhaps a year longer. It was therefore approximately 584 B.C. when he disappeared from the scene of action.

What happened to Jeremiah is not known. His age, in the

later sixties or seventies, would suggest that he might well have died a natural death. Yet it is not impossible that he was ushered out of the way by violence, even in old age as in the case of Isaiah, because his people wanted peace and would no longer tolerate his discordant voice. Whatever his end, it was significant that for more than four decades even his enemies were overawed by him and never quite dared to take his life.

Looking back in retrospect, we see that the career of Jeremiah was an exciting one. There was hardly ever a dull moment.

It must not be assumed that the whole story about Jeremiah's work and preaching has been told in these pages. The problem of selection has been difficult. What has been given is only a small part of what might have been presented if space were available. This realization should make us all the more conscious as to the great contribution this prophet has made to the cause of religion.

Christians are particularly interested in the many parallels between the teaching episodes in the life of Jeremiah and those of Jesus. Both cleansed the temple. Both predicted the destruction of the temple. So one might continue on almost indefinitely from item to item. It is now held by most reliable scholars that the ministry of Jesus was only one year in length. Contrasting with this short period were the forty-two or more years of active work on the part of Jeremiah. It was inevitable that, in the course of those many years of service, he should have encountered a large per cent of the situations faced by Jesus. It was a tribute to this prophet that, in New Testament times, many people believed that Jesus was in reality Jeremiah come back to life (Matt. 16:14).

There were other prophets who in particular respects surpassed Jeremiah. When the whole picture is considered, however, including the length of his service, the greatness of his effort, the vigor of his teaching, and the constancy and severity of the persecutions to which he was subjected, there can be little cause to dispute the judgment that he was the greatest of all the pre-exilic prophets. We can understand why many Jews and Christians, particularly ministers and rabbis, regard Jeremiah as their favorite prophet.

Jeremiah was God's hammer (Jer. 23:29), pounding away at the task of forging a new civilization. Although he did not succeed as he would have liked in his own day, such a man lives for the ages. In later times he has been more appreciated than in his own generation. Today his influence continues to go on molding life into something which grows better with the centuries. He may have been a rebel — but he was God's rebel. He was a man whose whole soul was on fire with the spirit of God.

Second Isaiah

17

Herald of Hope

AT THIS POINT THE SCENE SHIFTS from Palestine and Egypt to the military camp of Nebuchadnezzar at Riblah, on the way to Babylon. We look in on those thousands of Palestinians who were captured when Jerusalem fell in the latter days of Jeremiah. Taken by force from their native land, they were compelled to leave their property and most of their personal effects behind. Bidding good-by to the world which they had known was a heartbreaking experience. It was a time of unspeakable sadness for those people when they were herded into captive bands and began their march through torrid heat over semi-desert caravan trails, the long distance of over six hundred miles, to a land of slavery.

Mass removal of entire populations is fraught with hardships, even under the best of conditions. The siege of Jerusalem had been terrible enough, but making that long trek in an almost starved condition to begin with, and given little food from day to day, was an experience of unspeakable torture. All were forced beyond their energies by their captors. Even the bodies of the most vigorous became wasted away. It was not possible to adopt the pace of the slow, or stop to take care of the sick and famished. These died along the way.

The chief lament, which might have been heard from the lips of those tormented people on that long trip might well have been "If we only had listened to our prophet and followed his advice! Jeremiah was right."

Among the Exiles

Psalm 137 gives a picture of one group as they arrived in Babylon. Huddled on the canal banks, they were waiting for their new masters to come and claim them. They had been able to bring along only a few of their belongings. Here these refugees sat, squatting among the packs which they had carried for hundreds of miles across deserts and hot lowlands. A few, who had been musicians in Solomon's Temple, had brought their harps as their choicest possessions. However, these were of no use to them here. Isolated from their country and their god, whom they thought they had left back in Palestine, and exhausted from their long and arduous journey, they were not in the spirit of song. So they hung their harps on the willow trees that grew by the water's edge. There these dejected-looking people sat weeping.

Some of the Babylonians came along and tried to make sport with them. These oppressors wanted to hear some of this Jerusalem jabber. They wanted to hear them sing some of the Palestinian ditties. Nevertheless, the harps remained on the willow trees. These exiles were in too doleful a mood to sing. After all the indignities that had been heaped upon them in transit, to require of them "mirth" and "song" seemed adding insult to injury.

Even with the passing of time, the pathetic cry of the Hebrew captives continued. Being subjected to slave labor was a special ordeal for those who had never done any physical work in Jerusalem, but had lived by exploiting others. Even for those among the exiles who made the best adjustment,

BY THE WATERS OF BABYLON

it was a most humiliating experience. What may well have been their typical cry was expressed in the quatrain,

I will say unto God my rock, "Why have you forgotten me?
  Why must I go mourning because of the oppression of the enemy?"
As with a sword in my bones, my adversaries reproach me;
  While they continually say unto me, "Where is your god?"

Psalm 42:9-10

Most difficult to bear were the taunts of the Babylonians. These tormentors said in essence, "Oh! So you were so bad that even your god saw fit to desert you? Who was your god anyway? And where is he located? Are you sure he is any god at all?" To have their religion and their deity insulted was almost more than they could endure.

For times such as this, a wholly new type of presentation was needed. As the prophetic movement shifted from Palestine to Babylonia, where there was a new environment and where wholly different conditions prevailed, the character of prophecy also was destined to change. Now the nation of Israel was torn asunder and was sick unto death. This was no time to remind these people of their pre-exilic sins or to heap blame upon them. The only task now was to nurse the dismembered nation back to life in order that its unique religious heritage might be preserved for posterity. So we must expect among the prophets of the exile only words of hope and cheer.

The Unknown Prophet

There were three prophets in the exile — Ezekiel, Habakkuk, and an individual whose name is not known. This last nameless person was by far the most important of the trio. For want of a better designation, he is usually called Second Isaiah. This title has been chosen because his writings are found in Chapters 35 and 40-55 of the book which bears the name of Isaiah. Some writers call him the Great Prophet of the Exile. Although this is a fitting designation also, we shall use here the more commonly employed title of Second Isaiah.

In the strict sense of the word, he was the first writing prophet. All before him were speakers who delivered their messages in public to groups of people. Even when Jeremiah produced his book, he was merely redictating to Baruch what he had formerly spoken in public. Second Isaiah was the first of the prophets to produce his work in the first place as a complete book or written document.

Why did this individual write his message rather than speak it? Why did he wish to remain anonymous? The answer to both questions is found in the nature of the times in which he lived. He might have been called the chief of the Hebrew underground. His message, from the Babylonian point of view, was a seditious piece of work. If the identity of the author had been known, it probably would have meant certain death for him. By writing his thoughts in a book he could express his ideas without unduly hazarding his personal safety. The author therefore desired that all attention should be concentrated on his message, and that none should be diverted to himself. In written form, this material could be passed from person to person as it circulated among the many settlements of exiles. Probably a number of copies were produced so that if the Babylonian authorities should intercept some, others would continue on their way, spreading the message of impending doom upon Babylonia and announcing that there soon would be an opportunity for the Hebrew exiles to return unto their homeland in Palestine.

Second Isaiah apparently produced his book at approximately 540 B.C. when rumblings of insurrection against the tyranny of Babylon were already being heard from Media and Persia. He could see the handwriting on the wall for the once-mighty Babylonian Empire. Inasmuch as the fall of Babylon took place only two years later, in 538 B.C., we can see how Second Isaiah stood poised on the brink of world-shaking developments.

Comfort

The main emphasis in this prophet's literary production was hope for the return of his people to Palestine. This is supported by a number of related but supplementary themes. His message was to a people who had spent almost fifty years of bondage in a foreign land where most of the distinctive things for which they stood were scoffed at. People who had suffered so greatly throughout the years needed cheer. Some of Second Isaiah's earliest words were devoted to comforting these Jewish exiles.

> "Be comforted. Be comforted, O my people,"
>   Says your God.
> "Speak consolingly unto Jerusalem,
>   And announce unto her
>   That her servitude is completed,
>   That her iniquity has been pardoned,
>   That she has received of the Lord's hand
>   Double for all her sins."
>
> *Isaiah 40:1-2*

There was a spirit of almost intoxicated optimism in Second Isaiah which contrasts sharply with the pessimism of the pre-exilic prophets. There was not a cloud in the sky. All was happiness, cheer, and anticipation of the wonderful era that he believed lay ahead. He was the most exultant character in the Bible. He gave himself to the task of raising the courage of the exiles and inspiring faith in the future. Another typical passage expresses this radiant optimism.

> Strengthen the weak hands,
>   And make firm the shaking knees;
> Say to those who are fearful of heart,
> "Take courage. Be not afraid."
>
> Then the eyes of the blind shall be opened,
>   And the ears of the deaf shall be unstopped;
> Then shall the lame man leap as a deer,
>   And the tongue of the dumb shall sing.

Isaiah 35:3-4a, 5-6a

The Highway to Zion

It must be remembered that Babylon was separated from Jerusalem by the barrier of the Arabian Desert. When the Judean people were carried into exile, they were taken in a circular route by the main highway which went around the north end of that desert. This meant that the road they took resembled a crescent. Such a circuitous way of getting there had increased the length of their journey by at least three hundred miles.

As Second Isaiah contemplated the return, he had no time for roundabout ways of getting back. He conceived that God would prepare for them a great thoroughfare extending directly across the desert in a straight line from Babylon to Jerusalem. Involved in this also was a grading project in which the hills would be razed and the valleys filled, so the path of this super-highway would be a level stretch of road-

way. We may listen to his own words as he described this
expected development to the amazed exiles.

> Prepare in the wilderness the way of the Lord,
>   Make straight in the desert a highway for our God.
> Every valley shall be filled in,
>   And every mountain and hill, graded down;
> Even the steep heights shall become level,
>   And the rough places, a plain.
> So shall the glory of the Lord be revealed,
>   And all flesh shall see it together,
> For the mouth of the Lord has spoken it.

Isaiah 40:3b-5

An even more idyllic supplement to this picture is shown in
Chapter 35 where God's landscaping of this highway is described, with the irrigation system which he would provide,
including pools of water. What was now desert would soon
be as luxuriant as the garden ground of Palestine on Mount
Carmel, or the flower lands on the Plain of Sharon.

> The wilderness and the dry land shall be glad,
>   Even the desert shall rejoice and bud forth;
> It shall blossom profusely with narcissus,
>   And shall rejoice with joy and singing.
> The glory of Lebanon shall be given unto it,
>   And the excellency of Carmel and Sharon.
> They shall behold the glory of the Lord,
>   Even the splendor of our God.
>
> For waters shall burst forth in the wilderness,
>   And streams in the desert.
> Even the glowing sand shall become a pool,
>   And the parched ground, springs of water.
> In the resting places where jackals lie,
>   Shall be grass, with reeds and rushes.
> And a way shall be there, even a highway,
>   And it shall be called The Way of Holiness.

No unclean people shall pass over it or use it,
    Wayfarers, even morons, shall not lose their way.
No lion shall be there,
    Nor shall any ravenous beast set foot on it.
There the redeemed shall walk,
    And the ransomed of the Lord shall return;
They shall even come with singing unto Zion,
    And with everlasting joy upon their heads;
They shall attain exultation and gladness,
    For sorrow and sighing shall flee away.

Isaiah 35:1-2, 6b-10

This was to be a protected highway. Only those who obeyed the laws of God, and were ceremonially clean, would be allowed to travel on it. Wild beasts would be kept from it so that travelers would be safe from their depradations. Because there were no side roads, no one would be able to lose his way. On this highway the redeemed from exile would travel on their return to Jerusalem.

It is difficult to know how these descriptions should be understood. Are the details, as they are described, to be taken literally? Or is this all poetic imagery, presented only for effect and to create enthusiasm for the return? Elements of both seem to be present. At least it can be said that this description of the highway back to Jerusalem was highly poetic and very vivid. It must have done much to create a desire for the return among a people who had grown somewhat contented in their new homeland.

Cheer to Jerusalem

Second Isaiah called upon the watchmen to climb the highest mountains in that part of the world and shout across the deserts to Jerusalem the good news that the hour of her redemption was at hand. Also, they were to shout to the other cities of Palestine that the time had arrived when they would also be rebuilt. As if these wasted cities could hear, and as if the human voice could carry those five hundred miles across the deserts, he called upon the announcers to shout with all their might.

> Get you up upon a high mountain,
>   And announce good tidings to Zion.
> Lift up your voice with strength,
>   Lift it up, and be not afraid.
> Proclaim to the cities of Judah,
>   "Behold your God!"
>
> *Isaiah 40:9*

In another passage he became even more exultant in shouting the good news to Zion, merely another name for Jerusalem. Here he spoke to the destroyed and dead city as if it were still alive.

> Wake up! Wake up!
>   Put on your strength, O Zion.
> Put on your beautiful garments,
>   O Jerusalem, the holy city.
>
> Get up, and shake the dust from yourself.
>   Resume your habitation, O Jerusalem.
> Loose the bonds from your neck,
>   O captive daughter of Zion.
>
> Break forth into joy and sing together,
>   You waste places of Jerusalem;
> For the Lord will comfort his people,
>   And bring redemption to Jerusalem.
>
> *Isaiah 52:1a, 2, 9*

With his high poetic imagination, Second Isaiah spoke as if the very stones and ruins of Jerusalem were alive. He was giving them his message of comfort and hope. As the former residents of this holy city ceased groveling in the dust and became freed from their bonds, they would return and rebuild the wasted city. This was his message of joy to Jerusalem.

Cyrus, the Liberator

These things were about to take place because of a conqueror from the East. Cyrus, king of Persia, was organizing a super-army and would soon march on Babylon. Second Isaiah pinned great faith on him. He believed Cyrus would be able to put down the Babylonian tyrant and bring about the liberation of the Hebrew exiles.

> I have raised up one from the north, and he comes,
>   From the rising of the sun I call him by name;
> And he treads upon rulers as mortar,
>   Even as a potter tramples the clay.

> For the sake of Jacob, my servant,
>   And Israel, my chosen one;
> I have called you by your name,
>   And titled you, though you know me not.

> I have raised him up in righteousness,
>   And I will make straight all his ways;
> He shall rebuild my city,
>   And shall let my exiles go free.

Isaiah 41:25; 45:4, 13

The faith which Second Isaiah placed in Cyrus is amazing. This comes to its highest in Isaiah 44:28-45:6. Cyrus is designated as the one who will perform all God's pleasure, including rebuilding Jerusalem and laying the foundations of a new temple. Cyrus is even called God's "anointed." The deity would be the advance guard for Cyrus, smoothing his way and crashing all fortresses before him so his conquest might be successful. Second Isaiah felt that this would eventually lead Cyrus and his people to become worshipers of the God who had prospered his conquest.

The Lyric Touch

By these various themes of expectation which Second Isaiah developed, he opened new horizons of hope for his people. He called them to stop groveling in the dust of exile, to stand on their feet once more, and to move on into a future that was radiant with possibilities. By planting within them the dream of returning to Palestine, reconstructing Jerusalem, rebuilding the temple, restoring the nation, and re-awakening their religion, this prophet became the herald of a new age.

Second Isaiah has rendered a distinctive service to all ages by imparting something of his invincible optimism. Through the centuries, the contagion of this spirit has played an important part in keeping within religion a heart of joyousness. Wherever people tend to grow discouraged, through hardships or slowness of progress in the cause of good — there the voice of Second Isaiah comes to cheer and inspire.

There is something musical about the writing of this prophet. His production is really a great prophetic symphony in words. He played about with his major and subordinate themes as a master composer. The words almost sing as one reads them. That is why Second Isaiah, of all writers in the Bible, has become the chief inspirer of musicians. The lyric character of his poetry has played an important role in bringing into existence numberless immortal musical creations which one hears in synagogue and church. In this way, the poetry of Second Isaiah has been amplified into the songs, hymns, cantatas, and oratorios of the ages.

18

New Thoughts About God

HOWEVER MUCH SECOND ISAIAH SUCCEEDED in implanting hope, and raising the spirit of man, he made equally significant contributions in another major area. This concerned man's thoughts regarding God. Even though the leaders of previous generations, especially the prophets Amos and Hosea, had made rewarding searches into the nature of God, Second Isaiah found plenty of places in which to fill out the picture. As each age that is religiously awake enters into new thoughts concerning God, so Second Isaiah pioneered in making some further discoveries that are notable with regard to the deity. He also succeeded in presenting these ideas so attractively that they have become adopted into the religious thought of mankind.

God, the Good Shepherd

It is usually thought that the concept of the good shepherd, which comes to highest development in John 10:1-39, is distinctive in the New Testament. By most people it is forgotten that it goes back to Second Isaiah and the Twenty-third psalm. Of these two, New Testament thought seems to have been influenced most by the figure of God, the good shepherd, as developed by Second Isaiah.

This prophet anticipated that the restored Palestine would

have no human ruler. To put it in another way, there would be no Messiah. During the period of the Hebrew monarchies, the kings of Judah and Israel had been such a disappointing lot that Second Isaiah made no room for them in his expectations regarding the future. He anticipated a theocracy in which God himself would rule. This prophet expected that the deity would descend from heaven in all his glory at Babylon, and would take personal care of the exiles from that point on. He would protect and help them as they sought to realize their new dream of returning to their native Palestine and restoring it.

> Then the glory of the Lord shall be revealed,
> And all mankind shall see it together. . . .
> Behold, the Lord will come as a mighty one,
> And his arm shall rule for him. . . .
> He will feed his flock like a shepherd,
> And will gather the lambs in his arms,
> He will carry them in his bosom,
> And lead gently those that have young.

> *Isaiah 40:5a, 10a, 11*

In these writings of Second Isaiah the barriers between humanity and divinity are removed so that God and man become one in common association. God is pictured here with kindness and concern for even the least. There is something intimate and touching in the way the exalted deity comes down and gathers the lambs in his arms, carries them in his bosom, and gently leads those who are in difficulties. This is simply a figure of how he protects and leads his people.

God, the Creator

Today people usually are not aware that the idea of one God is a relatively new belief for mankind. The way in which, from century to century, man came to conceive of ever greater and greater deities is a long story.

On this subject there has been very much loose thinking. Until recently it has been assumed by almost everyone that Moses was a monotheist, i.e., that he believed there is only one God in the universe. Those people have never looked carefully at the first commandment which reads, "You shall have no other gods before me" (Ex. 20:3). Moses himself made a brass serpent-god and had the people worship it (Num. 21:9). Moses's actions, and subsequent Israelite practice, lead to the conclusion he allowed his people to worship as many gods as they wished, so long as they kept the worship of their tribal deity Yahweh supreme.

Friends of Egypt usually insist that Pharaoh Akhnaton, who lived at approximately the same time as Moses, was also a monotheist. Best Egyptologists of the present day regard this likewise as far from the truth. This pharaoh attempted to unite Upper and Lower Egypt in a firm unity. He conceived that this was not likely to succeed unless the people of all the land had one religion and worshiped a single god. So he banned the worship of Egypt's many sectional gods, and deities of special function, and decreed that the sun god Aton should receive sole veneration. His establishment of Aton worship as the only cult in Egypt was a political measure. He never went to the point of denying existence to other gods outside Egypt.

Creation stories are found in very early times. Even each idol worshiper usually insisted that his special god had created the world. Such statements were not meant to be taken literally but were in the nature of exaggerative compliments paid the several deities, as a man today may say that his wife is "the only one in the world."

In early creation stories, at least one of two limitations is usually present. In most instances a number of gods are involved in the creative process. Also, ordinarily, only a small portion of the world is included within the range of vision. Both these limitations are illustrated by the second, but much older, creation account in our Bibles (Gen. 2:4-3:24).

In this Garden of Eden story there are found the man-god, the serpent-god, the tree-god who dispenses immortality, the tree-god who dispenses wisdom, the two cherubim who were guardian deities, and the gods of the upper regions with whom the man-god consulted. Even Adam and Eve would have become full-fledged deities if they had only been able to go to the other god-tree and had eaten one bite of its fruit. Also, there is no formation of the world in this story, but only the creation of life on one small desert oasis. When most readers of the Bible unquestioningly assume that these two chapters describe the creation of the world by one God, we can see how wishful people are in their determination to find monotheism in the remote past.

Some will say, "Surely Amos, Hosea, Isaiah, and the other eighth- and seventh-century prophets believed that there was only one God in the universe." Even this is not true, for those religious leaders, forward-looking as they may have been, were not monotheists.

At the time of these prophets, development had advanced to the point where idols and local deities had given way, among people of progressive thought, to belief in national gods. Each country had its own deity. Yahweh, sometimes written Jehovah, was the god of the Hebrew people in Palestine. Similarly, each neighboring nation thought a special deity controlled its territory. Chemosh was the god of Moab; Molek, of Ammon; Rimmon, of Syria; Dagon, of Philistia;

etc. When people crossed national boundaries in those days, they automatically changed gods. The prophets up to this point lived in that thought world, and in most respects shared that view.

They had begun to advance slightly beyond it by conceiving that Yahweh was concerned regarding immoral conditions in Palestine's neighboring countries, and could step over the line on occasion to punish these offenders. On the reverse side, when Yahweh became outraged with the conduct of his people, he would in rare cases incite these nations to come across the border and give the Israelite people a much-needed chastening.

Second Isaiah went beyond all this by showing that there are no national gods. He looked upon it as absurd to think of heaven's being divided, as had been assumed up to this point, into rival jurisdictions corresponding to those on earth. This great thinker gave good-by even to the traditional god Yahweh. From this time on the term *Yahweh* gradually disappears as the more inclusive designation *God* comes into general use.

The pre-exilic prophets had spent considerable of their time trying to get their people to abstain from the worship of other gods. Second Isaiah went one step farther here also by asserting that these did not exist and were nothing more than figments of the imagination. There is only one God, and beside him there are no others. In and of himself, this one deity has created all things that are in existence. In so far as the nearer Orient and the Occident are concerned, it seems to have remained for Second Isaiah to make this discovery that there is unity under God in our universe.

Apparently this prophet could imagine himself back at the beginning of things, watching God mark out the circle of

the earth, stretch the sky over it as a curtain, pace off the
heavens, weigh the mountains on his scales, and measure every
ounce of ground in the world. Even the lakes are but handfuls
of water which he has placed in position. There is a highly
poetic touch in this description.

> He it is who sits above the circle of the earth,
>   And the inhabitants thereof are as grasshoppers;
> Who stretched out the heavens as a curtain,
>   And spread them out as a tent to dwell in.
>
> Who has measured the waters in the hollow of his hand?
>   And meted out the heavens with a span?
> And apportioned out the dust of the earth by measure?
>   Or weighed the mountains with scales?
>   And the hills with balances?
>
> *Isaiah 40:22, 12*

These beautiful concepts, and the unity which he discovered
in the make-up of things, found expression in the story of
creation, first written in its present form a hundred years after
his time, which has been placed at the beginning of our Bibles
(Gen. 1:1-2:3). Since the days of Second Isaiah it has been
possible for people to conceive in the fullest sense of *God
the Creator*.

The question may be asked as to why Second Isaiah was
the first person in the Near East to discover that there is only
one God in the universe. Presumably it was to no small degree occasioned by his travel, which is one of the most
broadening of influences. With Second Isaiah it was forced
travel. He had lived in Palestine, had passed through other
countries during the route of exile, now was living in Babylon, and had his mind upon Persia and Media. He may even
have had occasion to visit these two eastern countries. This

item of travel, plus perhaps other factors of which we are not aware, gave Second Isaiah wider horizons of experience than those which had been enjoyed by the pre-exilic prophets. This made him a spiritual pioneer, in the sense that he was the first truly world-minded person in the Bible.

God, Source of Knowledge

Second Isaiah was perhaps the first Hebrew philosopher. He began to think not only of physical origins but also of first causes with regard to the immaterial. The wonder of the creation proved that God was wise and had knowledge, but where did he get his wisdom? Who taught him?

> Who has directed the spirit of the Lord,
> Or, being his counselor, has taught him?
> With whom did he counsel, and receive instruction?
> And who taught him in the way of justice?
> Who imparted to him knowledge,
> And showed him the way of understanding?

Isaiah 40:13-14

The answer to this series of questions was a decisive "No one." Here God appears as the first cause and origin of all the higher qualities of life. God is the source of all knowledge, wisdom, and standards of justice. As God was the creator of the material world about us, he was also conceived by Second Isaiah as the author of the arts, sciences, and those spiritual qualities of life which raise man above his savage ancestry and make him civilized. For all these higher developments of life, mankind is indebted to God, *the great untaught,* who is responsible for furnishing the world of man's mind with its rich cultural heritage.

God, the Director of History

A third area in which Second Isaiah expanded man's idea of God concerned the matter of history. Were the happenings of history dependent, as people then thought, upon the outcome of conflicts between the gods of the nations? Or was it a matter of mere human chance, as many people are inclined to think today? Second Isaiah was convinced that, as there is unity in the physical world, there also is a unity in the ongoing of human affairs. Even though history may be largely in man's hands, when it goes too far astray, there is something in the justice of God which steps in and brings it right again.

> He gives power to those who are faint,
>   And to him who has no might, he increases strength. . . .
> He brings down princes to nothing
>   And makes the judges of the earth as nought.

> *Isaiah 40:29, 23*

It is important to realize that when modern poets write of "One Increasing Purpose" or "one far-off divine event toward which the whole creation moves," they are indebted, whether consciously or not, to Second Isaiah who first gave to this idea its full expression.

No Sacrifice

Up to this time the offering of animal sacrifices was the most basic rite in religion. People believed that if they roasted a lamb, or heifer, or bullock, the smell of the roasting meat would rise up to God. As he enjoyed the appetizing odor, it would place him in a good mood toward the worshiper. The pre-exilic prophets had protested against the offering of vegetables, grains, and animals by people who had no regard for morals, but they had not objected to the institution of sacrifice as such. It remained for Second Isaiah to pioneer also in calling for the abolition of all material offerings.

This decision was arrived at along a different line from that on which the pre-exilic prophets had been proceeding. The elimination of material sacrifices was made inevitable by reason of Second Isaiah's more exalted idea of God. If God is such a great deity, animal sacrifices would be futile. He implied that all the wood in the world would not be sufficient for the fire, and all the animals in creation would not be enough to make an offering that would do justice to God's greatness (Isa. 40:16). If no sacrifice worthy of the deity could possibly be presented, it would be better to refrain entirely rather than keep insulting him with their paltry offerings. With Second Isaiah the idea of God had advanced to the point where it had completely outgrown the idea of altar fires.

This was a revolutionary concept, and was slow in taking effect. In the restored worship after the exile, people forsook the advices of Second Isaiah in this regard and degraded the temple again into something which looked and smelled like a slaughterhouse. With the destruction of Jerusalem in 70 A.D. this cult of animal sacrifice came to an end. Since then, the custom has largely disappeared from the religions of the Near East and the Western world. For higher spiritual worship, which is not dependent upon the offering of material produce, we stand indebted ultimately to Second Isaiah and his more exalted concepts of deity.

No Idolatry

Throughout all earlier time, the worship of images had been almost as much a staple in religion as the practice of material sacrifice. The people of the Northern Kingdom had always used images in their worship. Even in the Southern Kingdom it was customary at many periods. Solomon's Temple itself was at times filled with images. Certain of the pre-exilic prophets denounced the pagan idols which had come to be worshiped by the Hebrews, but hardly anyone objected to the use of images in worshiping the Hebrew god Yahweh. Here too, it was left for Second Isaiah to become the first decisive voice in the Bible to be raised against the institution of image worship as such.

In approaching this subject, Second Isaiah showed that he had a sense of humor. Instead of denouncing the worship of idols by talking himself red in the face, he began to joke about them. He used gentle irony, poking fun at those who trusted in images. When he resorted to this technique, the death sentence against the institution of image worship was written.

He told how a man proceeded when he wanted to make an idol. He would go to a foundry and have the workmen cast the image in cheap metal. Then he would put his god under his arm and carry it to the shop of the goldsmith who would overlay it with gold leaf. As he went down the street he still thought it did not look quite good enough for a god, and so he stopped in with another smithy and had a silver necklace forged for it. After these were through with their work of creating this god, he took it home and nailed it fast on his god shelf, or little temple, so it could not be moved. These workmen, whose vocation it was to make gods, took pride in their workmanship and encouraged each other. The poor man, who could not afford such expensive deities, usually chose a piece of wood that he thought would not be likely to rot, and had a god carved out of it (Isa. 40:18-20; 41:7).

Again he told how a man cut down a tree. Some of it was used for firewood in his heating stove to warm himself. Part of it was set aside for fuel in the oven with which to bake his bread. Another piece of that same tree he fashioned by his skill into a god, and then he knelt before it and worshiped it as the giver of all good things, saying, "Deliver me, for you are my god" (Isa. 44:12-17).

At times Second Isaiah abandoned his humorous approach for more serious words (Isa. 44:9-11), especially in what might be called the dramatic climax of his attack on those who worshiped idols.

> Turned back and utterly put to shame
>> Shall be those who trust in graven images;
> Who say unto molten images,
>> "You are our gods."
> Behold all their works are nothing and worthless,
>> Their molten images are but wind and nought.
>
> *Isaiah 42:17; 41:29*

Under the influence of this prophet, an individual or group of editors went through the prophetic writings, inserting at appropriate places passages in condemnation of idols. Undoubtedly Second Isaiah was largely responsible for the fact that, when the Hebrews returned to Palestine, they never took up again in any extensive way the worship of images.

Israel, God's Servant

By his many new concepts, Second Isaiah reached a higher level of religious attainment than had ever been achieved in surrounding nations, or even by the Israelite people themselves. What was to be done about this? There could be only one answer. People far and wide must be given an opportunity to share in this spiritual achievement.

It was fitting that Israel should be the bearer of the good tidings. These new insights had come about by reason of the adversities undergone by these people during the exile. They had been refined in the crucible of suffering. Now it devolved upon them to share their higher religion with all peoples. Apparently God was entrusting Israel with this task.

This responsibility which rested upon them was a humbling experience. For more than half a century these exiles had been crushed and downtrodden, as the least of the nations. Normally these would have been the last people in the world of whom it could be expected that they would be turned suddenly into the spiritual teachers of humanity. Yet that was exactly what was happening as the insights of Second Isaiah began their leavening work. This prophet summed up the imperative of Israel's mission to mankind in the concept of the Lord's servant.

> Behold my servant, whom I uphold;
>   My chosen, in whom my soul delights;
> I have put my spirit upon him,
>   He will bring forth justice to the nations.
> He will neither cry out, nor speak loudly,
>   Nor cause his voice to be heard in the street.
> A bruised reed he will not break,
>   And a smoking wick he will not quench.
> He will bring forth justice in truth,
>   He will not fail, nor be discouraged
> Until he has established justice in the earth,
>   And even the isles will await his law.
>
> *Isaiah 42:1-4*

This new world-transformation, which was about to take place, would not be built on force. The heralds of Second Isaiah were not to use high evangelistic methods, with yelling, shouting, and street meetings to entice people toward their views. Nor were these announcers going out to destroy other religions as King Josiah had done in his reform. They were to proceed in quietness, and with a divine composure. Their gospel of the one God would be so appealing that all peoples would flock to it. Its right to the allegiance of mankind would lie in its establishment of justice wherever it should be spread in the earth.

This was a sobering challenge which came to Second Isaiah and his fellow Israelites. Would they be able for it? Could they suddenly be plummeted out of slavery and at once become the spiritual leaders of mankind? Second Isaiah believed that, with God's help, this would be possible. As they had known the terrors of slavery, they would be fitting subjects to bring the gospel of liberation to all mankind.

> I, the Lord, have called you in righteousness,
>   And I have strengthened your hands.
> I will keep you, and give you for a covenant to
>   Mankind, and for a light to the nations.
> To open the eyes that are blind,
>   And to bring out the prisoners from the dungeons,
> Those who sit in darkness, from the prison-houses.
>
> *Isaiah 42:6-7*

This was to be a world mission. Second Isaiah was certain that, as the veil should be lifted from the eyes of all humanity, the people of the nations would gladly accept. Inasmuch as they were all one under God, there was no longer any valid reason for distinctiveness among the several peoples. His was one of humanity's first visions of one world joined in pursuit of peace, for he beheld all nations united in common worship. In this way Second Isaiah gained the concept of a world religion.

He expected that this religious awakening would not stop until it had spread to the ends of the earth. He pictured the people in the isolated regions of central Arabia, in the mountain fastnesses, on the ships at sea, and even the dwellers on the remote isles of the seas, all joining in common chorus, praising God and affirming their allegiance to him.

> Sing unto the Lord a new song,
>   And his praise from the ends of the earth.
> Those who go down to the sea in its fullness,
>   Even the islands, and those who inhabit them.
> Let the wilderness, and its cities, give praise,
>   Even the settlements which inhabit Kedar;
> Let the inhabitants of Sela sing
>   And shout from the top of the mountains.
> Let them give glory to the Lord,
>   And declare his praise among the isles.

Isaiah 42:10-12

This was the first great call to evangelism in the Judeo-Christian tradition. It sprang from the feeling that one must share the light which has been given to him. Only in this way can higher religious perspectives in any age be saved for the future. Jesus must have had the same feeling when he said, "Even so, let your light shine before men, that they may see your good works, and glorify your father who is in heaven" (Matt. 5:16). Second Isaiah planted into our tradition the consciousness that any religion, which is worthy of the name, must be a missionary religion.

This prophet's insistence on a shared religion, that works to bring all mankind into the ways of God, has been perverted at times by Judaism into the repulsive doctrine of "the chosen people." Instead of Israel's being called to execute a difficult assignment at a critical point in history, this has been misconstrued as God's declaring his preference for these people throughout all time. In its exclusiveness and narrowness, this is the exact opposite of Israel's place in the world task as conceived by Second Isaiah.

Many branches of Christianity have also perverted the spirit of Second Isaiah at this point. Some have done it by their arrogant insistence that their particular group has a monopoly on religious truth, and first mortgage on heaven. With others it takes the form of a narrow and fanatical evangelism that goes out with an excessive mania to convert and save lost souls, but misses the deep and noble spirit of Second Isaiah.

This great prophet conceived that religion was not a monopoly to be enjoyed but a blessing to be shared. He did not approach his world mission in the spirit of, "You're wrong. We're right. Come over into our camp." It was not his purpose to blow out the least flickering light or break the most frail reed upon which people had come to rely (Isa. 42:3). Instead of destroying their several religious traditions, he proposed to transcend these lesser loyalties and merge them in common allegiance to the one and only God. In this way he gained a vision of the kingdom of God upon earth.

Second Isaiah and Jesus

Even though this Great Prophet of the Exile did not look through the centuries to leaders in the far distant future, there is a close connection between him and Jesus.

At his baptism Jesus was overshadowed with a sense of mission, but he was uncertain as to what specific form it should take. To solve this problem he sought seclusion for some forty days in the wilds of Judea, wrestling with his conscience and with his God. Strangely, the accounts of the temptations are not complete (Matt. 4:1-11; Luke 4:1-13). They mention the three types of ministry which he declined to choose, but neglect to state what he finally adopted.

If that account of Jesus on the mount of questioning were complete, it would probably have something like the following ending. In his continuing search for a type of ministry that would seem most worthy, Jesus apparently turned to the greatest of Second Isaiah's "servant psalms" (Isa. 52:13-53:12). There, in the concept of the suffering servant, Jesus found his whole plan of procedure laid before him. This idea of triumph through suffering, rather than through conquest or resistance, was something new, and it appealed to Jesus.

In those mountains of Judea, Jesus resolved that he would not be lord but servant. He would not have people minister to him, except in the barest essentials, but would spend his life ministering to the needs of others. As Jesus left that place of meditation and proceeded to his public work, he went reinforced by the program, spirit, and inspiration of Second Isaiah. It apparently was the pull of Second Isaiah which caused him to make unusual use of that choice collection, repeat its statements as texts for his sermons, and treasure it as his special Bible.

Jesus has been only one of the many whom the spirit of this prophet has nurtured. From age to age both Jew and Christian have found in Second Isaiah a source of inspiration and hope, as he points the way toward a higher God and a peaceful humanity.

Jonah

19

The Runaway Prophet

IN ACCORDANCE WITH THE EXPECTATIONS of Second Isaiah, King Cyrus of Persia succeeded in conquering Babylon in 538 B.C. Cyrus was a benevolent ruler and decreed at once that the people in exile might return to their native homelands. This provided the opportunity for the Jewish people to go back to Palestine. The first small group made the trip to Jerusalem immediately, and others followed.

Reaction

For those who returned, it was a most disillusioning experience. It was difficult to live on a heap of ruins. The land had been wasted by erosion while they were away, so that it was now almost impossible to raise crops. Neighboring people had moved in and had taken possession of their land. After eighteen years of struggle, the prophets Haggai and Zechariah in 520 B.C. found the returned ones very sad. A makeshift temple was built but this, and what buildings had been erected, were destroyed in the crisis of 485 B.C. when the other populations tried to put an end to this encroachment on their land. When Nehemiah arrived from Babylon in 445 B.C. he found the walls of Jerusalem still in ruins. The hardships they encountered embittered these returned ones.

The arrival of Ezra in Jerusalem in 458 B.C. was of

strategic significance in turning the Jewish community from the way of Second Isaiah. Ezra was a narrow legalist and bigot. By his writing the "law of Moses," as now found from Exodus to Numbers, he fastened a system of taboos and ritualistic services to Judaism which were completely foreign to its true spirit. He purged the family life of his people and forced them to divorce all who did not have full Jewish blood.

By bending the Jerusalem community to his views, Ezra almost completely nullified the spirit and teachings of Second Isaiah. Thus Judaism degenerated from a noble universalism to exclusivism and hate for all other people. The exile may have been a great hardship, but the triumph of Ezra's reactionary and anti-foreign influence was the greatest calamity which has ever befallen the Jewish people.

After the exile, there were several prophets who were rather typical of the period. They were Haggai, Zechariah, the author of Malachi, Obadiah, and Joel. After the pre-exilic and the exilic prophets, these were a great disappointment. They had a little of the prophetic spirit — enough so they have come to be called prophets. However, they were more priestly than prophetic. Conduct played little part in their considerations. They were more interested in tithes, offerings, altars, temples, and the whole ritualistic side of religion.

A New Prophet

An exception to this was a prophet untimely born — the last in the great succession. This was the author of the book of Jonah. He strove to revive the spirit and teachings of Second Isaiah with its good feeling toward all peoples. His book was a vigorous challenge to Ezraism in all its forms. Its story shows a Palestinian people who had degenerated to the point where they hated all Gentiles.

The book of Jonah (350-250 B.C.) pictures the low state to which the returned Israel had descended as a result of two or three centuries during which they glorified themselves but looked with disdain upon all others.

Thus far, prophetic books have been composed of the words, actions, and thoughts of historical characters, recorded either by themselves or by their followers who heard and admired these great leaders. By contrast, the book of Jonah is an entirely different type of presentation. It is a work of fiction. All the historical prophets were highly honorable men, but "the fictional prophet Jonah," as he appears in this story, is perhaps the most unregenerate villain in the whole Bible, all the more offensive because of his high religious pretenses. The prophet Jonah is the chief character in the story. The author's name remains unknown.

By contrast with historical writing, which records the happenings of the past as they have occurred, fiction can be purposeful writing. Though its plot and happenings may not be historically true, great fiction, such as the book of Jonah, is uniquely fitted to focus attention upon ideas and views that are true and typical in a given situation. Truth may be dramatized more clearly when the author can control his characters, and their circumstances, than if he is forced to report the unconnected data that usually appear in real life, where chance incidents that intervene serve to becloud the central issue an author may be attempting to dramatize.

One chief characteristic of great literature is its ability to inspire the reader's imagination. At this point the Jonah story is particularly rich. Knowing that it is a book of fiction rather than literal fact, it may be permissible to allow our imaginations rather free expression in reconstructing and elaborating the story.

The Prophet's Flight

This tale opens in the northern part of Palestine at a town called Gath-hepher, only a few miles north of Nazareth. In that small village lived Jonah the son of Amittai who was quite a pretentious prophet (II Kings 14:25). One day, perhaps in a vision while he was asleep, Jonah received a special message from God, commanding him to

> Arise! Go to Nineveh, that great metropolis,
> And preach against it,
> For their wickedness has come to my attention.

> *Jonah 1:2*

Jonah did not like the idea of going to such a far city and preaching to the Ninevite people. They were the most cruel and ruthless warriors the world had ever seen. They were regarded in Palestine as a heathen people, because they worshiped hundreds of gods and idol images. He was afraid if he should go they might repent, and this was the last thing he wanted. He looked upon these foreigners as the scum of the earth. He didn't want them rubbing elbows with him when he went to worship. He wouldn't want them to sit in his pew. He knew his god Yahweh must have lost his senses or he would not have thought of bringing foreigners into the religious fellowship of his select people. This would spoil everything. So Jonah decided he would not go.

Yet he was unable to rest easy over the matter. He had disobeyed his god, and that was regarded as a serious matter in those days. It was considered risky enough to disobey a sane god, but it was far more dangerous to ignore the commands of a god, such as Jonah's, who had lost all sense of propriety. Jonah was afraid his erratic god would bring some form of calamity upon him for not carrying out this commission. The disobedient prophet finally began losing sleep at night, worrying over what might happen.

One day he thought of a clever scheme. He decided to leave the country, because it was dangerous to remain where his god Yahweh would be able to punish him. If Jonah could only get out of Palestine, he felt he would be safe. After some time Yahweh probably would forget about this incident. Then Jonah could slip back into the country unnoticed and all would be well.

Those were the days when the idea of one God who enfolds all the world, as taught by Second Isaiah, had become largely forgotten among the people of Israel. They had reverted to worshiping the Hebrew national god Yahweh, whose jurisdiction, as they thought, did not extend beyond the boundaries of his particular nation.

As this prophet seems never to have had a sea voyage, he thought this would be an opportunity to take a cruise on the Mediterranean, and get a much needed vacation. So he packed a few belongings and proceeded down the road toward Joppa, the seaport of Palestine.

In spite of this joyful prospect, his heart was heavy and he grew more troubled the farther he went. What if his god Yahweh should see him fleeing the country, and stop him before he could get away? This might mean double punishment — once for his disobedience in failing to preach before the Ninevites and once for trying to flee.

Perhaps he would better turn around and go to Nineveh after all. No, he just could not think of preaching to such despised people. So he must go on, danger or no danger. Fear gave way to anxiety as he thought, "What if there is no boat in port when I arrive there? If I must wait for some days, Yahweh will surely look my way at some time and see me. Then it will be his rage to pay."

Propelled by ever greater fears, Jonah walked faster and faster. As he came over the last obstructing dune on the seacoast highway, he suddenly became exultant as he saw a Tarshish vessel at anchor in the harbor. These were the largest ships afloat in those days, the type used to sail the wide stretches of the Mediterranean Sea. Yes, he would have a real trip, and go with them to far-off Spain at the ends of the earth.

What if Yahweh should stop him before he could get on board? That was the great danger now, for his god might accidentally be looking. Jonah hastened his steps even more and almost ran in order to get there before Yahweh might get wise to this situation. If planning to get him, the deity would probably wait until Jonah was almost on the boat before seizing him. What if the boat should sail before he could get there? His fears became ever more terrifying, he grew tenser and tenser, and ran faster and faster. When he finally arrived at Joppa he probably raced by the ship's office at top speed, afraid to take time for inquiring as to the fare. He rushed on the ship frantically, all out of breath.

Sure enough! He made it. As he took his feet off the soil of Palestine and went up that gangplank, all Jonah's cares and fears vanished in an instant. He was safe, for now he was no longer under the jurisdiction of the god of Palestine. Since Jonah had made a successful escape from Yahweh's territory, that misguided deity could do nothing to him from this point on.

Soon the boat sailed away, and it was a moment of great joy for Jonah. He had outwitted his god, and that is no mean

"And Jonah Took Ship to Tarshish"

accomplishment for any man. As the ship moved from port, we can see Jonah on the stern, waving good-by not only to Palestine but also to his god. "I beat you this time. You can't get me now." Jonah chuckled over how he had made such a clever escape "from the presence of Yahweh" (Jonah 1:3).

Having had little sleep for days, Jonah at once went below deck to his assigned room, and was soon fast asleep.

Storm at Sea

It was not long until things began to happen. A terrific storm descended in the path of that ship. The sailors were thrown into consternation by it. The first thing they did was to pray, kneeling on deck as they called to their several deities for relief from the storm. After this prayer meeting, in which they all participated, they cast overboard the merchandise and baggage that was on the ship. They were willing to suffer all this financial loss in order that they might safeguard their human cargo.

Then we can imagine one of the crew saying, "What's become of that suspicious looking character who came on the boat at Joppa? Where is he? Why isn't he here by our sides praying that this portent of doom be taken from us?"

The captain went down to Jonah's room and, imagine it, he found him asleep. He woke up the prophet and said virtually, "Man, what are you doing, sleeping through a storm like this when all our lives are in danger? You ought to be praying. Dress! Get up on deck, and join us in prayer. Perhaps your added petition may do the trick, so that we may yet be saved."

By the time the captain and Jonah arrived on deck, the sailors had already decided that they must determine the cause of this deadly storm. In those days, before modern gambling had developed, dice were used only to determine the will of deity. In this particular situation the interested circle gathered around as the captain cast the lot on deck. All eyes became fixed on the sacred dice as they fell and lay there. The men were in breathless expectation. Who would be identified as the villain for whose cause this storm had descended upon them? As soon as it was announced that the lot had fallen on Jonah, all eyes became focused on him.

The sailors tried to be considerate of Jonah and attempted to strike up a conversation with him. They wanted to know what wrong he had committed, but they were hesitant about asking him outright. So they inquired whether he had any variant explanation as to why this tragedy of impending death had come upon them.

In a further effort to show their friendliness, and enter into conversation, they plied him with questions as to his occupation, his home, his race, and his country. However, Jonah was so repulsed by them that he could not think of speaking to these low-down *salts* of the sea.

As the silence caused by his failure to answer became embarrassing, Jonah might have been heard to say under his breath, "Well, you trash, if you must know, I guess I'll be forced to degrade myself by speaking to you." We can imagine that he prated on deck before them in the most arrogant manner as he said,

> I am a Hebrew,
> And I worship Yahweh, the God of heaven,
> Who has made the sea and the dry land.
>
> *Jonah 1:9*

These words, about a great exalted God of all the universe, formed an excellent statement of faith. How could such noble concepts issue from the lips of this fleeing prophet? These wonderful words were probably part of the little creed which he had been taught as a boy in the course of his religious instruction, and he had memorized it. He had remembered it through the years, and now was repeating it. The trouble was that for Jonah they remained only empty words. He had never stopped to think what they meant. If he had, he would not have been sailing on this Tarshish galley.

In theory, Jonah was worshiping the God of heaven and earth, who had made the sea and the dry land. In practice, his religious horizon had moved out no farther than that little sectional god Yahweh, who was supposed to rule only over the land of Palestine. Jonah is a signal example of those many individuals who, in religion, profess one thing, but live another. He not only did not practice what he preached, but had never even begun to comprehend the implications of the words which passed so lightly from his lips.

This is the reason why Jonah was unable to pray. Praying to the heathen gods, before whom these seamen were presenting their petitions, would have been beneath his dignity. He could not pray to his god Yahweh, because he knew he had left him back in Palestine. Jonah had thought he was clever in successfully exiling himself from his god for a season. Now he found himself in a dire predicament, with no deity upon whom he could call.

What crime had Jonah committed? In spite of their trying to get him to speak regarding this matter, he refused to talk on that subject. By his strange actions the sailors were beginning to suspect that he was trying to flee from his god because of some act he had committed. So they asked him what they should do that they might not all be carried to their death with him. He seems to have given no response even here. He was the type of person who would cause a whole shipload to perish with him rather than go in contrition to his deserved fate alone.

By this time matters were becoming serious. The waves were mounting higher and higher. Unless something radical was done, and quickly, doom for all seemed assured. In desperation the sailors began talking about throwing Jonah overboard as a last resort. Yet they had such high regard for human life that they could not think of bringing such a calamity upon their ill-fated passenger, even though his actions and the evidence of the lot had convinced them that he was guilty.

As Jonah overheard this talk about throwing him overboard, the fleeing prophet became somewhat alarmed. He finally decided it might be best to talk. Traditionally Jonah's words at this point have been regarded as the positive suggestion of a humbled prophet. Probably they are to be understood as a question, giving the last arrogant stand of one who dares these wretches to throw such a *very important person* overboard.

> Take *me* up?
> And cast *me* forth into the sea?
> So the sea may be calmed for you?
> And you think this great tempest
> Has come upon you because of *me?*

> *Jonah 1:12*

As a final resort, the men used their last remaining energy striving desperately to row back toward land so they could deliver their victim alive. The more they tried, however, the higher the waves mounted, and the more hopeless the effort appeared. Finally, in desperation, they decided to do the unpleasant deed.

Strange as it may seem, the sailors were receptive and had been overawed by Jonah's statement about this wonderful God of the universe. As they huddled together on deck for another prayer meeting, they all addressed themselves to the God about whom Jonah had unwittingly informed them. How the prophet must have scorned these vile seamen for having the audacity to pray to his god!

These crewmen requested that they might not all perish for the sins of this one man. They recognized that this was a dreadful deed which they were about to commit. They feared they would be held accountable by God for murder. Yet they begged earnestly that the deity would not reckon it as such. They implored God to pardon them for the deed which, in desperation, they felt compelled to perform.

We can imagine how Jonah must have felt as the sailors finally came over and laid hold on him. Unceremoniously, they took the unrepentant quack prophet and cast him overboard into the water. Immediately the sea became calm, and thereby they knew that they had disposed of the right man.

This experience overawed the sailors. They stood in amazement and reverence before this God of the universe who had such power. They were still fearful that he might take revenge upon them for this cruel act of casting one of his creatures into the sea. So they gathered in a group on deck once more in the act of prayer, presenting their petitions for mercy to this God of heaven and earth whom Jonah had declared unto them. The small gods to whom they had once prayed seemed forgotten in the enthusiasm of their new allegiance as they knelt there.

Relieved of this troublesome passenger, the sailors made ready to resume their trip. Bearings were taken, the course was set, and the vessel began once more to proceed uneventfully on its way. As this Tarshish ship receded from view toward the westward, we see a crew of sailors who were joyous over the new and greater God with whom they had become acquainted through this awful experience.

Deep-Sea Adventure

Beneath the surface of the Mediterranean Sea things were happening also. According to the story, God had prepared a fish especially for the occasion, and it was there at exactly the right moment to swallow Jonah when he struck the water. One can imagine this renegade prophet's thoughts as he felt himself slipping into the gullet of that sea monster.

Think of the difficulties suffered by that fish in trying to digest this tough morsel! In the stomach of that great fish the digestive juices reacted on Jonah, trying to soften him. Hour after hour he was churned about in this digestive mael-strom with no appreciable effect. He still seemed as hard as ever. Not until the process had been continued for seventy-two hours did this hard-shelled passenger become sufficiently humbled that he could pray.

It was a moment of rejoicing for God when he began to hear a voice coming from that fish's belly. He must have been so delighted that, at the first sound of a prayer from that quarter, he ordered the fish to proceed toward land and disembark its human cargo. The Palestinian coast was soon reached, and the accommodating fish vomited up Jonah, catapulting him onto the dry land.

After gaining his balance and bearings, we can see Jonah, bleached and emaciated, beginning to move in the direction of home. In light of all that had happened, he was likely ashamed to show his face to anyone. We can imagine him avoiding the highways, sneaking home through fields and byways that no one might see him. Perhaps he slipped back into Gath-hepher by night.

As the days wore on, he commenced to show himself in public. Things gradually began to seem like old times. Perhaps he resumed his custom of loafing with the men at the "corner store." Finally, in response to their constant questionings, he let it out one day as to what had happened to him during his period of absence.

Jonah was rather surprised to find himself gradually moving into the focus of popular attention. He was called upon to tell of his adventure to person after person, and group after group. In the course of time he came largely to forget about the humiliating aspects of that experience as all manner of people came to see and hear him.

Even though he had a big enough tale to start with, as with all fish stories he saw to it that it grew with each telling. Jonah soon found himself revered by people far and near. He was sitting on top of the world. He was glad he had gone toward Tarshish rather than Nineveh. So the prophet settled back to enjoy the halo of a hero-adventurer for the remainder of his days, basking in the glory of an admiring public.

20

Shadows of Hate and Love

IT WAS NOT LONG until there came to Jonah, perhaps one night in a dream or vision, almost those same words of God which he had heard at first:

> Arise! Go unto Nineveh, that great metropolis,
> And preach unto it the message that I bid you.
>
> *Jonah 3:2*

This caused the heart of Jonah to sink, and his world crashed about him once more. What greater calamity could have befallen him? He knew he was not likely to achieve anything by arguing, or trying to flee this time. Much as he disliked the prospect of such a mission, there could be no question but that it would be best to go immediately, and have it over with.

Repentant Nineveh

Jonah was soon on his way toward that famous capital of Assyria. During the journey, there occurred to him a new thought which brightened his horizon considerably. Perhaps he would get to see Nineveh burn. Watching such a great city go up in smoke would be worth all the sacrifice he was making in order to take this trip. He convinced himself that this was what Yahweh would do if the people did not repent, and he was quite certain they would not. So the remainder of his journey was for Jonah a triumphal march of joyful expectation.

In this story, Nineveh was so large that it required three days to walk diametrically across the city. After arriving and entering through one of the gates, Jonah walked a whole day, which brought him a third of the way through the metropolis.

Now for his unpleasant task! Even though it went against his better judgment, he concluded there was no escape from carrying out his appointed duty. He must suppress his pride and swallow this bitter pill of preaching to these despised people. The sooner he could get rid of this disgusting assignment, the better!

But what if these people should repent on his hands and invite themselves into his religion as those crude sailors on the Mediterranean Sea had done? That would be a pretty mess, for millions of people were at issue in this situation. He for one would not want anything to do with religion if such a trashy lot were going to join it. Perhaps he could do something about this too. He had better not preach the message exactly as God had outlined it to him. It would be too dangerous. They might accidentally repent, and that would be outrageous.

As evening time came, and most citizens of Nineveh were around their supper tables, very few people were in the streets. Perhaps, Jonah thought, he might as well get this off his chest before having his evening meal. Then he would be able to enjoy it better. He did not want to preach to a large audience, for someone in it might accidentally repent. At the moment, he seemed to notice practically no one around. This was his chance. So we may imagine he placed his hand partly over his mouth and mumbled,

> Yet forty days, and Nineveh shall be destroyed.
>
> *Jonah 3:4*

Things did not work themselves out according to plan. The trouble was that someone was near enough to overhear what he had spoken. This person told others, and they in turn passed the word along. Soon the whole city was in an uproar. Everyone who heard the message of doom put on coarse sackcloth as a sign of mourning. Before that evening was over, every person in that vast metropolis had repented, from the greatest of them to the least.

Even the king came down from his throne, laid aside his royal robes, and clothed himself in sackcloth. He sat on the city dump and threw ashes over his head, the greatest possible demonstration of mourning in those days. From this ash heap the king issued a decree which was signed also by all his nobles. It was proclaimed throughout Nineveh, and read as follows:

> Let neither man nor beast, herd nor flock, taste anything;
> Let them neither take food nor drink water;
> But let them be covered with sackcloth, both man and beast,
> And let them pray unto God with all their might;
> Also, let every one of them turn from his evil way,
> And from the violence that is in his hands.
> Who knows, but that God will change his mind and relent,
> And turn away from his fierce anger, that we perish not?
>
> *Jonah 3:7-9*

The Angry Prophet

When Jonah saw that the people were repenting, he became angry. This was a nice mess, he thought. To have those
people repent was the last thing in this world that he desired.
He wanted to see them get burned up. Jonah had been an
underprivileged child, for he had never seen a first-class fire
in all his life. He had always arrived on the scene too late,
after the fire was burned out. Here he had gone to Nineveh
with the happy prospect of watching a big metropolis being
consumed, and seeing several million people *sizzle and fry*.
Now that prospect was all spoiled by their repentance.

With that bitter disappointment Jonah's world crashed
about him again. If he could not see these people burn, then
for him there was nothing more left in life that was worth
living for. In his displeasure and anger he even turned on
God, and denounced the deity to his face. Jonah virtually
said, "I just suspected that you were of this sort. That's
why I tried to flee to Tarshish in the first place. You're
nothing but a chicken-hearted deity, with a wishbone for a
backbone — afraid to stand up to these wretched Ninevite
people and give them what they deserve. Fooled by a little
feigned repentance! I repeat, if I can't see those millions
of Ninevite people get burned up, I have nothing left in life
to live for. If these people aren't going to be destroyed, and
are going to be in my religion, I would be better off dead than
alive. So take my life" (Jonah 4:2-3).

This reaction of the supposed prophet, to God's accepting
the repentance of the Ninevites and resolving to save them,
was inconceivable to the deity. To God, Jonah's actions
seemed absurd. Most preachers have their "blue Mondays"
because their Sunday sermons have so little effect. Here was

the most successful preacher of all time. He had converted
several million people by mumbling a sentence that, in the
Hebrew which he spoke, consisted of only five words. Con-
trary to what would normally have been expected, he was
furious because his preaching had some response.

After the first flush of his anger, Jonah took second thought
with regard to the matter. "Surely," he must have concluded,
"Yahweh will come to realize that this is a fake repentance,
and he will yet burn up those people. Yes, he'd better come
around to seeing things my way."

This renewed prospect of seeing Nineveh consumed gave
Jonah a new lease on life, and he began to beam with optimism once more. He wanted to take no chances of missing
this great sight when the fire and brimstone should fall, as
in the days of Sodom and Gomorrah. Therefore he went
out the east gate and chose for himself a high sand dune at
a comfortable distance, although near enough so he could
see and hear everything as it transpired. He wanted to be
sure that he should have a box seat for the big show which he
still had faith to believe was coming.

The Gourd Vine

On the top of that sand dune, Jonah constructed a crude
booth to shield himself from the sun's heat. Under this little
hut he waited day after day, hoping the fire would fall, as
it had done centuries earlier on Sodom and Gomorrah. Probably he almost starved himself, because he feared that if
he should go into Nineveh to buy food he might get caught
and miss the big show.

This picture of the waiting Jonah, tense, and with every
expectation centered on the destruction of his fellow men,
made God smile once more. This situation was so absurd

that it was amusing. Consequently God thought he would have a little fun with Jonah, and play with him a trifle in the hope that he might regain a little bit of reason and wholesome regard for others.

One night, while Jonah was asleep, God caused a spacious gourd vine to grow up over his shelter. The deity made this to attain maturity in one night, so it became a great overshadowing canopy.

When Jonah awoke the next morning and saw the vine, he was overjoyed. During that day he was sitting on top of the world once more. He took this as a sign that the deity had changed his mind and had come to look upon things in Jonah's way. He concluded this gourd vine was sent to protect him from the intense heat of the burning city. This proved that God had seen the light at last, and was going to destroy Nineveh. That prospect made this the most joyful day of Jonah's entire life. He almost worshiped that gourd vine, and all he thought it signified.

After one day spent in this heaven of joyful expectation, the following morning saw Jonah's world crash about him once more. On that day God used a three-way squeeze on the prophet. He caused a cutworm to sever the stem, and that luxurious gourd plant soon became a browned and shriveled vine. Then God summoned the sirocco, that burning wind from the desert, with its blowing sands that almost blasted Jonah from his lookout. In addition, God turned on the sun to full power, and as its rays beat down and scorched Jonah's bald head, it was too much for him to bear.

The prophet construed this as a sign that Yahweh had changed his mind once more. Apparently this deity had decided again that he would not destroy the city. The sun and wind became so hot that Jonah fainted. As he revived and thought over all this, he became indignant that a god should be so wishy-washy and afraid to take drastic measures. Think of a deity who could be fooled by the fake repentance of these heathen people!

Reverting to his boyhood technique, Jonah threw himself into a tantrum so as to get his own way. He reminded Yahweh again that if he couldn't see those Ninevites burn, there would be nothing left in life for him to live for. So he invited God to kill him on the spot and get him out of his misery. It was either burn them or kill him. This was his ultimatum to his god.

The amused deity tried to reason with Jonah, using the gourd vine as a basis. He reminded the prophet how pleased he had been with that plant. Jonah had loved that vine because it had given him shade, comfort, and joy. God tried to get the sulking prophet to see that he took delight in Nineveh as Jonah had taken pleasure in the gourd, only far more. The gourd was only a green vine but in Nineveh there were human beings, millions of them. Nineveh was God's gourd vine. In fact, each person within that metropolis was as a gourd vine to God, in which he took special delight. In final analysis, every individual, even in Nineveh, was infinitely more precious in the sight of God than all the gourd vines that had ever grown.

Of utmost consideration were the cattle in the city, and the one hundred and twenty thousand infants below the age of three years. Even if all the adult people of Nineveh had been bad and worthy of death, the presence in the city of the live stock and innocent children were sufficient to prevent God, with his divine compassion, from destroying it. Nineveh, every person residing there, and every animal within its bounds, represented a piece of God's workmanship. He was trying to show Jonah how absurd it would be for the deity to destroy his own handiwork, in which he took such satisfaction.

Jonah was in no mood at this time to learn any lessons. He was in such a rage that no reasoning was possible. We are not told what eventually happened to him. That is left to each reader's imagination. All we know is that, as the curtain falls and the story closes, we still see the angry sulking Jonah sitting on his sand dune, continuing his one-man strike against God, trying to force the deity even yet into destroying Nineveh.

The Allegory

What has seemed like a simple tale is in reality far more than a story. It is an allegorical epic. It does not give the adventures of a real individual but casts the history of the Hebrew people into the form of a story. As the allegory is resolved, the meaning of the book becomes apparent.

Jonah in reality represents the prophet-nation which was called upon during the early days in Palestine to share her exalted religion with all mankind. In this, Israel shirked, preferring to keep her spiritual heritage a monopoly of her own rather than bring it to the attention of other nations. So there developed within her people a feeling of superiority and exclusivism. She degenerated to the point where she had forfeited her right to exist among the sovereign states of the world.

The tempest was in reality the storm of militaristic conquest which, at the hands of Assyria and Babylonia, descended upon the calm sea of Israelite existence. Throwing Jonah overboard represents the hurling of God's prophet nation into the sea of exile. The great fish which swallowed Jonah was in reality the Babylonian monster which finally gulped down the prophet-nation. The three days and three nights in the

belly of the fish signify the three exiles of the Hebrew people
— Israel in 722 B.C. and the people of Judah in 597 and
586 B.C. The vomiting out of Jonah is a designation of the
return from exile in 538 B.C.

The latter part of the story describes Israel in post-exilic
times. Stimulated by the wonderful ideals of Second Isaiah,
with his exalted concept of Israel's mission to all mankind,
immediately after returning from exile the nation had a
second chance to fulfill her destiny. However, the opportunity
was not seized. She soon degenerated, under the influence of
Ezra, into national exclusivism and hatred of all foreigners.
The community of Israel was purged of all foreign blood as
Hitler was later to purge the Germans of all Jewish blood.
Families were broken up as all non-Jewish partners were
driven from the community. So the history of post-exilic times
was an orgy of hate against foreigners, all of whom came to be
regarded as despised Gentiles and heathen.

The book of Jonah was written anonymously by some
author who probably guessed what would happen to him if
his name were known. It was produced in the hope that this
story might contribute toward reversing the tides of hate, and
might influence the author's fellow countrymen into adopting
attitudes of brotherhood and regard toward all peoples. The
book ends with a question, because it was not certain at the
time of writing whether this process of degeneracy was to
continue, or whether the people would see the light and yet
turn into ways of friendship and love.

Teachings about God

This story shows one of the last stages in the classic conflict
between the old idea of national gods and the newer concept
of one God for all the universe. Jonah held to the newer

concept in theory but in practice he was still following the old beliefs. His experience on the Mediterranean Sea should have proved to him that his old god, Yahweh of Palestine, whose influence was confined by national bounds, was but a figment of the imagination. By that experience he should have come to see that there is only one God in the universe, and that national bounds mean nothing to the deity.

We may laugh at the absurd belief which Jonah held, but the world even today is far from having outlived it. In the First World War our opponents prayed to the god of the Central Powers while we prayed to the god of the Allies. In the Second World War the Axis nations worshiped a totalitarian god while the democracies worshiped a democratic god. At mid-century, the Russians were worshiping a communist god and the democratic powers were worshiping an anti-communist god. The white people of the world worship a white god. The Negroes worship a Negro god. The yellow people worship a yellow god. Employers worship the god of capital. Laborers worship the god of labor. Catholics worship a Catholic god, Protestants worship a Protestant god, and Jews continue to worship the god of Israel. The Arab god speaks Arabic, the Jewish god speaks Hebrew, and the god of America speaks English. And so it goes.

We of the present day may not be conscious of the littleness of the gods we worship, but neither was Jonah. When we come fully to take stock we must begin to realize that we still follow pretty much the belief about God held by Jonah. We no longer have our gods regimented strictly on a national basis. We have created them to serve the various areas of race, international coalition, class, and social status. Although there may be a slight improvement, our partial worship of our partial gods is only slightly less absurd than the antics of Jonah. If we were really to believe in one God, we would radically alter our attitudes and manner of procedure.

Far more important than the teaching of the Jonah story with regard to the magnitude of God is its pioneering contribution with regard to the nature of God. It must be remembered that people in the early part of the Bible believed in a god of caprice and vengeance, who was not bound by moral scruples. He could do bad or he could choose to do good, and he was unaccountable. Amos took a long step in advance when he showed that God is not beyond the demands of right and wrong, but is bound by them as much as are people. In other words, God is a god of justice, and he demands just actions on the part of his worshipers. Hosea advanced beyond this and came to conceive that God is a god of love. It remained however for the author of the book of Jonah to give us the highest concept of the nature of God in the Old Testament as he proclaimed the deity.

> A gracious God, and merciful;
> Slow to anger, and abundant in loving-kindness;
> And one who relents when it comes to punishing.

> *Jonah 4:2*

This picture of a compassionate and merciful God, who takes no delight in punishing his people but does everything possible to avoid it, is one of the most revolutionary concepts of God in all the development of religion. The God of the book of Jonah is a deity whom one would like to face. The old terror of God has disappeared and we have in its place that outgoing compassion and mercy about which Jesus was to speak so much. It was here too that Mohammed got his most frequently quoted phrase, "God, the Compassionate, the Merciful." Those who continue to believe in a god of wrath and vengeance would do well to read, and reread thoughtfully, the book of Jonah.

Teachings about Man

The teachings about man in this story are even more revolutionary than the discoveries about God. If God is the God of all the universe, and if he is merciful and compassionate, then there must be some radical readjustments in human relationships. This book shows that there are no segments of humanity that can be called heathen or pagan. All people are good, wherever they are. And, as in the case of this story, those who are looked down upon as the despised of the earth are frequently better, at least potentially, than their despisers. Those who regard people outside their group as heathen, Gentiles, or pagans must guard lest their own self-righteousness and bigotry reduce themselves to an even lower level.

This book asserts that there is a natural responsiveness in all people. In those days no group was thought of as lower than those crude salts on that Tarshish galley in the Mediterranean Sea. Yet even they responded quickly when new religious concepts were presented to them. The Assyrians were the most warlike and brutal people in ancient times. Yet our author showed that even such supposedly callous people also respond quickly to new truth when it confronts them. The author of this book had faith in man as well as faith in God. He had seen enough of people to know that there is no such thing as a depraved person or nation. People usually are as they are because of circumstances. When they are presented with an attractive alternative, they will usually seize it. When man has half a chance, he is naturally responsive to better modes of life.

Even in his remote day, this writer had the foresight to see, through the vision of religion, the conclusion which modern science has proved true — that there are no basic differences between peoples. Every segment of mankind has that same potential ability to produce and advance, if they only have the opportunity. There are no inferior races. Racial retardation is largely the result of chance and circumstance. We ought therefore to think, as the author of Jonah, in terms of the possibilities of the several peoples rather than in terms of the conditions into which they may have become mired by force of geographical or economic circumstances.

In the mentality of the book of Jonah there is no place for such deprecatory epithets as sheeny, Chink, Dago, wop, *et al.* This is the book of one world, and in a world that is one, such invidious distinctions have no place. This story shows that there is only one humanity. If carefully studied, it should bring us far on the way toward achieving this oneness among all mankind which is so sorely needed in our time.

The Swan Song

The story of Jonah is the swan song of Hebrew prophecy. As that bird's last effort is supposed to be its sweetest, so this final expression of the prophetic spirit in Old Testament times is in many respects on a higher level than anything found in even the exalted work of the preceding prophets. The tragedy of ancient times was that the book became largely ignored as people degenerated even more into exclusivism and narrow bigotries. The tragedy of modern times is that attention has been so monopolized by the whale, or big fish, that the message of the book has been almost lost. Yet it still stands as the final and highest expression of the prophetic spirit in the Old Testament, and offers its messages of help toward bringing about a recreated humanity, a world of love and brotherhood in which prejudice and hate shall be no more.

Prophets of
Later Centuries

21

The Continuing Succession

IT MUST NOT BE THOUGHT that the prophetic spirit came to
an end with the closing of the Old Testament. Wherever there
are people and whenever religion is due for higher perspectives,
the prophetic spirit usually finds expression anew. In each
time of need there is someone with a pioneering vision who
steps forth and points out clearly the outlines of the upward
way.

John the Baptist

At the beginning of the New Testament, after several centuries of deadening narrowness and bigotry, there appeared
the dramatic figure of John the Baptist (Luke 3:1-22).
Dressed simply, with only a coarse camel's hair garment
and a leather girdle, and living on food which he found in
the wild, this prophet spent his time preaching by the River
Jordan and baptizing his converts. His was a fiery message.
He called the people "offspring of vipers" and ridiculed their
reliance upon their blue-blood Abrahamic ancestry. He announced that all who were not following in the pathway of
right would be "hewn down and cast into the fire." The
multitudes which gathered to hear his preaching were terrified at his message and cried out, "What must we do?" He
demanded that they share the material things they possessed,

together with abstinance from all forms of violence and exploitation.

John was even bold enough to attack King Herod for his immorality, particularly for taking his brother's wife and living with her. However, this was more than that depraved king would tolerate. John was interfering with matters of state. So Herod had him seized and placed in prison.

Sometime later, when King Herod had a birthday, he made a luxurious banquet for all his lords, high captains, and chief men (Mark 6:21-29). The daughter of this new wife Herodias, whom he had illegally married, was brought in and danced for the company. Herod was so swept off his feet by her performance that he offered her anything she might ask, even unto half the kingdom. After going out and consulting with her mother, she asked for the head of John the Baptist. A soldier was sent to the prison and soon returned with the trophy. The bloody head was brought and served up on a platter to the daughter who in turn presented it to her mother Herodias. With this sorry ending to the ministry of John the Baptist, another name was added to the role of the prophet-martyrs.

John was especially significant because he did much to inspire Jesus who came to his preaching and was baptized by him. With all due respect to Jesus, it must be remembered that it was John who produced the great religious awakening which formed the beginning of the New Testament development. He was the prophet of a new age.

Jesus

Whatever else may be said of Jesus, he too was a prophet. Beginning his ministry after John the Baptist was thrown into prison, he in a sense continued that movement. He felt that he was also resuming the succession of the Old Testament prophets. His frequent references show how deeply he was indebted to them. He found the ideal of the humble suffering servant in the fifty-third chapter of Isaiah. This was adopted by him as the main program of his ministry.

Jesus said on one occasion that he came to fulfill the law and the prophets (Matt. 5:17). This has usually been understood in the shallow way that they foretold his coming and that he satisfied those predictions. Jesus meant far more by this statement. As already suggested, in the introductory part of this study, it would express his meaning better if the two parts of the key word were reversed — i.e., he came to "fill full" the law and the prophets. In other words, he regarded it as his task to continue, advance, and enlarge the work which they had started.

It was evident to the people of that day that Jesus was a prophet. When he asked the disciples who the residents of Palestine thought he was, he received significant answers. Certain ones said he was John the Baptist come back to life. Others regarded him as the prophet Elijah returned to earth. In some quarters there was the feeling that he was the prophet Jeremiah. There were other minority views which asserted that Jesus was one of the other Old Testament prophets risen from the dead (Matt. 16:14). The two men on the road to Emmaus on Easter evening spoke of him as "Jesus the Nazarene, who was a prophet mighty in deed and word before God and all the people" (Luke 24:19). When Jesus returned to his Nazareth home he referred to himself as a prophet when he said, "A prophet is not without honor save in his own country, and among his own kin, and in his own house" (Mark 6:4). Apparently nothing pleased Jesus more than to be called a prophet, for he was in the prophetic succession. He differed from those before him not in essence, but only in the degree of his spiritual attainment.

The way of life which Jesus charted and lived, is only vaguely comprehended even yet. He was a religious pioneer who forged far ahead of the previous prophets. There is enough dynamite in his teachings to blow up many an unworthy segment of our life if the power that is latent in them were only released today. His Sermon on the Mount offers the Magna Carta of religion. The regret is that its implications are so seldom comprehended.

With respect to the death which he met, Jesus also stood in the succession of the prophets. As he looked at Jerusalem from the Mount of Olives, he was overcome with emotion as he exclaimed, "O Jerusalem, Jerusalem, that kills the prophets and stones those who are sent unto her" (Matt. 23:37). He had premonitions of impending tragedy before he went there. He knew it would probably mean death if he should preach his message of righteousness in that den of iniquity. Nevertheless, he showed that typical courage of the prophets in knowing no retreat but preaching where his message was most needed. Following the pathway of duty, he went to a glorious martyr's death. As Moses and the other prophets have continued to be the inspiration of Judaism, so the prophet of Nazareth remains the light of the Christian world.

Mohammed

The working of God's spirit is fortunately not confined to any one people or any one faith. The Muslim religion has had its prophets also. Of these Mohammed was chief, and occupies somewhat the same position among them that Jesus holds among Christians. Mohammed acknowledged his deep indebtedness to the prophets of the Old Testament and to Jesus. He regarded himself as continuing their work and elaborating upon it. His watchword was, "There is one God and Mohammed is his prophet."

To appreciate Mohammed it is necessary to know what religion was like in his country. Worship in Arabia at that time was mostly of a crude polytheistic type. People worshiped gods in stones, trees, and bodies of water. The greatest contribution of Mohammed lay in his vision of one God. He went about denouncing idolatry and helping the people get rid of their gods. Lone-handed, he established among them the worship of the one God, called Allah in the Arabian language. Mohammed's work has not achieved perfect results, for certain traces of the old order continue. It must be granted, however, that he created in Arabia a religion so monotheistic, or unitarian if that name is preferred, that most forms of Christianity appear by comparison as crude polytheism.

To appreciate the comparative greatness of Mohammed it is necessary to realize how degenerate was the brand of Christianity that was being preached and practiced in Arabia in the days of this prophet. In the minds of contemporary Christian preachers, the Biblical facts had become but a vague memory. They were identifying Miriam, the sister of Moses, with Mary, the mother of Jesus. The trinity that was preached in Arabia by Christians consisted of God, Jesus, and his blessed mother Mary.

The Arabian people were always prohibitionists. They clung tenaciously to that primitive Semitic belief, represented in the Old Testament by the Nazarites and Rechabites, that the use of intoxicating liquors is wrong. The Christians tried to break this, and became the bootleggers of Arabia. So it must be borne in mind that, inadequate as it may have been, the religion proclaimed by Mohammed was very much higher than the perverted brand of Christianity which was common in those days, a religion that had degenerated into polytheism and immorality.

When we understand the notable contributions which Mohammed made toward raising the religious perspectives and moral levels of the Arabian people, we can see why the residents of Muslim lands are unwavering in their loyalty to his name and the faith which he developed among them. Indeed Mohammed was a prophet, and a great one.

Mahatma Gandhi

The line of prophets is by no means confined to the Jewish, Christian, and Mohammedan traditions. The inspiration of the prophets was the spirit of progress, and no nationality, age, or religion can claim a monopoly upon it. Wherever faiths have vitality, one can know that it has been supplied, or is being furnished, by pioneering leaders who are devoted to keeping religion abreast or ahead of the times. This has been true from the ancient era of India's sages to the most modern day.

The greatest prophet of the late nineteenth and early twentieth centuries has been found in the Hindu tradition in the person of Mahatma Gandhi. Although influenced by the prophet of Nazareth, he has remained basically a son of India.

It is to the shame of the Christian world that it should have been left to Hinduism to give mankind its greatest teacher of non-violence in modern times. Gandhi was the prophet of "soul-force." This, he insisted, is more powerful than any physical might, and in the end will accomplish more than wars or rumors of wars. By using this new weapon Gandhi has become the world's most invincible conqueror, bringing even the British Empire to her knees in two great struggles.

During his stay in South Africa as a young Cambridge-trained lawyer, the depressed condition of his fellow Hindus attracted his attention. He forfeited his $15,000 a year income from legal practice and identified himself with their cause. By the British he was kicked out of hotels, thrown off railway trains; he was insulted and abused. Yet he triumphed in that struggle. The terrible poll tax, which amounted to virtual slavery, was removed. By his program of non-violent effort he won equal rights for the Indian people of South Africa.

The greatest battle of Gandhi's life consisted in winning independence for India. On the basis of soul-force he succeeded remarkably in uniting the spirit of his people. By civil disobedience campaigns, passive resistance, boycotts, and hunger strikes, he finally succeeded in bending the British Empire toward his wishes. He was assassinated before his dreams came fully true, but that deed of violence served only to dramatize his life. That event so drew attention to his ideals that it stopped the violence in India and assured the fulfillment of his program. Never before had a great nation been set free with such a practical absence of bloodshed. This vindicated his judgment that soul-force is a more powerful weapon for achieving freedom than violence or war. His triumphs in Africa and India have extended even beyond his country, for he has lit the light of freedom in all south-Asiatic countries. He has become the prophet of freedom and peace in the modern world.

Gandhi was also the prophet of the poor. He accepted the

challenge to lead his country out of her superstitions and poverty. Although born into fabulous riches, with his father the prime minister of an Indian native state, he forfeited all this, and the great wealth that was destined for him, in order that he might redeem the lost segments of mankind. He did not stop with being the prophet of the common man. He became the prophet of the world's outcasts and untouchables. He found India a land in which people of the low castes were not admitted to the temples. He himself was not allowed to enter because of his association with them. By reason of his efforts, he left India a country in which all, however lowly, may worship in the temples. By identifying himself with these outcasts, he raised them up until today they are being treated as people.

Seldom has any individual been so revered and so hated. As a symbol of liberation for India's vast suppressed masses, he was thronged wherever he went. People crowded merely to touch him or snatch some blessing as he passed. To them it was the experience of a lifetime to be near this "Great Soul." They gathered by thousands at railroad stations to see his train go through. By the high caste people of his country, and by Britain, he was hated as no other person. Winston Churchill called him "that naked little fakir." Few people in the world have been so often jailed as he. Numerous of the best years of his life were spent behind bars. He seemed to be a man of defeat. Yet no one in the modern religious world has scored such triumph.

As an old man, he presented a spectacular appearance. Wearing only a loincloth, with spinning wheel under his arm, and living on a diet of goat's milk, vegetables, and fruit, he was also the prophet of the simple life. He had such passion for truth that he would not even use "false" teeth except when eating. Weakened by fasts, imprisonments, and violence of mobs, he weighed less than a hundred pounds. Although he was forced to sit while speaking, because of not having sufficient strength to stand, this feeble and almost toothless old man has been perhaps the most powerful person in the modern world. The various facets of his prophetic significance are well summarized by the individual who said of him, "In all the world I think I have never seen a man so honest, so fearless, so gentle, and so lovable." We can understand why the people of India have called him Mahatma Gandhi, which means "Great Soul Gandhi."

The Wider Fellowship

John the Baptist, Jesus of Nazareth, Mohammed of Arabia, and Gandhi of India are only four of the numerous prophets outside the Old Testament. Although these are especially illustrious, many others have ranked very highly.

All faiths have had their prophets. Otherwise, religions would never have come into being. Also, an occasional prophet is necessary, during the course of a religion's development, to keep it alive and growing, and to prevent fossilization.

In most ages, the prophets come infrequently. They rise up in times of great need or crisis. Usually there is only one at a time in any country. Even so, when the spiritual leaders from all lands are considered together, it is possible to speak of a great continuing succession. This has been particularly true with regard to those who have carried on the spirit of the Hebrew prophets.

Judaism has had its great liberal, Rabbi Hillel, who in

spirit was somewhat like Jesus. At the dawn of modern times the Jewish people have given to the world the philosopher Spinoza who helped lay the foundations for our modern interpretation of the Bible. Roman Catholicism has had its Saint Francis, the prophet of poverty, and Savonarola, the prophet of religious reformation at the dawn of modern times.

The Protestant reformers constitute a great galaxy of prophets. It is to the glory of Protestantism that it has been so richly blessed with the prophetic spirit. The curse of this movement lies in the fact that whenever a prophet has appeared, the followers of such a one have taken for granted that they must draw aside from the main Christian procession and form a new sect. In this way Protestantism has considerably dissipated its rich heritage.

In modern times there have been many prophets on what might be called the periphery of religion. Galileo, with his first telescope, was the prophet of the unfolding heavens and the infinite spaces. Darwin was the prophet of the laboratory sciences, giving a whole new orientation to man's perspective. He gave new meaning to the term "eternity" by showing that life has developed gradually from age to age. Although people in most churches considered him an evil and destructive influence, he was in reality tracing the footsteps of God. Pasteur, with his discovery of germs, became the prophet of modern medicine. In the same way Florence Nightingale and Clara Barton became the angels of the battlefields and the founders of the Red Cross.

This is only the beginning of those who might be mentioned. It is a source of regret that limitations of space do not permit even short treatment of the many prophets of religion, and those on the periphery of religion, particularly in modern times, whose contributions have been woven into the basic fabric of the civilization which we enjoy.

Mighty Men of God

Whatever the age in which the prophets of religion have labored, or the specific fields in which they have rendered their distinctive services, it is possible to see certain factors characteristic of their work.

The prophets were reformers, in the sense of re-formers. In each generation they have worked to re-mold the life of their day into something more worthy.

The mainspring of the prophet's urge was his vision of right and truth, and his unwavering devotion to it.

By reason of the fact that right is on the side of progress and wrong makes for regression and ruin, the prophets were men of the progressive spirit. They constantly have envisioned ever greater things beyond, and have striven to attain them. Whatever the age, they occupy the most advanced position in pushing out and widening the horizons of good.

The prophets were men of courage, proclaiming the right and condemning the wrong at all times, even hazarding their lives for these principles. Stationed in the front lines, they have borne the brunt of battle in the eternal conflict with the forces of wickedness.

Far behind the prophet follow the timid souls who are afraid to back him up. The more he advances and moves into the forefront of the world's progress, the greater becomes the distance between him and their sluggish pace. In so far as this world is concerned, the better the prophet, the more friendless he will be. His only consolation is that he knows he is a friend of God.

Recognizing Them Today

It must not be assumed that all the prophets lived in ancient, medieval, and early modern times, or that we find ourselves in a period when they are significantly absent. The prophetic spirit has not died, but is very much alive in our world today. There are prophets living in our midst. The trouble lies in our not being able to detect them. It is very difficult for any age to recognize its own prophets.

By contrast with the millions of people living today, the contemporary prophets may be few in number. Yet, when added together, they make a considerable company. To point them out and cite their contributions would be another study.

To discover who these prophets are is something that must be learned by practice. They are usually not the people who wear the medals, or receive testimonial dinners, or have their names heralded as heroes in the press. Only among their followers, who also have glimpsed their vision, are they revered. Outside this small circle they are more often the victims of bitter hatreds. They are usually maligned as dreamy idealists, impractical, brain-trusters, atheists, unpatriotic, subversive, or even traitors.

It is easy to understand how the forces of corruption abominate the prophets who would destroy their opportunities for illicit or tainted gain. Whether derived from crime, prostitution, liquor, gambling, political corruption, exploitation by religious professionals, or dishonesty in business, the recipients are willing to spend almost any sums that may be required to turn the populace against the accusing prophets. Such interests invent all manner of derogatory names and discrediting stories, spreading these from mouth to mouth and over the pages of the press. After people hear and read these malicious remarks often enough, they come to believe them.

In spite of all the propaganda which may be directed against the prophet, it seems inconceivable that the masses should allow themselves to be regimented into opposing those prophets who would really bring benefit to them. Here the working of the average mind is an important consideration. It is a regrettable fact that most individuals fear the future and are afraid of change. In their complacency, most people either worship the present or long for the past. In living for the future, the prophet speaks a language which the average person does not understand. So the masses can often be fooled into thinking that the prophet is bad and destructive.

Today people have grown in one way more humane, but in another way more cruel. In only rare cases do we kill the prophets in these times. Instead, they are smeared and slandered until their influence is weakened and they become powerless. It is important that people should learn not to be fooled by those who, for selfish reasons, malign the prophets.

Only after the prophet dies do the eyes of people usually come gradually to be opened. With the passing of time, most men begin to catch a glimpse of what the prophet had envisioned, and begin to speak well of him, or even to revere him. It is one of the supreme tragedies of life that mankind is afflicted with this peculiar brand of bewilderment which enables us to recognize the good in the past while remaining blind to it in our own age.

A Growing Fellowship

Inasmuch as the prophets were purposive speakers and writers, the biographical aspects of their experiences must not blind us to the heart of their messages. One comes really to appreciate these spiritual pioneers only when something of their sense of values sweeps over into ourselves. This study achieves its purpose to the extent that readers catch the spirit and vision of the prophets and come to stand, at least to some degree, in that grand succession.

The voices of the Israelite prophets still come to us across the centuries, calling us to greater activity in advancing the moral and spiritual side of our materialistic world. When the average person takes his stand by the side of the prophets, in struggling for the right and truth which they have glimpsed, a new day for civilization will have dawned.